ANCIENT PHILOSOPHY

ANCIENT PHILOSOPHY

A Companion to the Core Readings

ANDREW STUMPF

broadview press

BROADVIEW PRESS – www.broadviewpress.com
Peterborough, Ontario, Canada

Founded in 1985, Broadview Press remains a wholly independent publishing house. Broadview's focus is on academic publishing; our titles are accessible to university and college students as well as scholars and general readers. With over 600 titles in print, Broadview has become a leading international publisher in the humanities, with world-wide distribution. Broadview is committed to environmentally responsible publishing and fair business practices.

The interior of this book is printed on 100% recycled paper.

Ancient
Forest
Friendly™

PERMANENT   100%

© 2019 Andrew Stumpf

Library and Archives Canada Cataloguing in Publication

Stumpf, Andrew, 1979–, author
    Ancient philosophy : a companion to the core readings / Andrew Stumpf.

Includes bibliographical references and index.
Issued in print and electronic formats.
ISBN 978-1-55481-392-6 (softcover).—ISBN 978-1-77048-674-4 (PDF).—
ISBN 978-1-4604-0630-4 (HTML)

    1. Philosophy, Ancient. I. Title.

B171.S78 2018   180   C2018-906437-4
                                                        C2018-906438-2

Broadview Press handles its own distribution in North America:
PO Box 1243, Peterborough, Ontario K9J 7H5, Canada
555 Riverwalk Parkway, Tonawanda, NY 14150, USA
Tel: (705) 743-8990; Fax: (705) 743-8353
email: customerservice@broadviewpress.com

Distribution is handled by Eurospan Group in the UK, Europe, Central Asia, Middle East, Africa, India, Southeast Asia, Central America, South America, and the Caribbean. Distribution is handled by Footprint Books in Australia and New Zealand.

Canada

Broadview Press acknowledges the financial support of the Government of Canada for our publishing activities.

Edited by Robert M. Martin
Book design by Michel Vrana

Front cover image, combination of: "Socrates, painted portrait (DDC0339.JPG)" (https://www.flickr.com/photos/home_of_chaos/2902081064) and "Socrates, painted portrait (DDC0335.JPG)" (https://www.flickr.com/photos/home_of_chaos/2900762433) by Thierry Ehrmann (https://www.flickr.com/photos/home_of_chaos/) Licensed under CC BY 2.0 (https://creativecommons.org/licenses/by/2.0/)

PRINTED IN CANADA

To Joseph Novak, my teacher and mentor in the ways of ancient philosophy for many years, and a good friend.

Contents

CHAPTER 6: NATURE AND FIRST PHILOSOPHY

CHAPTER 7: GOOD PEOPLE AND GOOD CITIES: ARISTOTLE'S *ETHICS* AND *POLITICS*

CHAPTER 8: HELLENISTIC PHILOSOPHY, CHRISTIANITY, AND NEOPLATONISM

Acknowledgements

I would like to acknowledge Gerry Callaghan for his exhaustive review of this text and numerous helpful suggestions, John Greenwood for hours of discussion and feedback, Stephen Latta from Broadview Press for guiding the process from start to finish, Bob Martin for his exceedingly careful reading of the manuscript, Leslie Dema, Michel Pharand, and the rest of the Broadview team, and finally an anonymous reviewer who encouraged me to add some things that have made this a better book.

Introduction

TO THE STUDENT

The Nature and Goals of This Book

You have in your hands (or on your electronic device) a selective survey of the writings of some of the most significant philosophical works from the Ancient, or Classical, period in the history of philosophy. As you read it, you will be exploring what some of the greatest thinkers in the Western tradition have said about such questions as, "What is real?" and, for that matter, "What is *really* real?" "Can we know anything?" "If we can know something, *how* do we know it?" "Do we have souls, and if so what are they like?" "Does God exist?" "If God does exist, what is God like?" "Does human life have a purpose?" "What does a good human life consist in?" In my discussion of these texts and the philosophical problems they deal with, I seek to achieve a balance between themes in the areas of Metaphysics (the study of reality) and Epistemology (the study of knowledge), and in questions of Logic (the study of the rules for thinking well) and Ethics (the study of good and bad human activity).

Assuming that you think such questions are worth trying to answer, you might nevertheless be asking yourself, "Why should I care about what ancient philosophers had to say about subjects like these?" Let me offer three reasons why studying the history of ancient philosophy is important and interesting:

1. The Greco-Roman world and its philosophy and culture can justly be called the cradle of Western civilization. We can come to better understand contemporary Western culture and thought by examining their historical roots.

2. Studying ancient philosophy can help us to see outside the box of our present culture's prejudices. Looking at things from a perspective outside our own can be a great stimulus to honing and developing our own views. And the ancients give us a carefully thought out and comprehensive perspective on some of the most basic human questions.

3. Finally, the message of these thinkers continues to speak to us today. People worked hard to preserve the writings of the great thinkers because they found in those writings insights they could use to guide their own pursuit of wisdom and happiness.

Besides the three reasons listed here, there is also the pure intrinsic fun of reading and thinking through these ancient texts! Well, *I* believe it is fun to read them, at any rate, and I hope I can convince you of that as we go along.

My hope, in providing this companion to ancient philosophy, is that it will serve as a useful guide to you as you read the original texts for yourself and gain exposure to some of the great classics of the Western tradition. But that means you will have to locate some good English translations of the relevant works. If you are reading this as part of a course, your instructor may have already done that work for you. If you are looking for an edition, please note that Broadview Press (the publisher of this book) has released excellent and inexpensive editions of some of the texts we will be examining (see my list of texts below). You can also locate at least some of the relevant texts online via the Internet. If you choose that route, I would recommend the Perseus Digital Library: http://www.perseus. tufts.edu/hopper/. Whether accessing the texts online or in print, it is important to use good, scholarly editions of the works. I will be indicating which trans- lations of each text I myself have used, so that may be useful to you if you can track down copies of them in a library near you. But there are many other good translations out there.

Approaching the great philosophical texts by reading the primary sources can seem like a daunting task. That's because it *is* a daunting task. In undertaking it, I find it helpful to think of reading old philosophical texts as something like learning a language. You need to pick up the basic conceptual "vocabulary" and learn the "grammatical" or "syntactical" rules for putting those ideas together and relating them to each other. This is one of the ways the present book aims to be helpful. In addition to summaries and extended treatments of key concepts and arguments, this text provides historical and philosophical contexts to help you situate and understand the original texts.

Another goal of this book is to get you to start thinking for yourself about the questions and topics our authors are dealing with, many of which remain important, relevant, and hotly debated questions and topics for us today. For this reason, each chapter begins with an introductory "big question" that presents a major theme of the readings covered in that chapter, and shows how it is a perennial issue of con- tinuing relevance today. If you are reading this text as part of a course on ancient philosophy, your classroom will hopefully provide you with a forum for dialogue and discussion of such topics. As a general rule, the more you engage in dialogue with other interested people over philosophical topics, the more you will get from your learning experience.

I do strongly encourage you to read the primary texts before reading this book, and if possible take notes while you're reading. If you do, you will be in a better position to appreciate and evaluate my treatment of the major themes and key arguments. Don't be too worried if you don't understand everything the authors are saying on your first pass through; one of my main reasons for writing this book is to help you to deepen and clarify your own understanding of the great works. The bigger hope is that this process will empower you to enter the great conversation that is Western philosophy.

History, Philosophy, and "Great Works"

This is a history of philosophy text. People who teach the history of philosophy sometimes emphasize the history more than the philosophy, and others emphasize the philosophy more than the history. In this book, I'm going to do my best to provide a balance of both fields. What does this mean for you? Part of what it means is that on the one hand I'm not going to be emphasizing minute historical details about the specific places and dates where and when the philosophers whose works we'll be studying lived. On the other hand, I *will* be trying to help you to get the big picture of how the different periods of history fit together, and a sense of how to situate a given thinker within the historical and cultural context in which he or she lived and thought. But again, all this will be done with an eye to helping you understand and wrestle with ideas and arguments.

As we'll see, the text covers a broad swath of history, around 1,000 years in fact. Obviously, we can't discuss all the philosophers who lived in all the different periods stretching from the first origins of Western philosophy in the fifth century BCE to the late Classical period in the second century CE. The hope is to provide you with a helpful introduction to the major themes and movements in ancient philosophy that will be independently interesting, and also to set you up for a more detailed study of the period should you choose to pursue it. To this end, I emphasize several significant areas in which later thinkers continue and develop the thought of their predecessors. In particular, I highlight the ways Aristotle engages critically with the teaching of his master, Plato.

As the title of this book suggests, the focus here is on the "core readings" in the Western tradition. Another commonly used expression for this is "great works." The suggestion that certain philosophical works are greater than others and more worthy of attention is of course a contentious one. Who decides which works are the great ones? What standard do we use to decide this? And why are the vast majority of these works authored by dead white guys? Doesn't this make the whole project an exercise in European ethnocentrism and sexism? These are all good questions. Thankfully, I can avoid answering them by appealing to the fact that there is solid scholarly consensus, with a long and prestigious history, that a fairly well-defined body of texts count as the great texts. That probably doesn't get me out of the hot water altogether. But at the very least it's a fact that if you want to be a serious student of philosophy in the Western tradition, you can't really avoid the texts we'll be considering.

Note on the Stephanus and Bekker Numbering Systems

If you are using a good edition of Plato's original texts, you will notice tiny numbers and letters appearing in the columns beside the text. These are the "Stephanus numbers," and they are standard among scholarly translations of Plato's writing. They refer to the pages (represented by the numbers) and page sections (represented by the letters) of a complete edition of the works of Plato published in 1578. The editor, Henri Estienne (Stephanus is a Latin form of his last name) arranged the text with each page sub-divided into five sections—hence the letters "a" through "e" for each page. If you come across a reference like, *Apology*, 20e, it indicates the fifth section of the twentieth page of the Stephanus edition of Plato's works. Whenever I cite Plato's writings in this text, I will do so using the Stephanus numbers. This means that you and I do not need to be using the same version of the text; the page numbers of the translations we are using will most likely be different, but the Stephanus numbers give us a common reference point. The rationale involved here is the same as that which led to the division into chapters and verses of the various books that make up the Christian Bible, so that different people can quickly locate a passage under discussion despite using different versions or printings of the Bible. (Stephanus did this too.)

When you begin reading Aristotle, you will notice similar—but slightly different—numbers attached to the body of the text. This time, the references are to the pages, columns (two per page, so either a or b), and line numbers of a complete edition of Aristotle's works produced by a man named August Immanuel Bekker. The maximum number of lines on a page of the Bekker edition is 40. A reference to that text will look something like this: 1258a29–36; in this case, it is a reference to lines 29–36 in the first column (column "a") of page 1258 of Aristotle's *Politics* in the Bekker edition. The Stephanus and the Bekker numbering systems accomplish the same function. Since these numbering systems are standard in the academic world, using these numbers will be a good habit for you to develop when citing Plato or Aristotle in your own papers.

List of Translations Used in This Text

1. The Greek Poets
   a. Homer, *Iliad*, trans. Stanley Lombardo (Indianapolis: Hackett, 1997).
   b. Hesiod, *Theogony*, trans. Robert Lamberton and Stanley Lombardo (Indianapolis: Hackett, 1993).

2. The Presocratics
   Quotations of the Presocratics are taken from *Readings in Ancient Greek Philosophy: From Thales to Aristotle*, 4th ed., ed. S. Marc Cohen, Patricia Curd, and C.D.C. Reeve (Indianapolis: Hackett, 2011).

3. Plato
   c. I have used the translations of Plato's *Apology*, *Euthyphro*, and the death scene from the *Phaedo* contained in *The Apology and Related Dialogues*, edited by Andrew Bailey, translated by Cathal Woods and Ryan Pack, and published by Broadview Press, 2016. These are available online at SSRN: https://ssrn.com/abstract=1023142 or http://dx.doi.org/10.2139/ssrn.1023142

d. The translations of the *Meno*, the earlier parts of the *Phaedo*, and
    the *Republic* which I have used are by G.M.A. Grube, as reprinted
    in *Classics of Western Philosophy*, 8th ed., ed. Steven M. Cahn
    (Indianapolis: Hackett, 2012).

e. Quotations from Plato's *Seventh Letter* are drawn from *Plato:
    Complete Works*, ed. John M. Cooper, trans. Glenn R. Morrow
    (Indianapolis: Hackett, 1997).

4. Aristotle

f. The translations I've used for Aristotle's *Categories, Posterior
    Analytics, Physics,* and *Metaphysics* are by Terence Irwin and Gail
    Fine as reprinted in *Classics of Western Philosophy*, 8th ed., ed. Steven
    M. Cahn (Indianapolis: Hackett, 2012).

g. I have made use of David Ross's translations of Aristotle's
    Nicomachean Ethics and *Politics*, published in Richard McKeon's *The
    Basic Works of Aristotle* (New York: Random House, 2009).

h. Selections from Ross's translations of these works can also be found
    in *Ancient Political Thought: A Reader*, ed. Richard N. Bosley and
    Martin M. Tweedale, and published by Broadview Press, 2014.

5. The Hellenistic Philosophers and Plotinus
    Unless otherwise noted, I have taken each of the translations of the
    writings of the Hellenistic Philosophers listed here from their reprinted
    editions in *Classics of Western Philosophy*, 8th ed., ed. Steven M. Cahn
    (Indianapolis: Hackett, 2012). Specific information on the translators are
    given below.

i. Epicurus, *Letter to Menoeceus* and *The Principal Doctrines*, both from
    Hellenistic Philosophy, ed. and trans. Brad Inwood and L.P. Gerson
    (Indianapolis: Hackett: 1988).

j. Epictetus, *Encheiridion*, from *The Handbook of Epictetus*, trans.
    Nicholas White (Indianapolis: Hackett, 1983).

k. Sextus Empiricus, *Outlines of Pyrrhonism*, from *Selections from
    the Major Writings on Skepticism, Man, and God*, trans. Sanford G.
    Etheridge (Indianapolis: Hackett, 1985).

l. Plotinus, *Enneads*, from *Neoplatonic Philosophy: Introductory
    Readings*, ed. and trans. John Dillon and Lloyd P. Gerson
    (Indianapolis: Hackett, 2004). Note that in one or two instances I
    have used Elmer O'Brien's translation from *The Essential Plotinus*
    (Indianapolis: Hackett, 1984).

A NOTE FOR INSTRUCTORS

This text provides a selective overview of Ancient Philosophy from the Presocratics through Neoplatonism, spanning a period between the fifth century BCE and the second century CE. It would serve well as a companion text to a "Great Works" course, or to an introductory History of Philosophy course, in which the relevant primary sources are made available to the students either in print or through online sources.

I deal with the primary sources by explaining the overall purpose and structure of the work(s) covered in each chapter, and by critically assessing key arguments within them. The book will be most useful as a way of stimulating student thinking about, and classroom discussion of, enduring philosophical arguments from ancient sources. Given this pedagogical aim, and in order to balance the competing goals of brevity and depth, I have not spent as much time on other features of the texts as might be desired. For example, I deal relatively briefly with some of the literary features of Plato's dialogues, and I generally refrain from giving exhaustive accounts of the relevant contemporary literature, opting instead for a more direct and simple engagement with the argumentative content of the primary sources. An instructor using this text may wish to supplement it by addressing further literary and contextual aspects of the writings in their lectures.

In addition to detailed reflections on one or more primary texts, each chapter includes:

(A) A historical introduction to the relevant period that contextualizes the texts to be examined in that chapter, and

(B) A "big question" section that highlights a major philosophical problem or theme broached in a central way by the relevant texts, and that shows its relationship to perennial philosophical debates.

Topics covered in the (A) section of each chapter include, for instance, historical information about Plato's Academy and Aristotle's Lyceum, or details concerning wars and the general political situation where relevant. As an example illustrating the function of the (B) section, I discuss in chapter three the fate of the notion of the "soul" originating in Plato and sources pre-dating him, and trace the subsequent history of this notion through Aristotle and into contemporary philosophy of mind via Descartes and the mind–body problem. Including such thematic discussions can enable students to grasp the ongoing relevance of these thinkers and the problems they engage in, as well as provide instructors with suggestions for topics of in-class discussion and debate. A major goal of the book is to make the historical texts come alive, and to give students a sense of entering into the two-and-a-half-millennia-long conversation that is the Western philosophical tradition.

While Plato and Aristotle take pride of place in the volume's content, I cover a broad range of other thinkers in greater or lesser detail. I include discussions of the major Presocratic thinkers relevant to an understanding of the Platonic and Aristotelian corpus set in relief against the backdrop of the Greek mythic poets. I also connect the Sophistic movement with the figures of Socrates and Plato and present the major movements within Hellenistic Philosophy along with the emergence of Christianity and Neoplatonism. Along the way, I provide aids to approaching historical texts, such as explanations of the use of testimonies and fragments in reconstructing the thought of ancient philosophers, and of how to use the Stephanus and Bekker numbering systems (see above) in reading the texts of Plato and Aristotle.

Specific thinkers and texts covered in greater or lesser detail within the volume's eight chapters include: Homer (*Iliad*); Hesiod (*Theogony*); Thales; Anaximenes; Heraclitus; Parmenides (*Poem of Parmenides*); Socrates; Plato (*Apology, Euthyphro, Meno, Phaedo, Republic*); Aristotle (*Categories, Posterior Analytics, Physics, Metaphysics, Nicomachean Ethics, Politics*); Epicurus (*Letter to Menoeceus, Principal Doctrines*); Epictetus (*Encheiridion*); Sextus Empiricus (*Outlines of Pyrrhonism*); Jesus; Paul; Plotinus (*Enneads*); Augustine. I situate each of the texts I discuss within the larger context of the work of its author and the broader philosophical movement(s) to which the author belongs. For instance, I introduce Aristotle's *Categories* and *Posterior Analytics* as representative texts within his logical organon, epistemology, and philosophy of science, and contextualize his view of the natural world within the scheme of Ptolemaic cosmology. I discuss Epicurus in relation to earlier Greek and later Roman atomists, display the influence of leading figures of Epicureanism, Stoicism, and Skepticism on later philosophical thought, and present Plotinus within the context of "pagan" and later Christian Neoplatonism, leading into Augustine and the Medieval era. The text emphasizes continuity and development, in which each figure can be understood to some extent as building on and engaging with the thought of his or her predecessors. This emphasis serves the pedagogical function of providing students with a narrative framework within which to situate and relate various thinkers to one another.

Timeline

Greek Epic Poets and Other Ancient Figures

— Abraham (c. 2000–1800 BCE)
— Moses (c. 1600–1393 BCE)
— Homer (800–701 BCE)
— Hesiod (around 700 BCE)

Pre-Socratics

The Milesians

— Thales (625–545 BCE)
— Anaximander (610–547 BCE)
— Anaximenes (?–525 BCE)

The Eleatics (Monists)

— Xenophanes (570–478 BCE)
— Parmenides (515–460 BCE)

Pythagoreans

— Pythagoras (570–495 BCE)

Pluralists (Atomists, etc.)

— Heraclitus (540–475 BCE)
— Leucippus (fifth century BCE)
— Empedocles (492–432 BCE)
— Democritus (460–370 BCE)

Sophists

— Protagoras (490–420 BCE)
— Gorgias (483–375 BCE)
— Thrasymachus (459–400 BCE)

The Golden Age

— Socrates (469–399 BCE)
— Plato (429–347 BCE)
— Aristotle (384–322 BCE)

Ancient Figures and Dates

— Aristophanes (450–386 BCE)
— Political Golden Age of Athens under Pericles (450–430 BCE)
— Peloponnesian War with Sparta (431–404 BCE)
— Founding of Plato's Academy (386 BCE)
— Alexander the Great (356–323 BCE)
— Founding of Aristotle's Lyceum (335 BCE)

Hellenistic Philosophy

Epicureanism

— Epicurus (341–270 BCE)
— Lucretius (99–55 BCE)

Stoicism

— Zeno of Citium (334–262 BCE)
— Cleanthes (331–232 BCE)
— Chrysippus (280–207 BCE)
— Cicero (106–43 BCE)
— Seneca (4 BCE–65 CE)
— Epictetus (55–135 CE)
— Marcus Aurelius (121–180 CE)

Skepticism

— Pyrrho (360–270 BCE)
— Arcesilaus (316–241 BCE)
— Carneades (214–129 BCE)
— Sextus Empiricus (160–210 CE)

Hellenistic Political and Religious Figures and Dates

— Julius Caesar (100–44 BCE)
— Rise of Roman Empire (31 BCE)
— Augustus Caesar (63 BCE–14 CE)
— Jesus Christ (4 BCE–30 CE)
— Paul the Apostle (5–67 CE)

Neo-Platonism

— Plotinus (204–270 CE)
— Porphyry (234–305 CE)
— Iamblichus (245–330 CE)
— Proclus (412–485 CE)
— Pseudo-Dionysius (485–528 CE)

Patristic Period

Church Fathers

— Irenaeus (120–200 CE)
— Origen (185–254 CE)
— Augustine (354–430 CE)

Early Medieval Political and Religious Figures and Dates

— Emperor Constantine (272–337 CE)
— Christianity adopted as official Roman religion (381 CE)
— Roman Empire split into Western and Eastern / Byzantine (395 CE)
— Fall of Western Roman Empire (476 CE)

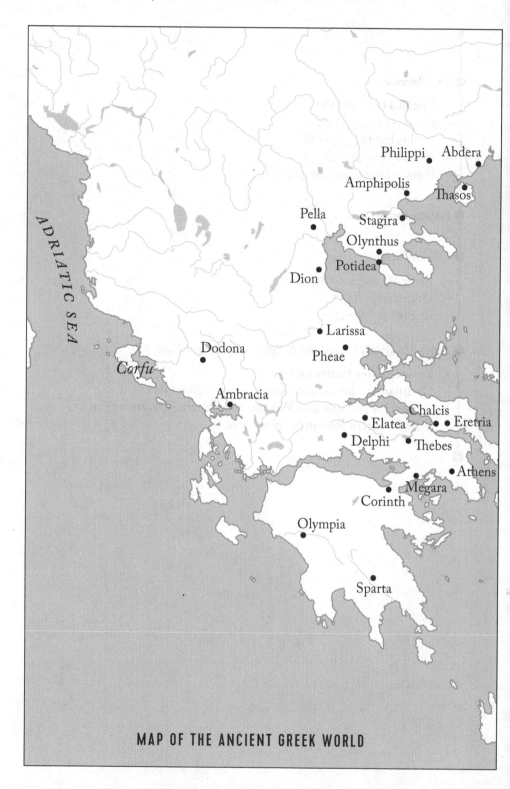

MAP OF THE ANCIENT GREEK WORLD

Byzantium

Perinthus

PROPONTIS

Maronea

Lesbos

Smyrna

Ephesus

Samos

Miletus

AEGEAN SEA

Rhodes

CYCLADES

DODECANESE

Rhodes

Crete

0   50   100 km

Chapter 1:

GREEK MYTH

AND THE

RISE OF PHILOSOPHY

Historical Context
Introductory Big Question: What Is Philosophy?
1. Greek Religion and Mythological Explanation
    a) Homer and Hesiod: Gods as Causes
2. The First Philosophers
    a) The Milesians
    b) Heraclitus and Parmenides
    c) The Atomists
    d) Enduring Themes from the Presocratics
3. Socrates, Plato, and the Sophists
    a) The Sophists
    b) Socrates and Plato
    c) Plato's *Apology* and Socratic Wisdom
    d) Plato: Early, Middle, and Late Periods
4. Conclusion

HISTORICAL CONTEXT

We are embarking on a whirlwind tour of nearly 1,000 years of the history of Western philosophy, covering the earliest beginnings of the philosophical tradition in ancient Greece all the way to the end of the Classical era and the start of the Medieval period in the Roman Empire. This chapter begins at the beginning, with a group of ancient Greek philosophers known as the Presocratics. As their name suggests, these were the philosophers who came before Socrates (well, that is true for the most part). They are defined, in relation to Socrates, as *"Pre-Socratics"* because of the foundational importance of Socrates (along with his student Plato) for the

Western tradition. The approach I'll be taking to these thinkers will reflect the historical consensus on the relative importance of Socrates, and will focus on themes in Presocratic philosophy that we will see playing out later on in the thought of Socrates, Plato, and Aristotle. By the end of this chapter, we'll have had a chance to think a bit about the life and philosophy of Socrates as well. But even the Presocratics themselves need to be situated in the context of the historical period preceding them. So we'll actually be starting our historical survey with a brief look at the Greek poets Homer and Hesiod. It's time to climb into your time-travel machine and buckle your seatbelts for a journey back to the roots of Western philosophy.

INTRODUCTORY BIG QUESTION: WHAT IS PHILOSOPHY?

I'll be starting off each chapter with a short commentary on a major theme that relates to the content of that entire chapter. Here is a central question of the present chapter: "What is the nature, and what are the goals, of the discipline we call philosophy?" Interestingly, this question about the nature of philosophy is part of the discipline of philosophy itself, which is one of the things that makes philosophy different from most other fields of study. Most engineers and computer scientists spend little time reflecting on the overall meaning and significance of engineering or computer science. By contrast, it makes sense that philosophy would be uncertain about what philosophy itself is, given that the way you answer the question "What is philosophy?" depends on the answers you give to many other philosophical questions. For instance: "What is the purpose of human life?" "What is a good human life, and how can a person attain it?" "What is real and what is possible for us to know?" "What kind of thing is a human being anyway?" "Is a human person merely one collection of material particles among other such collections, or is there something more to being a human person?" "Does God exist, or are we alone in the universe?" "If God does exist, does God interact with or care about us?" Different people answer these interrelated questions in different ways, and as a result they understand philosophy in different ways. Some think of philosophy as a technical discipline whose role is to solve abstract theoretical problems. Others view it as primarily an attitude of openness to reality, or even as a way of life, verging on the mystical urge to become one with the universe. For some, the boundaries between philosophy and religion or spirituality are porous; for others, there is a hard and fast divide between them that cannot be crossed.

Regardless of these differences, philosophy is commonly understood to be the most general of all fields of study. It asks the biggest and broadest questions that human beings can ask. If you are like me and you want to know *everything*, then philosophy is a good bet, since it is practically impossible to know everything; but in philosophy you can at least study everything in a general way. Philosophy is also arguably the most critical of all disciplines. Philosophers do not remain content with commonplace views, but critically assess and examine even the most basic assumptions we hold in our search for ultimate explanations and answers. This is part of the reason why practically-minded people tend to think of philosophers as rather useless at best, and as troublemakers at worst.

The idea of a search for ultimate answers brings us to the Classical concept of philosophy, itself originating in the thought of Socrates, Plato, and Aristotle, as "the love of wisdom." Understood in this way, philosophy is the *desire for* and *pursuit of* **wisdom**, rather than its attainment. As such, it suggests a way of life lived in active pursuit of the goal of wisdom, rather than merely the analysis of an abstract set of doctrines and propositions. But what is wisdom? What is this goal that the philosopher pursues? Classical thought understands wisdom as having a theoretical side and a practical side. Theoretically, wisdom is the state of knowing the ultimate causes of things. On the practical side, it involves knowing what a good human life—in other words, *happiness*—consists in, and how to reach it. In both its theoretical and its practical aspects, the possibility of wisdom depends on our ability to grasp the *truth* about these matters. Today, truth is a hotly debated concept that people understand in various ways, or even deny altogether. For the most part, the Classical Greek thinkers accepted that it is at least *possible* for us to know the truth, even if we only get a partial view of it. And this makes intuitive sense. After all, if it's impossible to reach the truth, why are human beings so driven to seek it out?

The idea that there might actually be answers to our deepest questions out there is at the very least intriguing. But the quest for truth is not unique to philosophers. Religion is another major human enterprise that has historically tended to seek out the ultimate explanations of things and to understand what human happiness consists in. In the next section, we will consider the way philosophy emerged out of a generally religious context, as a relatively new way of proceeding in the search for the ultimate truths.

1. GREEK RELIGION AND MYTHOLOGICAL EXPLANATION

It is a commonplace to state that Western philosophy and science began with the Ancient Greek-speaking thinkers known to us as the Presocratic philosophers. The story begins with a wise man named Thales in a city called Miletus in Ionia (part of present-day Turkey) who famously predicted a solar eclipse in 585 BCE. Thales and the other Presocratics began a revolutionary new approach to thinking about the world. What distinguished these men from their predecessors in a way that warrants these claims? Many have seen the Presocratics as representing a movement away from religion and mythology toward reason and rational argumentation. There is something correct about this way of describing the situation, but it is also ambiguous in a way that can easily lead to misunderstanding.

Procession of Twelve Gods and Goddesses: Hestia, Hermes, Aphrodite, Ares, Demeter, Hephaestus, Hera, Poseidon, Athena, Zeus, Artemis, Apollo. From a Greek marble carving of unknown date

For one thing, it is not true that before Thales came on the scene nobody knew how to use reason and people were straightforwardly irrational. Prior to the Presocratics, people still held beliefs that were more or less justified, given the state of information available to them, and could draw inferences from those beliefs to other beliefs. But with the Presocratics, the *starting points* and *methods* employed by reason underwent a significant shift. For another thing, it is not the case that once the Presocratics got going, they left religion and mythology behind. From Thales all the way through to Aristotle and beyond, Classical Greek philosophical thought operated with a sense of the divine; for these first great philosophers, an understanding of God or the gods was frequently (even usually) an integral part of the wisdom the philosopher was seeking. *What really distinguished the first philosophers from the earlier writers and thinkers was their willingness to rework and rethink inherited conceptions of the divine.*

In what comes next I will first give some indications of the way in which pre-Presocratic authors, in particular the poets Homer and Hesiod, used myth and religious conceptions as ways of explaining phenomena. After that, I'll be taking you on a brief tour through the Presocratic thinkers themselves to illustrate the ways in which their approach to explaining the world differed from that of the poets. Given the necessary limitations of this survey of the history of Western philosophy, the present discussion will serve to set the stage for the thinkers we'll be mainly concerned with in most of the rest of the book, namely Socrates, Plato, and Aristotle.

a) Homer and Hesiod: Gods as Causes

The *Iliad* and the *Odyssey*, written by the Greek epic poet known to us as Homer (around 850 BCE—dates uncertain), give us some of the earliest surviving written material in Western culture. For the Greeks of the later period in which Socrates, Plato, and Aristotle lived, these texts played a cultural and educational role similar to the role the Bible played in Medieval Europe, or to the role played by the works of Shakespeare in the West until relatively recently. Both the *Iliad* and the *Odyssey* relate events connected to the Trojan War, which may be familiar to you (in a woefully inaccurate form) from films like *Troy* (2004), which starred Brad Pitt as Achilles, the Greek hero and demi-god around whom much of the action of Homer's *Iliad* revolves.

The *Iliad* has been described as a reflection on the causes and effects of the wrath of Achilles. Here is the opening line: "Sing, O goddess, the anger of Achilles son of Pereus, that brought countless ills upon the Achaeans." Throughout the poem, gods and goddesses show an interest in, and capacity to make things happen to, mortal human beings. For instance, different gods and goddesses support or oppose warriors from the Trojan or the Greek side. At one point the god Apollo deceives Achilles by appearing to him as a Trojan soldier, and as a result, the Trojans escape defeat in that part of the battle. We clearly have here a way of *explaining* things (historical events), and so a way of using *reason* to understand the phenomena being considered. But these explanations appeal to divine beings as causes. This leads us to ask, "Isn't it irrational to explain what takes place in the human sphere by appealing to the actions and intentions of divine beings?" Not necessarily. Given that a person believes that divine beings like those described by Homer exist, it would hardly seem right to call that person "irrational" for believing that divine beings can influence human affairs. "But," you might respond, "isn't it irrational to believe in divine beings like the Greek gods and goddesses in the first place?" Again, I think the answer is "It depends."

It would probably be irrational for someone living in twenty-first century North America to believe in the Homeric gods. The evidence we have available to us supports the non-existence of those beings. But would it have been irrational for someone living in ancient Greece to believe in them? Even if we say that such a person's beliefs would be *false* (since the Greek gods do not exist), that does not necessarily make it *irrational* for her to hold those beliefs. Roughly speaking, we are justified in believing a statement, even if it is false, when the evidence available to us supports it. A typical Greek would have heard about the gods in stories from trusted sources like their parents and relatives, and would have had the existence of the gods reinforced by society at large through various religious ceremonies, and by their own experience of prayer and of life's events, of which the accounts of the gods would have helped them to make sense. The gods were basic to the meaning and values that made up ancient Greek culture. That being the case, it would have seemed entirely reasonable to the average Greek to accept the existence of the gods, and to think their actions were part of the explanation of why things happen.

Homer tended to focus on the ways the gods impacted human life and events; Hesiod has them playing explanatory roles on a much bigger stage. Hesiod's seventh-century BCE poem *Theogony* provides a **cosmology**—an account of how

Homer (eighth–seventh century BCE)

the cosmos (world or universe) came to be the way it is now—by telling about the origin and nature of the gods. Hesiod begins with an extended description of the way he received his information, namely by **divine revelation** from the Muses, the daughters of Zeus, the king of the gods. These Muses, he says, "breathed in me an inspired voice so I might celebrate what will be and what has been, and they bid me to hymn the clan of the blessed ones who always are and to sing of them first and last" (lines 32–34). Around lines 104–15 Hesiod requests that the Muses tell him "how the gods and Gaia first came into being and rivers and boundless sea raging with swell and the shining stars and wide Ouranos above." In the course of their account, the Muses describe how Chaos and Gaia were the first to be created, and how all the other major and minor deities were produced from them, either asexually or sexually.

The goddess Gaia is a personification of the earth, and she first produces Ouranos, a male god who personifies heaven. Among the deities produced from these primordial figures we find Pontos (god of the sea) and Okeanos (the ocean god). Hesiod is giving us two things at the same time: a series of myths about divine beings *and* a description of the origin of the cosmos. Clearly, this mythic poet held a view of nature as imbued with divine meaning and presence. One of the strangest parts of Hesiod's account is the story of how Kronos hated his father Ouranos and, at the request of his mother Gaia, cut off his father's genitals and threw them into the sea (lines 175–80). Giants and Nymphs were produced from the blood that spurted from Ouranos's severed manhood onto the land, and in the sea his body parts generated a foam from which Aphrodite (goddess of erotic love) emerged. While it would be nearly impossible for a contemporary North American to take these stories seriously as literal historical or factual accounts, we can nevertheless appreciate the drive toward understanding the big picture, and the ultimate causes, that is embodied in them.

All this goes to show that before the Presocratics, the way people explained events cannot simply be called irrational. Taking Homer and Hesiod as representative of the mythological, religious approach to understanding the world, we can see that the intentions and actions of the gods could be invoked in explaining both how the world came to be the way it is (the question of origins) and why things now happen the way they do (the explanation of ongoing phenomena). But such explanations cannot properly be called scientific or philosophical. The move toward what we might call *scientific* rationality begins with the Presocratics.

2. THE FIRST PHILOSOPHERS

What distinguished the earliest Greek philosophers from the poets and religious thinkers who came before them? We can answer in brief by pointing to two key characteristics of the Presocratics. First, the Presocratics attempted to explain the phenomena of the world around them by appealing primarily to natural (as opposed to supernatural) realities. Second, they relied on experience and argument (as opposed to divine or poetic inspiration) to establish their claims. I have organized this section with the goal of showing how these two characteristics apply from Thales up to Democritus, who was a contemporary of Socrates and Plato. (By the way, it is worth pointing out that the term "Presocratics" is a bit funny since at least a few of the thinkers in this category lived around the same time as Socrates.) Despite the two characteristics mentioned above, the early philosophers were far from being atheists. Although they tended to reject traditional ways of thinking about the gods, they continued to believe in a divine reality. One of the few direct quotations of Thales we possess (from Aristotle's *On the Soul*, 11a22) has him claiming that "all things are full of gods." The early Presocratic thinker Xenophanes of Colophon (b. 570 BCE) gives the most direct attack on the anthropomorphic deities of the tradition represented by Homer and Hesiod. But he concludes from this not that no gods exist, but that the true conception of the divine is the idea of a single being completely unlike human beings, who (according to a testimony from Simplicius) "without effort ... shakes all things by the thought of his mind."[1]

Before getting further into a discussion of the trajectory of Greek philosophy leading up to Socrates, it is worth pausing to take stock of the situation we historians of philosophy are in as we try to find out what the Presocratic philosophers thought. Obviously we do not possess the original manuscripts of their writings, which were produced so many centuries ago. In fact, given how long ago these people lived and wrote (and given how expensive and difficult it was to reproduce written works prior to the invention of the printing press in the 1440s CE) it is astonishing that we know anything at all about their ideas. Much of the time we do not even have copies (of copies of copies ...) of what the philosophers themselves wrote. What we do have are **fragments** (sayings or passages found in copies of copies of the writings of later authors which are thought to be direct quotations of the original authors) and **testimonies** (paraphrases of the sayings and views of the original thinkers also found in later authors). For this reason, studying the thought of

---

1 Cohen et al., p. 22.

a given Presocratic thinker is a bit like trying to reconstruct a 1,000-piece puzzle from three or four pieces (the fragments) along with descriptions by other people of what the puzzle once looked like (testimonies). (By way of comparison, note that, given the relatively greater importance the ancients placed on preserving the works of Plato and Aristotle, we are much more confident that our critical editions of their works reflect fairly closely what they originally wrote.)

You might take the situation concerning the views of the Presocratic philosophers as an exciting challenge (if you're an optimistic sort of person) or as a frustrating obstacle (if you're a more pessimistic type). Actually, the comparison I just made to reconstructing a puzzle probably leans unrealistically toward the side of optimism. We cannot even be certain that these fragments are in fact parts of the original puzzle. The sources from which we gather our bits and pieces of evidence are written by authors who have their own agendas, and they quote from or paraphrase the earlier authors within that context. One such source is Aristotle, who often wanted to show how all thinkers who came before him were fumbling toward the very views which he himself would later express. How likely is it, we might wonder, that he presented their views with impartial objectivity?

Now that we know that we may not know very much at all about the views of these thinkers, without further ado, let's move on to a discussion of the views themselves.

a) The Milesians

Discussions of the Presocratics standardly begin with a group of three men from the city of Miletus in Ionia in the sixth century BCE. Although this city was on the other side of the Aegean sea from Athens, its citizens were allied with Athens. **Thales** (625–545 BCE) is generally acknowledged to have been the first philosopher in the Western tradition. One of the seven sages of ancient Greece, Thales famously predicted a solar eclipse in 585 BCE. But his star-gazing also gained him the reputation of being impractical and absent-minded; Plato recounts a story about Thales falling into a well while staring up at the stars, only to be mocked by a servant girl (*Theatetus* 174a).

One of the big ideas of the Milesian philosophers was that some single unifying principle lay beneath the diversity of physical things. For this reason we can refer to them as *materialistic monists*, that is, people who believe that in the final analysis there is only one sort of material reality that everything else is made of. These men asked, "How do different things (tomatoes, snails, mountains) come to be and perish?" Such things clearly must come to be *from* some prior reality, and when they cease to be, they must also cease to be *into* something else. But what might that basic, underlying something be? Thales seems to have thought it was water. In his view, everything comes from water and returns to water. Water is the unifying cosmic principle that explains how change takes place within the natural world.

We can only speculate about Thales's reasons for coming to this conclusion. But with his student **Anaximander** (d. 547 BCE) and with **Anaximenes** (d. 525 BCE) after him, the basic idea of a single, unifying principle becomes clearer. Anaximander argued that water was too definite a thing to act as the basic underlying stuff out of which everything in the universe emerges. Instead, this basic stuff had to be without any definite character, in order that it might take on the character of anything that comes out of it. For Anaximander, the only thing that could do the job was the *apeiron*, which can be translated as "the boundless" or "the indefinite." Anaximenes had his own idea of what the basic stuff of the cosmos consists in; he says it is air. He reasoned that since air is capable of compression and expansion, it gives us not only a more precise sort of stuff than the nebulous *apeiron* of Anaximander, but it also allows us to describe the processes (condensation and rarefaction) by which the one basic stuff becomes other things—the denser elements of water and earth, or the more rarified element of fire. In the thinking of the Milesians, both the realities and the causal mechanisms appealed to in these large-scale attempts to explain and understand the nature and working of the natural world are themselves thoroughly natural, leaving aside the appeals to supernatural divine beings that we found in Homer and Hesiod.

b) Heraclitus and Parmenides

The next thinker who offered what looks like a solution to the problem of change and the unity of the natural world was **Heraclitus** of Ephesus (540–475 BCE), who claimed that everything comes from and returns to fire. "All things," says Heraclitus, "are an exchange for fire and fire for all things, as goods for gold and gold for goods."[2] Plato, in his dialogue entitled *Theatetus*, depicts Heraclitus as ascribing to the view that all physical reality is in flux, that is, constantly changing. While this account gets at one side of the story—fire is constantly burning and hence in constant, dynamic motion—the other side of the story is that in the course of its constant burning fire remains the same—it continues to be fire. So there is also a constancy and order to the universe, which Heraclitus referred to as the *logos*. To grasp this two-fold picture of reality as changing and remaining the same, I find that it helps to think of the flame of a candle. As long as the air in the room is calm, the flame looks like a motionless source of light. But of course we know that the very constancy of the flame is also at the same time an energy-rich process of motion (what we now call combustion). This view of reality expresses Heraclitus's theory of the unity of opposites, a theory that he presents in short, pithy proverbs or riddles, such as "The road up and the road down are one and the same," "We step into and we do not step into the same rivers. We are and we are not."[3] The same view appears again in a quotation in

2   Cohen et al., p. 31.
3   Cohen et al., p. 30.

which Heraclitus shows disdain for the poet Hesiod: "Most men's teacher is Hesiod. They are sure he knew most things—a man who could not recognize day and night; for they are one."[4]

I mentioned Plato's depiction of Heraclitus as an adherent of the flux theory (everything is constantly changing). Plato contrasts Heraclitus with **Parmenides** of Elea (b. 515 BCE), who held exactly the opposite view: according to *The Poem of Parmenides*, nothing ever changes. For Parmenides, change is simply an illusion. This surprising conclusion follows, Parmenides believes, from claims made earlier in his poem. The poem describes Parmenides being taken by chariot to meet a goddess, who then guides him through the distinct ways of truth and of seeming. The way of truth (or, we might say, the way of *reason*) is also the way of *being*, since it is not possible to think about non-being. The goddess asserts: "the same thing is for thinking and for being," and "[t]hat which is there to be spoken and thought of must be."[5] For this reason, she tells us, we must always hold back from thinking "that things that are not, are."[6] From this starting point, Parmenides infers that reality is eternal, indestructible, indivisible, and unchanging. Reality or Being could not have begun, nor could it end, for that would involve non-being (a time when being was not). But non-being is unthinkable. Hence reality is timeless. Change would also require non-being, since when something changes, what existed at one point ceases to be and is replaced by something else that comes to be, presumably out of non-being, since beforehand the reality in question *was not*. The conclusion follows, Parmenides thinks, that there is no such thing as change. Instead, reality can be thought of as a massive, perfectly homogenous block of pure Being. It can best be represented as a sphere, since everything on the circumference of a sphere is equally distant from the centre, and in Being, there is no reason for any aspect of it to be different from any other aspect. For, again, if that were the case, we would be involving non-being in our thinking.

The views of Heraclitus and Parmenides, as well as those of the Milesians, sound somewhat unusual to our ears. "Nothing ever changes?" You may be thinking to yourself, "What could be less likely?" Granted, few contemporary thinkers would be inclined to think that everything is really water or fire either. But even if we reject their conclusions, we should not simply dismiss the views of the Presocratics without appreciating the problem they were wrestling with. They were trying to discover, at the most fundamental level, what reality is like, and how different aspects of reality come to be the way they are. Crucially, they wondered how to account for the changes we observe around us every day; by what natural processes and causes are these changes produced? These are problems that have been with us ever since, and it would not be too much of a stretch

---

4 Cohen et al., p. 30.
5 Cohen et al., p. 37.
6 Cohen et al., p. 38.

to say that they are the same problems the natural sciences have been trying to answer right up to the present day. So we have to applaud these thinkers for asking the right questions, and for getting on to the rudiments of a method for answering them. The **Atomists**, the last group of Presocratic thinkers we'll be discussing, give us answers to these questions that feel a lot more familiar to the way we think about things today.

c) The Atomists

The Greek Atomists can be seen as combining the views of Heraclitus and Parmenides. Like Parmenides, they believed that reality was constituted by something unchanging and eternal. But while Parmenides claimed there was only one such entity, the Atomists said there were many. For this reason they are among the group of Presocratics known as **Pluralists**. Unlike the Monists, the Pluralists believed that physical reality is made up of many different basic forms. The Atomists called the building blocks of reality *atoms*, a word meaning "uncuttables." Like Heraclitus and unlike Parmenides, they understood change to be a real and fundamental aspect of reality. They accounted for this change in terms of the combining and disjoining of atoms. According to the Atomists, all composite things (things that have parts) come to be out of the interactions between the basic indivisible atomic parts of physical reality. In this way, they provided an ingenious solution to the problem of change that had so driven the earlier Presocratic thinkers. Change could be accounted for without appealing to non-being, since everything that comes to be (composite bodies) comes to be from things that always exist (atoms).

Among the first of the Atomists are **Leucippus** (fifth century, exact dates unknown) and his student **Democritus** (b. 460 BCE in a city called Abdera). Democritus was a contemporary of Socrates and Plato, and Aristotle engaged with his views at some length. According to Democritus, the cosmos is composed of atoms and the void—the empty space in which the atoms move. (It does have to be admitted that the void of the Atomists looks pretty much like nothingness, so that it isn't really entirely true to say that they could account for change without non-being.) Atoms cannot be seen, but they have different sizes and shapes. They collide randomly and become entangled with each other because of the tiny hooks or other structures on their surfaces, and this combination results in the generation of the macroscopic physical bodies we see around us (e.g., rocks, lakes, plants, and animals) and the entire physical cosmos.

As we will see later on in our presentation of Hellenistic philosophy, Epicurus also elaborates an atomistic system derived from Democritus. Perhaps more than any other ancient thinkers, the Atomists took explanation by reference to physical or natural entities to the extreme, leaving very little place for the activities of supernatural beings. Yet Democritus and later Epicurus both find some room for the gods, though only as physical bodies composed of especially fine atoms. The thoroughgoing materialism of the Atomists stands out in strong contrast to most of the thinkers we'll be considering later on. The first of these, Socrates and Plato, will be the subject of the next part of this chapter, following some concluding remarks on the Presocratics.

d) Enduring Themes from the Presocratics

Several of the themes we've come across in our tour of the Presocratics will be popping up again in later parts of this course, so it is worth summarizing them here in brief as we conclude our short tour of the earliest Greek Philosophers.

Theme 1: There is a difference between appearance and reality. To understand what reality is really like, we have to go beyond what our senses and common-sense opinions tell us. The Presocratic thinkers and their followers are both very interested in answering the *metaphysical* question, "What is really (or ultimately) real, and what is merely apparently real?" In the course of attempting to answer this question, they are also forced to face the *epistemological* questions of how we can know what is real and what methods are appropriate to achieving genuine knowledge of reality.

Theme 2: The picture of the gods inherited from Homer and Hesiod must be revised. None of the Presocratics outright denies the existence of a divine reality. Even the materialistic Atomists cannot fairly be described as atheists. But neither do they simply repeat the stories of the poets about the gods. Instead, they use rational criteria to yield accounts of what the gods are like rather than relying on poetic or divine inspiration. This rethinking of the divine will be apparent in Socrates, Plato, and Aristotle, and again in later Hellenistic thought and in the Neoplatonism that was influential throughout the Medieval era.

Theme 3: We come to understand the nature of things and their causes by means of reasoned argument. This theme relates to both of the previous two. Reason and argument are the tools we need to penetrate beyond the appearances offered by our senses and opinions to the underlying reality of things. And the correct philosophical and scientific methods will show us how to make use of reason and argumentation to produce an understanding of whatever can be understood by human beings, including what the divine aspect(s) of reality are like. Questions about the role of philosophy and science in knowing the ultimate things will be with us throughout the rest of the course.

On the basis of these three themes, we can see the Presocratics as forming part of a common philosophical tradition that leads through Socrates, Plato, and Aristotle, right through the Medieval, and arguably through the Modern period. Of course there are also major differences that must be considered when we look at specific movements and individual thinkers from these later periods. This book will indicate points of continuity and divergence as we move across the centuries that make up the Classical period of Western philosophy.

3. SOCRATES, PLATO, AND THE SOPHISTS

In this section, I'm first going to discuss another group of ancient thinkers called the Sophists, about whom we need to know something in order to understand much of what Socrates and Plato are talking about. In the second part, I provide some background information about the historical figures Socrates and Plato and their relationship to one another. In the fourth part, I discuss one of Plato's works, the *Apology*, in order to highlight key aspects of Plato's portrait of Socrates.

a) The Sophists

The word "sophist" derives from the Greek word for wisdom (*sophia*). Roughly translating, then, we can think of these travelling teachers of wisdom as "wise guys." Active in the fifth century BCE as travelling educators, the Sophists have had a bad reputation throughout history since their own time, largely because of Plato's depiction of them. In one of his later dialogues, Plato defines a sophist as someone who practices the art of preying on rich young men for the sake of taking their money in exchange for the imparting of skills that make them *appear* to be wise (*Sophist*, 226a). That does not sound like a particularly flattering job description! The Sophists were paid well by their clients. They taught their students to speak persuasively and win arguments using debating techniques and rhetoric. These were particularly important skills in the Athenian society of the day, where political assemblies and courts of law were a significant part of life. It was common to criticize the sophists by saying that they "make the weak argument stronger" (*Apology* 18b). This most likely referred to their ability to take any position in a debate and, by using rhetorical tricks, to successfully defeat their opponent.

This brings us to the nub of the complaint Plato had against the sophists. Someone who argues just for the sake of winning arguments (and teaches others to do the same) does not really care about attaining the truth or becoming wise. As far as philosophy is concerned, in Plato's eyes, these men were mere pretenders. As Plato presents him, Socrates is just the opposite. He is willing to sacrifice his time, his career, even his very life for the pursuit of wisdom and truth. He is the paradigmatic lover of wisdom. But as we will see when we consider Plato's *Apology*, many people thought there were enough similarities between Socrates and the Sophists to identify him as one of them. These would have painted a different picture of Socrates.

I won't be able to go into details about the individual Sophists, several of whom appear in Plato's dialogues (in fact, four of his dialogues are named after individual Sophists). Instead, I will discuss one Sophist and let him stand as a representative of the others. The one I'm referring to is **Protagoras** (490–420 BCE). Protagoras is most famous for holding to a version of **subjective relativism**, the view (roughly) that truth depends on perception, so that whenever something is true, it is only true *for someone*. As a result, something may be true for me (because I perceive it as true) but not be true for you (because you perceive it as false). Protagoras's famous saying goes like this: "A human being is the measure of all things, of those things that are, that they are, and of those things that are not, that they are not" (reported in Plato's *Theatetus*, 151e). If all truth is relative to the individual, as Protagoras appears to be claiming, it follows that there is no way things are in themselves, objectively, independently of individual perceptions and beliefs. A consequence of this view—which comes up in Plato's *Republic* in the speech of Thrasymachus, another Sophist—is that morality becomes a matter of convention, so that there is no objective right or wrong. Socrates, along with Plato and Aristotle, will reject all of this, claiming that an absolute truth does in fact exist, and that morality is not purely conventional. The Sophists' apparent rejection of objective truth fits in nicely with their emphasis on skills that enabled people to win arguments, a pursuit that Plato predictably rejects as unworthy of a true philosopher.

Socrates (469–399 BCE)

b) Socrates and Plato

In the minds of many people, Socrates is the founding father of the discipline of philosophy as we know it, at least in the Western tradition. While the Presocratics focused on "natural philosophy," which was basically an early and rudimentary form of physics, with Socrates we find the first truly significant development of the major branches of philosophy proper: Logic, Metaphysics, and Ethics. This is an impressive accomplishment, given that as far as we know, Socrates himself never wrote anything down. Because of this, everything we know about Socrates depends on what others wrote about him. Our main source for information about Socrates is Plato, who was a student of Socrates. Plato wrote for the most part in the literary form of dialogue. Most of his works read almost as plays that could have been performed, and Socrates is nearly always the main character. In his dialogues, Plato explicitly contrasts Socrates with the Sophists. As I mentioned earlier, not everyone agreed with Plato's presentation of his teacher and hero. In fact, the comic poet **Aristophanes** (c. 450–386 BCE) wrote a play entitled *The Clouds*, in which he depicts Socrates as both a paradigmatic sophist and a natural philosopher in the Presocratic style. Walking with his head literally in the clouds, teaching people tricks to win arguments, Aristophanes's Socrates also instructs people to give up the worship of traditional gods and worship the clouds instead.

There were indeed significant similarities between Socrates and the Sophists. As we will see when we start working through some of Plato's early dialogues, Socrates was, like the Sophists, a sort of educator who spent most of his time engaging in discussion and debate on topics having to do with ethics. In these early dialogues, we often find Socrates refuting his discussion partners' views, often leading to frustration and even anger on their part. You could fairly easily understand how a person watching Socrates in action might conclude that he belonged to the same species as the Sophists who were haunting Athens and other Greek cities of the day. One of the main purposes of Plato's *Apology*, to which we will turn shortly, is to defend Socrates's reputation against the charge of being a Sophist. If you haven't read the *Apology* yet, it would be a good time to do so before reading further.

c) Plato: Early, Middle, and Late Periods

Before discussing the content of the *Apology*, I should make one more remark about the different periods in Plato's writings. There is significant consensus among scholars that Plato's dialogues can be grouped into early, middle, and late periods. The **early dialogues**, like the *Euthyphro*, which we will be looking at in the next chapter, arguably come closest to representing the historical Socrates. It would be an oversimplification to see these early dialogues as mere written recordings of conversations that Socrates actually had with people in and around the public places of Athens. Plato presents these conversations with a high level of dramatic skill and philosophical flair. Nevertheless, they probably do give us a window through which we can get a good idea of Socrates's life and activity. These early dialogues follow a pattern: Socrates typically questions his interlocutors (conversation partners) about their understanding of a certain term or position (for example, "What is holiness?" or "Can virtue be taught?" or "Is it always better to be just than to be unjust?"). Almost invariably, Socrates examines the answers provided by his discussion partner and shows that they are unsatisfactory. He systematically refutes his interlocutor's claims, showing that the definitions offered are too specific, or that the views proposed contradict other things the interlocutor believes. This method of examining a person's beliefs and opinions using questions and answers is what we refer to as the **Socratic Method**. It can also be called the elenchic method, after the Greek word *elenchus* meaning "refutation," since it did not tend to yield positive results but only the negation (or rejection) of various views and opinions. The early dialogues typically end inconclusively; Socrates does not provide answers to the questions raised by these dialogues: he simply lets things rest with the refutation of the mistaken views of others.

By contrast to the early Socratic dialogues, in the **dialogues of Plato's middle period**, to which the *Meno*, *Phaedo*, and *Republic* belong, Socrates begins to expound positive doctrines and theories and to provide answers of his own to the questions raised. This difference has led scholars to conclude that the Socrates of the middle period acts less as a window into the historical Socrates and his activities, and more as a mouthpiece for Plato to express his own views. For this reason,

Plato (429–347 BCE)

people sometimes refer to the middle dialogues as "Platonic" dialogues, as opposed to the earlier, "Socratic" dialogues. In some of these middle dialogues, Socrates turns from the ethical focus of the early period to examine logical and metaphysical topics. The **Theory of the Forms**, which we will discuss at some length in later chapters, is a particularly important example of this.

We can distinguish **Plato's late dialogues** from those of the middle period by the feature of self-criticism, and by the expansion of the views that Plato (via the character of Socrates) expressed in the middle period. Sometimes the views Plato presented in the middle dialogues come under attack by other thinkers in the dialogues of the later period. For instance, in the *Parmenides*, we find a young Socrates in discussion with the great Presocratic philosopher, Parmenides. Socrates presents the Theory of the Forms in much the same way it appeared in the middle dialogues, but Parmenides raises objection after objection against the theory, leaving Socrates more or less speechless. Parmenides then takes over the conversation, and embarks on some highly complicated speculation about the nature of the one and the many. We will not be looking at any of the late dialogues, but if you study Plato in greater depth, they are required reading for a complete understanding of this multifaceted thinker.

The view of Plato's dialogues I have just been discussing is not the only possible view, but it is one that many scholars find helpful. It pins the historical person known to us by the name of Socrates to the earlier works of Plato, and depicts him as a man devoted to debate and discussion in search of answers to some big ethical issues. Since the way of life the Socrates of these early works embodied was in many ways very similar to that of the Sophists, Plato faced a difficult task in distinguishing Socrates from that group. He took up this task in the first "great work" of Western philosophy we're going to be looking at, namely, the *Apology*.

Table 1: Plato's Dialogues

EARLY	MIDDLE	LATE
Apology	*Cratylus*	*Critias*
Charmides	*Euthydemus*	*Sophist*
Crito	*Meno*	*Statesman*
Euthyphro	*Phaedo*	*Timaeus*
Gorgias	*Phaedrus*	*Philebus*
Hippias Minor	*Republic*	*Laws*
Hippias Major	*Symposium*	*Parmenides*
Ion	*Theaetetus*	
Laches		
Lysis		
Protagoras		

Note that these classifications are disputed. A number of other texts are also sometimes attributed to Plato, including the *First Alcibiades*, *Clitophon*, and *Menexenus*.

d) Plato's Apology *and Socratic Wisdom*

Plato's *Apology* is the defense speech Socrates gives at his own trial. As a result, it contains little in the way of dialogue. The trial and execution of Socrates provides the dramatic backdrop for several of Plato's dialogues besides this one, including the *Euthyphro* and the *Phaedo*, which we'll be looking at in later chapters. For Plato, these events marked the epitome of the injustice of the Athenian society of his day. And given that they involved the trial and death of his greatest hero and mentor, it is not surprising that Plato often took the opportunity to ponder on their implications.

In the defense speech, Plato has Socrates respond to two groups of charges. The first, explicitly brought against him by the prosecutor Meletus, is the charge of impiety. Socrates, says Meletus, disbelieves in the traditional Greek gods and invents new gods, and he spreads this impiety among the youth of Athens, thus corrupting them. The second group of charges, reflecting almost exactly the portrait of Socrates presented by Aristophanes, accuses Socrates of being both a Sophist and a natural philosopher of the Presocratic variety. At that time, these charges would have implied that Socrates was an enemy to the tried and tested religious traditions of Greek culture and possibly to the social order itself. These last charges were more serious and difficult, Socrates says, because they involved deeply rooted, unspoken prejudices against him, based on the reputation he had acquired in the course of engaging in constant philosophical conversation and debate. To defend himself against the charge of being a Sophist, then, Socrates had to provide the background story of how he came to live a life of dedication to philosophy.

This story began when a friend of Socrates named Chaerephon visited the oracle of Delphi—a prophetess of Apollo, the Greek god of music, healing, light, and truth. His friend asked the oracle whether there was anyone wiser than Socrates, and the oracle replied that no one was wiser. Hearing this, Socrates made it his aim to disprove the oracle by finding someone who was in fact wiser than himself. He started by examining the political leaders (whom, one would hope, have some measure of wisdom), and found that although many of them viewed themselves as wise and knowledgeable, in fact none of them really knew what they were talking about. From there he went on to question the poets, and then the craftsmen, and found—to his dismay—that none of them possessed wisdom. Of course, in the process of questioning all these people, Socrates made a fair number of enemies. It seems, unsurprisingly, that the people of Athens did not enjoy being made to look like idiots in front of their friends and the crowds of people who followed Socrates around!

Socrates concluded from all this that the oracle was correct, and that he was indeed the wisest of all. But this was not because he possessed any great knowledge of truly important things. Rather, his wisdom consisted in knowing that he did not know anything of real importance. The only reason his condition was preferable to that of other people was that, while neither he nor they possessed true knowledge, other people thought that they did, while Socrates was at least aware of his ignorance (*Apology*, 21d). So we get the famous saying of Socrates that wisdom consists in knowing that you don't know anything.

We have to take Socrates's claim to not to know anything with a grain or two of salt. Clearly Socrates knew many things. For instance, he knew that his name was Socrates and that he was not a Sophist. He retained a good deal of information about history and poetry and other topics. More significantly, Socrates's lack of wisdom did not prevent him from holding very strong convictions about what was good for himself and for the people of Athens. Consider the following remarks Socrates makes in a later stage of his defense speech:

> I cherish and love you, men of Athens, but I am more obedient to the god
> than to you, and so long as I have breath and am able I will not cease seeking
> wisdom and appealing and demonstrating to every one of you I come across,
> saying my customary things: Best of men, you are an Athenian, of the greatest
> and most renowned city in regard to wisdom and power. Are you not ashamed
> that you care about how you will acquire as much money as possible, and repu-
> tation and honor, while you do not care or worry about wisdom and truth and
> how your soul might be as good as possible? (29d–e)

Socrates not only believed the things he was saying here, but was willing to back them up with his very life. What sort of things can we say he held to be true from this passage and elsewhere in the speech? For one, he believed that wisdom, truth, and the condition of a person's soul were of higher value than material possessions and honour. For another, he believed that he had been ordered by a god (Apollo) to follow the philosophical lifestyle he was following. Socrates regarded his devotion to philosophy as a divinely appointed mission; in his eyes, the philosophical life was also a deeply religious life. Finally, Socrates asserts that "there has never been a greater good for the city than my service to the god" (30a), because Athens was like "a great and noble horse that's somewhat sluggish because of its size and needs to be provoked by a gadfly" (30e). Socrates was this gadfly, a messenger sent by the god of reason and truth to provoke and stir up the people of Athens from their slumber, and to get them to realize that they were neglecting the things that were most important for human life. For this reason, in deciding to execute Socrates, the people of Athens were really only harming themselves.

The last point relates to another famous saying of Socrates from the *Apology*, namely that "*the unexamined life is not worth living*" (38a). What does Socrates mean by the examined or unexamined life? Before reading further, you might want to stop and ponder the following question: What do *you* think about this statement of Socrates? Does it seem true to you or not? Why or why not?

Immediately before making this claim, Socrates had stated that "it is the greatest good for a [person] to discuss virtue every day and those other things about which you hear me conversing and testing myself and others." The examined life, then, is the life in which you submit your beliefs and opinions about what a good human life and good human actions amount to, to critical testing in conversation with others, with a willingness to be corrected and to change your mind if necessary. An *unexamined* life, by contrast, involves refusing to test or question your own beliefs, assuming you are right and acting accordingly without ever trying to see if you might, in fact, be wrong. This is the state of ignorance that Socrates found in all the people of his society who had the reputation of being wise. According to Plato, it is this state of ignorance that resulted in Socrates's conviction and eventual execution, since people preferred to get rid of Socrates rather than have to face up to the truth about themselves.

Reflecting on the importance of the examined life also helps us to understand in a somewhat deeper way the significance of the Socratic Method (the method of *elenchus* or "refutation"), and the way Socrates differed from the Sophists. Although Socrates did often engage in refuting the beliefs and views of others, he did not do this for its own sake. In his view, and in Plato's, having one's false beliefs challenged and tested was a necessary first step to becoming educated. People who think they already know something will not be motivated to learn anything new. So they first need to recognize their own ignorance before learning can take place. What truly differentiated Socrates from the Sophists is that the latter claimed not only to possess wisdom themselves, but to be able to impart this wisdom to other people in exchange for money. As we have seen, Socrates claimed that he was far from possessing any wisdom himself, let alone capable of transmitting it to others. Nevertheless, he did act as an educator at least in the sense that he could help people to realize the extent of their own ignorance. And if they were willing to accept this, they would then be in a much better position to learn and become wise. If anyone's beliefs could withstand philosophical testing by Socratic refutation, those beliefs could be deemed solid and trustworthy.

At this point we can take a minute to ask ourselves how this relates to us. Most of us, if we are honest with ourselves, know what it's like to persist in our own ideas without truly listening to challenges raised by other people who think differently. We are offended when our cherished beliefs are questioned. We prefer to retreat into the wishy-washy pseudo-tolerant attitude that everyone can believe whatever they want. You don't challenge my beliefs, and I won't challenge yours. Don't get me wrong—I'm not suggesting that we should not respect other people's differences and understand that they have reasons for believing what they do. But it has been shown again and again that human beings tend to be unwilling to admit their own ignorance and mistakes. Arguably, thinking that we know something when we really don't, and being unwilling to examine ourselves and each other about our beliefs on what is most important, lead to all sorts of problems and injustices, from the level of interpersonal relationships with friends and family, to the level of massive social conflict and civil war. What Plato's Socrates represents is an alternative to this situation. But are we willing to accept his challenge and open our minds to think about wisdom, virtue, and truth, with a willingness to have our own beliefs questioned and examined? This willingness is, for Socrates and for Plato, the place where true philosophy, the love of wisdom, begins.

"The unexamined life is not worth living."
(Socrates, as described in Plato's *Apology*, 38a5–6)

---

4. CONCLUSION

Western philosophy emerged from a religious and mythologically oriented culture and consciousness. The first philosophers, the Presocratics, distinguished themselves from the religious poets not by giving up talking about the divine, but by emphasizing naturalistic explanations of phenomena, and by seeking to rationalize their conclusions from observation of, and reflection on, the natural world around them. They appealed to principles of reason rather than (or at least in addition to) divine inspiration as the source of their claims. Plato takes up several of the problems and themes of the Presocratics in his philosophical dialogues. He also engages with another significant group of intellectuals of his day, the Sophists. One of the main goals of Plato's *Apology* was to defend his teacher Socrates, who almost invariably takes centre stage in Plato's dialogues, against the charge of being a Sophist. In the course of doing so, Plato contrasted Socratic wisdom and the spirit of true philosophy embodied in Socrates, to the pseudo-education promoted by the Sophists. Socrates's lasting challenge consists in his claim that an unexamined life is not worth living.

In the next chapter, we will continue our investigation of Plato's dialogues, beginning with a typical early Socratic dialogue, the *Euthyphro*, and then moving into the middle period with Plato's *Meno*. In the latter, we will start to see Plato emerge a bit more, as the figure of Socrates begins to do more than refute the misguided views of others, and to present his own positive arguments for various positions. In particular, Socrates, or Plato speaking through Socrates, argues that all learning and acquiring of knowledge is actually a process of remembering or recollecting things that our souls already possess. This and many more exciting problems await us as we delve further into the thought and work of one of the very greatest minds of all time.

Chapter 2:

DEFINING VIRTUE: PLATO'S *EUTHYPHRO* AND *MENO*

HISTORICAL CONTEXT

For the next few chapters, we'll be lingering around the time period in which Socrates and Plato lived. By the time Socrates was born in 469 BCE, Athens was already on the rise as a major political and cultural force in the region. Athens enjoyed its **"Golden Age"** under **Pericles** between 450 and 430 BCE, during which time the great **Acropolis**—a temple to the goddess Athena—was reconstructed. (You can still visit the ruins of the Acropolis today, and they are still pretty impressive.) Around the age of twenty, Socrates entered the Athenian military and participated in the **Peloponnesian War** (431–404 BCE) against Sparta for about ten years. Plato, born in 428, grew up during this period, likely coming under the influence of his mentor and hero Socrates in his teenage years. The city of Athens was devastated by the Peloponnesian War, but made some recovery afterward and continued to be something of a cultural and philosophical centre well into the **Hellenistic period**, which begins with the death of **Alexander the Great** in 323 BCE and ends with the rise of **the Roman Empire** in 31 BCE. After Socrates's death in 399 BCE, Plato fled from Athens and stayed in Megara for some time. He later returned and founded his famous school, **the Academy**, around 386 BCE. Part of what Plato hoped to accomplish through this school was to train politicians in philosophy. As we will see when we come to discuss Plato's *Republic*, Plato was putting into practice his (entirely reasonable!) belief that the only way to have a truly just society would be to have philosophers for rulers. Plato's Academy went through several stages during its 900+ years of history, until it was finally closed under the Christian Roman emperor **Justinian** in 529 CE.

The ruins of the Acropolis in the early twentieth century. Photograph by Frederic Boissonnas

INTRODUCTORY BIG QUESTION: THE QUEST FOR DEFINITIONS

In Plato's early, or Socratic, dialogues, we find Socrates again and again questioning others about the meanings of words, in order to stimulate them to become better educated about key ethical concepts: "What is justice?" "What is beauty?" "What is friendship?" This explains Aristotle's description of Socrates's interest in definitions:

And when Socrates, disregarding the physical universe and confining his study to moral questions, sought in this sphere for the universal and was the first to concentrate upon definition, Plato followed him and assumed that the problem of definition is concerned not with any sensible thing but with entities of another kind; for the reason that there can be no general definition of sensible things which are always changing. These entities he called "Ideas" ... (*Metaphysics*, 987b)

The question of how to define terms has been with philosophers ever since. In conversation about some topic (let X represent the topic), it is characteristic of a philosophically-minded person to say things like, "That depends on what you mean by X." Philosophers like to have their terms spelled out as clearly and carefully as possible. In Socrates's view, getting an accurate understanding of key ethical ideas was crucial for the purpose of living the good life; if a person was confused or mistaken about virtue and goodness and the other components of the good life, how would they be able to live out such a life? Since living the good life is the most important goal a person can have, the quest for clarity about what this good life consists in takes on a particular urgency for Socrates.

The search for definitions that Plato inherited from his teacher, Socrates, occupied much of Plato's attention, and resulted in his famous Theory of the Forms. (We'll have a lot to say about the Forms in upcoming chapters.) In the quotation from Aristotle I just mentioned, Aristotle links Socrates's interest in definitions to Plato's "Ideas," which is another way of saying "Forms." Several questions naturally arise in this context: What counts as a good definition? Is there a right method for acquiring definitions of terms? Furthermore, is knowing the definition of something the same as knowing the thing itself? What does it mean to know what something *is*, anyway, and how can we be sure that we do know it? These are the sorts of questions that fall under the branch of Philosophy called **Epistemology**, which means the study of knowledge.

Before going further, stop and think about a few questions. *Assuming that you know at least a few things (for example, "beavers are mammals," "the sum of 2 and 2 is 4," "the moon is not a cheeseburger"), how did you come to know these things? And how do you know that you know them?* (And how do you know that you know that you know ... alright, you get the idea.) In the two dialogues of Plato we'll be looking at in this chapter, the *Euthyphro* and the *Meno*, epistemological questions like these will take centre stage.

1. THE *EUTHYPHRO*: SOCRATIC METHOD IN ACTION

In Plato's *Apology*, we saw Socrates in the middle of his trial, giving his defense speech. The *Euthyphro* takes place outside the court, *before* the trial, where Socrates happens to run into the man after whom the dialogue is named. Euthyphro was a priest who was also on his way to the law court, not to face charges, like Socrates, but to *lay* charges against someone else. The someone in question was Euthyphro's father, whom Euthyphro was accusing of murder. Euthyphro explains to Socrates what had happened: One of Euthyphro's father's slaves had killed another of his slaves. Hearing this, Euthyphro's father had tied up the murderer and thrown him into a ditch while he went to find out from the authorities what he should do. Meanwhile, the murderer died of exposure and thirst. After the initial stage-setting, the rest of the dialogue consists of Socrates engaging Euthyphro in the question-and-answer discussion I described in the last chapter as the Socratic Method of refutation (*elenchus* in the Greek). Recall that Plato's early dialogues give us the best representation of the actual historical person of Socrates. Studying this dialogue gives us some insight into what it would have been like to see Socrates at work, acting out his mission from Apollo, in the context of the Athenian society of the day. As you observe Socrates at work testing and refuting the beliefs of his fellow Athenians, try to see how effective his elenchic method is—does it help his interlocutors to acquire knowledge or at least to come closer to being wise?

a) Defining Holiness

As noted earlier, Socrates often appears in Plato's dialogues looking for definitions of terms or concepts, that is, for answers to questions of the form, "What is X?" The concept under examination in the *Euthyphro*, is the concept of "piety" or "holiness" (*eusebia* in Greek). For Socrates, awaiting a trial where he is being accused of impiety or unholiness, having an understanding of the concept of holiness had a good deal of practical value. If he knew clearly what holiness was, then he would have a much better chance defending himself against the charge that he was unholy. Socrates expresses his excitement at having chanced to meet Euthyphro, since Euthyphro the priest claimed to know a good deal about the holy and the unholy. Indeed, Socrates says, Euthyphro must have very precise knowledge of what holiness is—otherwise he would never be confident enough to take his own father to court. So this was a perfect chance for Socrates to learn!

The fact that Euthyphro was prosecuting his own father is worth thinking about a bit further. For one thing, in many cultures, including that of ancient Greece, the notion of piety or holiness had to do not only with a person's respect for and duty to the gods, but also to their parents. Like the gods, a person's parents provided and protected and educated them, and in return deserved honour and respect (think of the fifth of Moses's Ten Commandments: "Honour your father and your mother"). At face value, Euthyphro's act of taking his father to court looked like a case of impiety or unholiness. For this reason, Euthyphro's claim that what he was doing was in fact pious would sound strange to Greek ears at least, if not to our own. Euthyphro, however, could justify his behaviour by appealing to the stories of the gods that came down to the Greeks from Homer and Hesiod. If you remember our earlier discussion of Hesiod's *Theogony*, Hesiod featured the story of Kronos, who, motivated by envy, castrated his father Ouranos. As Euthyphro points out, Zeus similarly overthrew his father Kronos after Kronos "unjustly swallowed his sons" (*Euthyphro*, 6a). In response, Socrates makes the telling, ironic comment: "Maybe this, Euthyphro, is why I am being prosecuted for this crime, that whenever someone says such things about the gods, for some reason I find them hard to accept?" (ibid.). Here we see Socrates expressing a sentiment that links him to the Presocratic thinkers, who also felt the need to revise the conceptions of the divine they had inherited from the poets. Surely a genuinely divine being would not behave the way Kronos and Zeus are said to have behaved in the mythological accounts of the poets?

Indeed, as we see from Euthyphro's definitions of piety, and Socrates's responses to them, the internal coherence of inherited ideas of the gods is a central focus of the *Euthyphro* as a dialogue. Socrates, eager to learn the nature of the holy, poses his definition question at 5d: "So tell me, what do you say the pious is, and what is the impious?" The first response that occurs to Euthyphro involves pointing out examples of holy acts, and the one that seems most obvious to him is his own holy action. So he says [definition #1], *"the pious is what I am doing now, prosecuting someone who is guilty of wrongdoing—either of murder or temple robbery or anything else of that sort,* whether it happens to be one's

Kronos Devouring His Offspring (*Saturno devorando a su hijo*), by Francisco de Goya (1819–23)

father or mother or whoever else—and the impious is failing to prosecute" (5d–e). Socrates is unhappy with Euthyphro's first attempt, because a definition should be sufficiently general to cover all cases. Pointing to a few instances of holy acts fails to account for what the holy is in general. Socrates needs a general formula in order to be able to identify instances of holiness and unholiness wherever they might arise. We can call this requirement for a good definition **the generality requirement**.

Euthyphro tries again [definition #2]: *"what is beloved by the gods is pious, and what is not beloved by them is impious"* (6e–7a). Euthyphro's second attempt successfully meets Socrates's generality requirement. According to this definition, any holy act or thing will possess the characteristic of being loved by the gods. But this time Socrates finds a different problem. The proposed definition fails what we can call **the coherence requirement**. Socrates gets Euthyphro to admit that the gods are in conflict with one another, as is clear from the accounts of them in Homer and Hesiod, which Euthyphro accepts. But the things that are most likely to cause conflict between two intelligent moral beings are disagreements over what is right or wrong, or what is good and bad. Given that a person will tend to love what he or she thinks is good and hate what he or she thinks is bad, we have to say that the gods will disagree with each other concerning what they love, or what is dear to them. But given that Euthyphro's second definition identifies the holy with what the gods love and the unholy with what the gods hate, we end up having to say that the gods disagree with each other concerning what is holy and what is unholy. Obviously, a good definition should not make it possible for something to be holy and not-holy at the same time, but that is exactly what Euthyphro's second definition does. Euthyphro's second definition turns out to be incoherent (it fails the coherence requirement), in that it leads to contradictions.

b) Looking for the Essence

Euthyphro then gives Socrates a third definition of "the pious" or "the holy." His third attempt is a modified version of the second, designed to remove the incoherence Socrates had pointed out. Instead of claiming that the holy is what is dear to *some* gods, Euthyphro now claims that [definition #3] *"the pious is what* all *the gods love"* (9e, my emphasis), so that whenever all the gods agree in loving something, that something is holy, and whenever all the gods agree in hating something, that something is unholy. Since agreement among the gods is now built into the definition, Socrates can't pull it apart by citing the fact that the gods sometimes disagree. In the case where gods disagree about whether something is holy or not, presumably, that thing would be neither holy nor unholy.

This time, Socrates takes a different approach to assessing the quality of Euthyphro's definition. He begins by asking the following question: "Is the pious loved by the gods because it's pious, or is it pious because it is loved?" (10a). Socrates tries to explain the import of his distinction by listing examples of active and passive: We can distinguish something carrying from something being carried, and something leading from something being led, etc. In every such case, the object that is receiving the action (the thing carried or led) possesses the relevant quality (being carried or led) because of the activity of another thing (the thing carrying or leading). Applying this to the cases of what is loved and what is holy, we see that these two concepts are different, so that they cannot be identical to each other, as Euthyphro's third definition requires. We can see this from the following statements, applied to each case:

1. The god-loved is god-loved because it is god-loved, that is, *because* the gods love it. (*The G is G because it is G*)
2. The holy, on the other hand, is god-loved *because* it is holy. (*The H is G because it is H*)
3. The god-loved is not god-loved because it is holy. (*The G is not G because it is H*)
4. The holy is not god-loved because it is god-loved. (*The H is not G because it is G*)

Pairing statements (1) and (4), and statements (2) and (3), we can see that opposite things are true of the god-loved (that which is dear to the gods) and the holy. The reason why the gods love holy things is because those things are (already) holy. So, prior to and independently of the gods' affections, what makes something to be holy is rooted in the nature of the holy things themselves. But what makes something have the feature of being loved by the gods is rooted in the volitional states of the beings who love it—what makes something to be god-loved is just the fact that the gods love it. The god-loved and the holy are indeed both god-loved, but for different reasons. This shows, Socrates thinks, that the two concepts are non-identical. And this shows that Euthyphro's third definition of the holy has failed to tell us *what* the holy *is*. We can call the requirement for a good definition that has not been met here **the identity requirement**. Socrates believes that a good definition must provide a formula that captures, in a complete and exclusive way, the identity of the term being defined. In other words, he wants a formula that expresses the **essence** of the thing in question.

It is common in philosophy and in speaking of definitions to explain what the "essence" of a thing is in terms of necessary and sufficient conditions. A **necessary condition** for X is a condition that must hold in order for X to be the case. For instance, air is a necessary condition for human life. Without air, the maintenance of human life is not possible. Air is not, however, a *sufficient* condition for human life, because more than air is needed to sustain human life. Food, water, and a certain temperature range are also needed. A **sufficient condition** for X is a condition that, if it holds, guarantees that X is the case. Being hit head-on by a fast-moving train is sufficient to bring about the death of most mammals. Given that a mammal has been hit head-on by a fast-moving train, you are guaranteed that the mammal in question is dead. But being hit by a train is not a *necessary* condition for mammalian death, since a mammal can die in many other ways, for instance, due to old age. In order to provide the sort of definition Socrates is looking for, we would have to provide a condition for X—in this case, for something's being holy—that is **both necessary and sufficient**. Clearly, this is a tall order. We find such definitions rarely. One common example is the definition of water as H_2O. Arguably, being H_2O is both necessary and sufficient for being water. If something is not H_2O, then it's not water. And if something is H_2O, then you've got a guarantee that it's water. This is because the chemical formula H_2O uniquely picks out water—it captures the *identity* of water.

Clearly Socrates's standards for a good definition, represented by the three requirements I have described (the generality, coherence, and identity requirements), give us a high standard that would be difficult to meet. We might object, "Is it really true that unless we can define something in a way that meets all these conditions, we don't know what the thing is?" Can't we know, for example, what a cheeseburger is so long as we can reliably point one out at McDonald's, even if we can't list off the necessary and sufficient conditions of cheeseburgerness? Recall Socrates's claim, in the *Apology*, that he does not know anything. Of course, Socrates knew many things in a rough and ready sort of way, and Euthyphro also presumably knew enough to get by in everyday life. But the question Socrates is interested in is the question of complete, or comprehensive, knowledge, the sort of knowledge of things one would expect God to have. It seems clear that Euthyphro does not have such knowledge of holiness. Socrates thinks that without this knowledge, a person should be hesitant to make bold claims, like the claim that one should prosecute one's father for murder for unintentionally causing a criminal slave to die. This sort of perspective raises interesting questions for us, too. We are often quick to pass judgement on other people. We identify others as being morally bad or evil, judging them by our own standards of good and bad. But do we really know what the good and the bad *are*? Could we provide a definition of what is morally good or bad that is capable of meeting Socrates's three requirements? If we can't, does that tell us something about the limits of our knowledge, and the need for us to exercise caution? Or is it okay to ignore such questions and forge ahead with decisions and judgements about good and evil regardless of our ignorance?

c) An Inconclusive Conclusion

After pinpointing the failure of Euthyphro's third attempt to define holiness, Socrates urges Euthyphro to keep trying. Socrates even tries to help him get on a track more likely to succeed by suggesting that perhaps holiness is a part of the virtue of justice. Euthyphro picks up the trail for a while but ends up bumbling his way back to his third answer again—which they had already agreed did not work. Socrates refuses to be discouraged. He tells Euthyphro,

> Then we must examine again from the beginning what the pious is, as I am
> determined not to give up until I understand it. Do not scorn me, but by apply-
> ing your mind in every way, tell me the truth now more than ever. Because you
> know it if anybody does and, like Proteus, you cannot be released until you
> tell me. Because unless you knew clearly about the pious and impious there is
> no way you would ever have, on behalf of a hired laborer, tried to pursue your
> aging father for murder. Instead you would have been afraid before the gods,

and ashamed before men, to run the risk of conducting this matter improperly. But as it is, I am sure that you think you have clear knowledge of the pious and the impious. So tell me, great Euthyphro, and do not conceal what you think it is. (15c–e)

To Socrates's dismay, Euthyphro says he's in a hurry and will have to meet Socrates's request some other time. Trying to locate necessary and sufficient conditions for being holy proves to be too tall an order for Euthyphro. As frequently happens in the early dialogues, the *Euthyphro* ends without providing an answer to the dialogue's main question, "What is holiness?"

If we were to read this dialogue as purely negative, in the sense of merely negating or refuting various answers, it would be easy to understand this Socratic conversation as the same sort of thing the Sophists were up to. The Sophists, you might remember, would engage in disputations and would win arguments using debating tricks, tripping up their opponents and making them look bad. Is this the lesson we should draw about Socrates from the *Euthyphro*, that Socrates is just like the Sophists? I don't think so. The Socratic method does include refutation as a component. But for Plato's Socrates, refutation is only a means toward education. It is a necessary first step to become educated to realize that you don't know what you thought you knew. Euthyphro doesn't get there. But the reader—that means you—has the opportunity to learn something even if Euthyphro doesn't. For one thing, many people in Socrates's day would have felt that defining holiness or piety as "what the gods love" made good sense. Plato's dialogue appears to show us that this common conception of holiness has some problems. But if that's not what holiness is, then what is it? Plato has not given us the answer, but he has given us a clue. Holiness has something to do with justice in the relations between human beings and the divine. Is there a way of pursuing this suggestion that would allow us to make headway, instead of collapsing as Euthyphro did?

The *Meno* shows even more clearly that what Plato actually does and says in his dialogues is not the end of the story. Plato is using this form of writing to draw his reader into a conversation as an active participant. When you read a Platonic dialogue you are supposed to start asking yourself questions. If what I always thought holiness was isn't really what it is, then what is it? Once you start asking such questions, you've arguably taken the necessary first steps on the journey toward a philosophical education.

d) The Euthyphro Dilemma

There is one last thing I'd like to point out before we move on from our consideration of the *Euthyphro*. Socrates's question, "Is something loved by the gods because it is pious, or is it pious because it is loved by the gods?" has been understood by thinkers after Plato to pose a dilemma. The Euthyphro Dilemma faces anyone who wants to suggest a basic connection between religion and morality.

This suggestion typically posits a connection between the will of God and the morally good, so that what is good (moral action for example) is identical to what God wills. Why is murder wrong? Because God says so. Again, check the Ten Commandments, number six. The view that God's will and morality are deeply related has different names: Divine Command Ethics and Divine Voluntarism being two of the most common. The Euthyphro dilemma appears to pose a significant challenge to any such position. It is called a dilemma because there seem to be only two options, but no matter which of the two options you take, you run into serious problems.

Substituting "moral goodness" for "piety" in the expression of the dilemma, we can put it like this: Either (a) what is morally good is good because God wills it, or (b) God wills what is morally good because it is good. But either option seems to be problematic. If we accept (a), and claim that goodness derives purely from the will of God, then morality seems to become arbitrary. If God had willed and commanded that people should torture kittens for fun, then it would be morally right for people to torture kittens for fun, because that would be God's will. But that just seems wrong! Let's say we accept the other horn of the dilemma, (b), instead. God wills what is good *because* it is good. The problem here is that now we are pulling apart morality and the will of God. What is good is good, we are saying, *in itself,* not because of the fact that God wills it. But that seems to mean that moral standards are independent of God, and this contradicts the original intention of the divine command ethicist, who claimed that morality and God's will were inextricably related.

Diagram 1

If…	Moral goodness is essentially tied to God's will	
Then either …	What is morally good is good because God wills it.	God wills what is morally good because it is (independently) good.
Which would mean …	Religious morality is arbitrary.	Religious morality is superfluous.

There have, of course, been a number of responses to the Euthyphro Dilemma through history by thinkers who wanted to maintain the link between God's will and morality. Some of them, wanting to preserve the absolute freedom of God, have accepted the first horn of the dilemma, (a), denying that there really is any problem involved in accepting (a). It just is the case, these trueblood voluntarists would say, that God's choice fully determines what is morally good, and that is the end of the story. We're glad that God did not command us to torture kittens, but if He had, then it really would have been the right thing to do. Others have rejected (a) and embraced a modified version of (b). Even if morality is in a sense independent of God's will, these more subtle voluntarists argue, that does not entail that morality is independent of God. Instead, we can say that God finds the reasons for willing and commanding what he wills and commands within His own nature, which is, in fact, good. This way, morality does not depend on God's arbitrary choice, but on something else about God's nature—say, His intellect or His character.

The question of the relationship between religion and morality is just one of the issues that comes down to us all the way from classical Greece, and was formulated with particular clarity by Plato. This partially substantiates the twentieth-century philosopher Alfred North Whitehead's assertion that "The safest general characterization of the European philosophical tradition is that it consists of a series of footnotes to Plato."[1] As we look at the next few dialogues, we will find a few more reasons to think that Whitehead may be right about this.

2. THE *MENO*: SOCRATES, THE TEACHER OF VIRTUE

I trust that you've been finding your reading of Plato enjoyable so far. Since this is a book about "core readings," part of what you're supposed to be getting out of it is a chance to actually sit down and read some of the best philosophical literature the Western tradition has to offer. Of course, you could skip the primary sources and just read the chapters of this book instead, but that would defeat the purpose.

Our next dialogue, the *Meno*, shares elements with the early or Socratic dialogues of Plato. Socrates is the leading character and he guides Meno through systematic questioning and eventual refutation of Meno's various attempts to answer the question, "What is virtue?"—and they fail to reach a conclusion about it in the end. The bulk of the dialogue actually centres on another, related question posed by Meno in the opening line of the work: "Can you tell me, Socrates, can virtue be taught? Or is it not teachable but the result of practice, or is it neither of these, but men possess it by nature or in some other way?" (*Meno*, 70a). As we will see, this question does get (some sort of) an answer at the end of the work, but I'll be arguing that we can't simply accept this "answer" at face value.

In other ways, the *Meno* is unlike the early dialogues. The Socrates who appears in the *Meno* goes beyond simply questioning and answering others, and actually proposes some views of his own, which actually seem to do some work in moving the conversation forward. These views include Plato's famous Doctrine of Recollection, as well as the belief in reincarnation and in the existence of human souls prior to our present lives. This positive presentation of views that the historical Socrates

---

1   Alfred North Whitehead, *Process and Reality* (New York: Free Press, 1979), p. 39.

likely did not hold himself has led scholars to put the *Meno* in the category of Plato's middle dialogues, or at least to see it as transitional between the early and middle periods. The *Phaedo* and the *Republic*, which we will be looking at in the next two chapters, will provide us with two clearly middle-period dialogues.

a) Plato and Meno on Virtue

We saw in our look at the *Apology* that Socrates was constantly concerned with questioning and examining himself and others concerning ethical concepts. The central ethical concept for the Greeks was virtue (*arete*), which can also be translated as "excellence." So it only makes sense that many of Plato's dialogues revolve around questions of how different virtues relate to each other, and other questions about virtue. A virtue is a positive character trait, and a vice is a negative character trait. When we say that a person is compassionate or intelligent, we are saying positive things about his or her character. When we say that a person is mean or stupid, we are saying negative things about his or her character. A person's character can roughly be understood as that person's tendencies to behave in ways that we would evaluate as positive or negative, resulting from the kind of person he or she is. For Socrates, character traits are features of a person's soul, rather than features of their bodies. Socrates discusses a number of virtues in the dialogues. Some of the central ones are the virtues of justice, courage, moderation, and wisdom. In another of Plato's early dialogues, the *Protagoras*, Socrates argues that all the virtues in the end boil down to a single thing, namely wisdom or knowledge. But other dialogues suggest different views about the unity of the virtues.

As I noted earlier, the *Meno* opens with the question of whether virtue can be taught. This question was particularly relevant in the Athenian society of the day that had been infiltrated by the Sophists, who claimed to be capable of teaching virtue, and were making some good cash at the expense of the young people of Athens. That Plato has the Sophists in mind is evident from the early reference to Gorgias, a very well-known Sophist under whom Meno himself had apparently been "learning." The first move Socrates makes in this dialogue is to claim that we can't know properly whether virtue can be taught unless we first have a clear understanding of what virtue *is*. Socrates makes this claim based on the general point that "[i]f I do not know what something is, how could I know what qualities it possesses?" (71b). At first glance, the point seems plausible. But its plausibility depends on how we understand "knowing what something is." If we mean by this "knowing something in any way at all," then yes, of course, we could not possibly know what features a thing had if we did not know the thing itself in that sense. But if Socrates means to say that we can't know the features of a thing unless we possess *a clear definition of the essence of that thing*, a definition that meets the three requirements for a good definition outlined in the previous section's discussion of the *Euthyphro*, then Socrates's point is questionable. Surely I can know that bunny rabbits are furry and can hop around even if I do not clearly grasp the essence of what it is to be a bunny, can't I?

For the sake of argument, let's allow Socrates to have his point, and see what follows. We must, then, ask the question, "What is virtue?" if we are to know whether it can be taught. In Meno's *first attempt to define virtue*, he distinguishes the virtue of a man, the virtue of a woman, the virtue of a child, of a free man, and of a slave. Socrates rejects this fragmentation of virtue into different sorts for different people for reasons similar to the reasons he gave for rejecting Euthyphro's first attempt at defining piety. Rather than giving examples of virtues, Meno should instead provide the single common form that makes all of the diverse virtues to be properly called virtues (72c). It takes Meno a while to understand what Socrates is looking for, but eventually he gives his second attempt at a definition of virtue [definition #2]: Virtue is "to be able to rule over people" (73d). But this definition falls apart very quickly because, as Socrates points out, it fails to cover the case of a child or a slave—clearly their virtue cannot consist in ruling over their parents or their masters.

Next, Socrates illustrates what he is looking for with a couple of examples. He defines shape in general as "the limit of a solid" (76a) and colour in general as "an effluvium from shapes which fits the sight and is perceived" (76d). Encouraged by these examples, Meno tries again to enunciate a general account of virtue, drawing from the words of a popular poet [definition #3]: "I say that virtue is to desire beautiful things and have the power to acquire them" (77b). Since Meno's definition contains two parts, Socrates takes each part separately, beginning with the desire of beautiful things. The problem here, Socrates argues, is that no one (whether virtuous or not) desires bad things, so desiring beautiful or good things can't distinguish a virtuous person from a bad one. In the background of Socrates's argument here is the famous Platonic view that **no one can knowingly do what is evil**. Stop for a minute and ask yourself, what do you think about this? Can a person choose to do something that they know to be bad, or not?

From one perspective, the view Socrates expresses here only makes sense. How, after all, could someone consciously believe that something was in no way good or desirable, but nevertheless continue to desire it? That would be totally incoherent. Desire *just is* for things we see as good. But the reality of our experience shows that people desire and choose things, apparently in full awareness that they are bad, all the time. Take smoking, for example. I'm sure you've seen the labels on cigarette packages, required by the Surgeon General, depicting horrendous pictures of smoking-induced illnesses along with verbal statements of the potentially devastating effects smoking can have on a person's health. Yet smokers continue to smoke despite these warnings, even while consciously acknowledging that smoking is bad for them. You could respond to this by arguing that even though smokers know smoking is bad for them, they nevertheless think it is good in other ways (the nicotine buzz, the satisfaction of a craving, the pleasurable social aspect of a smoking break with friends or coworkers, etc.). Perhaps this can explain how someone can coherently desire to smoke in a way that is consistent with Plato's view that no one knowingly chooses what is bad for them. I can't hope to settle this issue here, but will simply note that Aristotle and Augustine are two later thinkers who disagreed with Plato on this point.

Having dismissed Meno's claim that virtue consists in desiring good or beautiful things, Socrates turns to the other part of his third definition, the claim that a virtuous person tries to acquire good things. Socrates disposes of this part by pointing out that it is very possible to acquire good things (like gold, silver, honours, and political positions) by unjust means. This shows that only some ways of acquiring good things are in fact virtuous, and they are precisely the ways that involve virtue, at least the part of virtue we call justice. But it is quite unhelpful to define virtue as the ability to do something in a virtuous way, or in a way that involves a part of virtue. Since we don't know what virtue is, we can't know what it means to acquire something in a virtuous way either.

b) The Debater's Paradox and the Doctrine of Recollection

At this point in the dialogue, Meno is stumped. He compares his experience conversing with Socrates to being stung by a torpedo fish, which is another name for an electric ray. Torpedo fish are capable of stunning their prey by means of an electrical discharge. Meno complains, "I have made many speeches about virtue before large audiences on a thousand occasions, very good speeches as I thought, but now I cannot even say what it is" (80b). And he attributes the cause of his present deficiency to Socrates: "you seem, in appearance and in every other way, to be like the broad torpedo fish, for it too makes anyone who comes close and touches it feel numb, and now you seem to have had that kind of effect on me, for both my mind and my tongue are numb, and I have no answer to give you" (80a–b). Socrates replies by saying he differs from the torpedo fish at least insofar as he makes himself just as numb and perplexed as the people he's talking to. Here we have another instance of Socrates's ironic claim not to know anything.

In spite of his own, and Meno's, perplexity, Socrates urges that they keep searching for the nature of virtue. Meno responds by asking Socrates a question that Socrates identifies as a **debater's argument**. The gist of it is "that a man cannot search either for what he knows or for what he does not know.... He cannot search for what he knows—since he knows it, there is no need to search—nor for what he does not know, for he does not know what to look for" (80e). From this, it is tempting to conclude that any attempt to learn something new is futile. But the claim that no one can ever learn anything is counter-intuitive. We have all experienced learning. And yet, as Meno's debater's argument paradox urges, learning does not seem to be possible. For any item of knowledge, X, either I know X or I do not know X. If I already know X, it makes no sense to talk about learning it again. And if I don't know X, how would I recognize or locate it in order to come to know it? A quick response to this argument would be to say, "Hold on a minute. Though I don't know *something* about X (say, X's genetic code), I may still know X in some other way that would be sufficient for me to identify X in order to come to learn more about it." Take the case of the blue dragon, a type of tropical sea slug. I'm betting you have not heard of a blue dragon before, and so it's fair to say you don't know the blue dragon. Now since you don't know it, how would you ever come to know it, since you wouldn't know it even if you found one? But do a google images search for 'blue dragon' and take a look at the image of a blue dragon. Now that you've seen an image and perhaps read a bit about the blue dragon, you would probably be able to identify one if you were ever snorkeling in a suitable tropical location. At that point, you could continue to learn more about the sea slug, maybe even uncovering its genetic code, if you had the right equipment and expertise.

Instead of giving a straightforward answer like the one I just gave, Socrates solves the debater's argument by bringing in a theory he had apparently heard from some priests and priestesses and from some poets. The view in question claims the following three things: (1) Our human souls are immortal and were in existence before we were conceived. (2) In their pre-existent state, our souls came to know everything there is to know. As a result, (3) When we learn in this life, we are simply remembering what our souls knew before birth. The upshot of this view is that *all learning that takes place in this life is recollection* of things we once knew, but have now "forgotten." Plato's **"Doctrine of Recollection"** gives us a way to escape the debater's argument, since it shows how a person can know something in a certain way, and yet not know it in another way. We all know what it's like to have a memory of something—the name of an acquaintance, for example—but to be unable to access it at the moment. You know the person's name, but you can't bring it to the level of conscious awareness. Then there is a mysterious flash and the name suddenly rises up from your unconscious mind and you remember. According to the doctrine of recollection, all learning is like this. Our souls already contain knowledge about everything. They acquired this knowledge "in the underworld," or Hades, the place where disembodied souls reside. (We'll be hearing more about this in the chapter on Plato's *Phaedo*.) In order to "learn," in our present embodied state, we need to engage in certain processes in order to draw the knowledge up to the surface.

Socrates goes on to demonstrate his proposal that learning is recollection by walking one of Meno's slave boys through a process of questioning and answering, in the course of which the slave boy "learns" the answer to a geometry question without being told the answer by Socrates. Socrates starts by drawing the following square (we'll call it square 1—see Diagram 2).[2]

Each line of this square is two feet, and its area is four feet (squared). Socrates now asks the slave to tell him the length of the line of a square whose area would be double that of square 1, that is, the line of a square with an area of eight feet. The boy, who has not been taught geometry, starts out thinking the line would have to be four feet—since the area has doubled, the length of the line should also

---

2 This image is a reproduction of a similar one in footnote 9 of G.M.A. Grube's translation of the *Meno*, reprinted on p. 80 of Cahn's anthology.

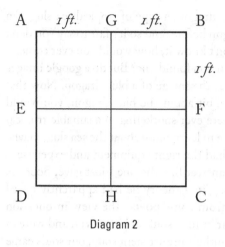

Diagram 2

have doubled, he thinks. But Socrates, by questioning, quickly brings him to realize that the area of a square with four-foot sides would be sixteen feet, not eight. The boy next attempts to make the line of a square eight feet in area to be three feet long, since it has to be longer than the line of square 1 (whose area was four feet squared) but shorter than the line of the square with four-foot sides. But the area of a square with three-foot sides is nine. The slave boy is perplexed and admits that he does not know the answer to Socrates's question.

At this point, Socrates, in an aside to Meno, asks whether the slave boy is not in a better position to acquire knowledge, now that he has realized his own ignorance. The boy has been numbed by the torpedo fish (Socrates's questions), but this is a *good thing*:

> Indeed, we have probably achieved something relevant to finding out how matters stand, for now, as he does not know, he would be glad to find out, whereas before he thought he could easily make many fine speeches to large audiences about the square of double size and said that it must have a base twice as long. (84b–c)

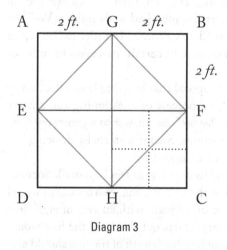

Diagram 3

Socrates then walks the slave boy through further questions until the boy realizes the answer for himself. The way Socrates and the slave boy reach the answer can be seen in diagram 3:

The side of a square with an eight-foot area can be found by starting with the ABCD square, whose area is sixteen feet, and dividing it into four equal parts, yielding four squares each of whose area is four feet. One then produces a square with an eight-foot area by cutting each of the four squares in half along the diagonal, producing the square EGFH. The diagonal line cutting any of these four-foot area squares in half is the length of the side of the eight-foot area square. The boy walks through the process with Socrates until he comes to accept this solution for himself. Socrates claims that the answer has arisen out of the boy's soul, showing that he had the answer in himself all along, and only needed some help to remember it. Of course, it looks suspiciously as though Socrates had merely led him along the way by his leading questions, which, at first glance, may not seem to be a case of the slave boy figuring out the answer for himself. And yet, Socrates only asked questions and did not tell the boy the answers. At each step, Socrates waited for the boy to see for himself what was correct.

c) Tying Down the Statues: Knowledge and True Belief

Having given his "proof" that learning is indeed possible, Socrates urges Meno not to allow himself to be halted in his search for the nature of virtue by the debater's argument. But Meno gives up the chase, asking Socrates to go back to the original question about whether virtue can be taught. Socrates somewhat reluctantly agrees, despite his earlier protestation that a person cannot discover the properties of a thing whose essence they do not yet understand. He suggests they proceed "hypothetically." The first hypothesis is that virtue is knowledge. If virtue is knowledge, then it can be taught, since all knowledge can be taught. Conversely, if virtue is *not* knowledge, then it will not be capable of being taught. Socrates quickly establishes that virtue *can* be taught using the following argument, which I am presenting here in a highly summarized form:

1. Every good thing is knowledge or depends on knowledge.
2. Virtue is a good thing.
Therefore,
3. Virtue is knowledge or depends on knowledge.
Therefore,
4. Virtue can be taught.

But a problem arises because Socrates also finds himself in possession of another argument that establishes exactly the opposite conclusion, using the same hypothetical method:

1. All knowledge, being teachable, has both students and teachers.
2. There are no teachers or students of virtue.
Therefore,
3. Virtue is not knowledge.
Therefore,
4. Virtue cannot be taught.

Socrates reaches the key premise 2 of the second argument, the claim that "There are no teachers or students of virtue," with the help of a third conversation partner, Anytus. (Note that Anytus is one of the men who brought forth the accusations against Socrates in the *Apology*. See *Apology*, 18b.) Socrates leads a reluctant and increasingly angry Anytus to admit that there are no teachers of virtue because even the best people of Athens were unable to instruct their children in virtue, which they surely would have done if it were possible. After issuing a warning to Socrates, Anytus drops out of the conversation around 94e. Socrates goes on to establish, through questioning Meno again, that the Sophists don't really teach virtue to others, even though they profess to do so.

Socrates and Meno then pursue a different line of thought. One way to guide other people is by having knowledge. But it is also possible to guide others even if you only have correct opinion. For example, let's say you have a friend who wants to visit the St. Jacobs Farmer's Market near Waterloo, Ontario, but does not know the way. You aren't from around there, so you don't know the way either. But you do a quick search online and determine the address for the market, and send the directions to your friend. It turns out that the directions you found on the Internet are correct, and your friend uses them and succeeds in getting to the Farmer's Market. As a result, she enjoys some delicious apple fritters. Even though you didn't know how to get there yourself, you acquired the correct opinion about how to get there, and so were able to benefit your friend. Nevertheless, even though you have the right opinion about the market's address, you are still not as reliable a guide as someone else who has driven there herself many times. That is to say, someone who knows the way to the market would be a more reliable guide overall than someone who only has correct opinion about it.

Socrates discusses the difference between knowledge and correct opinion by using an analogy. The mythical sculptor Daedalus was reputed to be so good at his art that his statues were exceedingly realistic. They were so realistic, in fact, that if you did not keep them chained down, they would run away. True opinions are like statues of Daedalus that are untied. They are not of much use, because, although beautiful, you won't be able to hold on to them for long. But possessing knowledge is like having one of these statues tied down and secured so that you can continue to enjoy its beauty long-term. Socrates gives a brief description of what it means to tie down an opinion so that it becomes an item of knowledge:

> For true opinions, as long as they remain, are a fine thing and all they do is good, but they are not willing to remain long, and they escape from a man's mind, so that they are not worth much until one ties them down by (giving) an account of the reason why. And *that, Meno my friend, is recollection, as we previously agreed.* After they are tied down, in the first place they become knowledge, and then they remain in place. That is why knowledge is prized higher than correct opinion, and knowledge differs from correct opinion in being tied down. (98a; my italics)

The difference between having knowledge and having true belief is that knowledge involves an explanation of why the thing you know is the way it is. If the best you can do is to give your friend a printout of directions to the Farmer's Market, without knowing *why* it says to turn left on Weber St., then your mental state is a relatively unstable one. If your Internet access ever gets shut down, you'll be left completely in the dark on how to get those apple fritters. If, on the other hand, you know how to get there yourself, then you can explain exactly why you have to turn on Weber St. You understand the relation of the various streets to each other, and the position of St. Jacobs in relation to Waterloo, and the position of the market relative to the town of St. Jacobs, etc. Your mental state, in this case, is much more reliable and secure.

d) Solving the Riddle of the Meno

The passage on the distinction between knowledge and true belief I just quoted is very important for understanding what Plato is doing in the *Meno*. An indicator of the passage's importance comes almost immediately after it, where Socrates uncharacteristically declares, "I certainly do not think I am guessing that right opinion is a different thing from knowledge. If I claim to know anything else— and I would make that claim about few things—I would put this down as one of the things I know" (98b). Here we have a stunning admission by Socrates of something he actually knows! Socrates and Meno move on to conclude, rather quickly, that because virtue cannot be taught (because there are no teachers of it), it is not knowledge but only correct opinion, and so virtue must be acquired by people in some other way than by instruction. Virtuous people, says Socrates, "are no different from soothsayers and prophets. They too say many true things when inspired, but they have no knowledge of what they are saying" (99c). Consequently, we have to say that virtue "comes to those who possess it as a gift from the gods which is not accompanied by understanding" (99e–100a).

Unlike most other Socratic dialogues, the *Meno* appears to give us an answer to the question it set out to investigate. Question: How is virtue acquired? Answer: It cannot be taught, but instead is acquired by divine inspiration, like the sayings of prophets or poets. But what are we to make of this "solution"? Is this what Socrates (or rather, Plato) really thinks? I think there are several reasons to believe that the answer the *Meno* gives us on the surface is not really what Plato wants his reader to take away from this dialogue. For one thing, Plato's Socrates points out at the end of the dialogue that clear knowledge of the way virtue is acquired would only be possible after first finding out what virtue itself is. This shows that Plato believes the conclusion is not something established with any great certitude. Secondly, if the conclusion of the dialogue is simply that knowledge cannot be taught but is a gift from the gods, that would contradict the many other places in Plato's works where he suggests that virtue *is* knowledge. It would also undermine the whole Socratic process of intellectually investigating the nature of various virtues. Why all the effort to know what virtue is if Plato thinks it really isn't knowable? This leaves us with a puzzle, or riddle: What does Plato really think about the teachability of virtue, and why does he end this dialogue the way he does? In the remainder of this part of the chapter I will explain my resolution of this riddle, and indicate some lessons on how to understand the roles of Socrates and Plato as educators.

First, the solution of the riddle. If Plato wanted to tell us that there are no teachers of virtue, and if virtue is not knowledge, then what was the point of the whole presentation of the doctrine of recollection, and of Socrates's demonstration with the slave boy? Furthermore, what was the point of the identification of recollection as the process by which a person takes a true belief and secures it so that it becomes an item of genuine knowledge? It is very important to remember the way Socrates emphasized that he was not *teaching* the slave boy anything during his demonstration. The slave boy acquired the knowledge about the eight-foot square from within himself, by recollection. Yet he did so only with the assistance of Socrates's questions. Without someone like Socrates to ask the right questions and to show him the error of his previous conceptions, the slave boy never would have been able to draw what he already knew to the surface. And, Socrates says, through repeated engagement in this sort of questioning process the slave boy would come to have as firm and secure a knowledge about such things as anyone else (85d). Plato sees Socrates as someone capable of "teaching" others without teaching them. That is to say, Socrates does not teach others in the sense of giving them information that they then absorb and repeat on a test. Instead, Socrates guides people in the process of recollecting knowledge from within themselves. Socrates himself was notably absent from the list of potential teachers of virtue that he and Meno discussed when investigating whether virtue was taught. But Socrates's method of "teaching" without teaching is very much present earlier in the dialogue.

The answer to the riddle of the *Meno*, I believe, is this: Plato's real view is that virtue is a type of knowledge, and can in fact be learned, though not in the same way a person learns other skills. It is learned through a process of examination that can lead a person to recollect, a process which the Socratic method of testing by question and answer relies on. When a person goes through this process successfully, she will be able to acquire correct opinions about matters having to do with virtue. If she goes through the process continually, she will be able to tie down her correct opinions more and more securely by gaining clearer and clearer insight into the reason why the virtues are the way they are, into their relationships to each other and to other items of knowledge. Like the person who has been to the St. Jacobs Farmer's Market many times, and driven around the surrounding area for many years, she will have a comprehensive grasp of what virtue is like, and will be able to implement it into her way of life, living in ways that are just, courageous, self-controlled, and wise. Of course, it is not enough to know that this is the way a person can acquire virtue—individuals must actually go through the process themselves. And this leads to my final remark on Plato's pedagogical approach in his dialogues.

If I'm right about the riddle present in this dialogue, and about the way Plato meant us to understand the dialogue's message, then why didn't Plato just tell us these things openly? Why the hidden message? At least part of the answer is that Plato himself in writing his dialogues was engaging in a Socratic form of teaching. Plato did not just present easy answers for people to read and memorize. Instead, he sought to draw his readers into the conversation, to challenge their preconceptions, and to get them to think for themselves. Plato understood that no true philosophical understanding can emerge unless a person is truly engaged in the search. In other words, you can't just be told by someone else about the deeper and more important things in life—you have to search it out and discover the truth for yourself. This does not mean that Plato believed anyone's opinions on a philosophical subject were as good as anyone else's. He thought there really was a truth of the matter—we will hear more about this soon as we examine his views on the Forms. But the truth had to be accessed *from inside* the knowing person. Plato described his thoughts on philosophical learning in his much-discussed Seventh Letter, where he says that he has never written down his own views about any important philosophical subject, because such things do not "admit of verbal expression like other studies." Instead, a person must acquire philosophical understanding by much conversation and by communing with the subject itself until understanding "is brought to birth in the soul on a sudden, as light that is kindled by a flame that leaps from one soul to another" (341c–d). Seeing Plato's writings as ways of evoking learning indirectly can make reading them seem annoyingly difficult. Plato would probably say that that's how it should be when we're talking about the most important truths of life and existence. And he would invite us, as Socrates does in the *Meno*, to pursue the investigation with a sense of excitement at the challenge.

3. CONCLUSION

In Plato's *Euthyphro* and *Meno* we are introduced to several epistemological issues. Reading the *Euthyphro* led us to consider what is involved in defining a term, and what criteria might apply to a good definition. It also raised questions about the relation between religion and morality, and about how we might come to know what piety or holiness—or good moral character more generally—consist in. The *Meno* challenged us to ask about the possibility of learning virtue, and of learning in general, and proposed the view that all learning is recollection as a solution to a paradox about learning. Plato also introduced us to the distinction between knowledge and true opinion, linking the process by which a person turns mere opinion into knowledge to the Socratic method that is capable of leading individuals to "recollect" the knowledge their souls already possess. We ended by considering Plato's own strategy for educating his readers philosophically by seeking to understand what I called the riddle of the *Meno*.

Questions concerning definition, learning, and the nature and acquisition of knowledge have been with Western thinkers ever since their first thorough treatment in the works of Plato. Such epistemological questions will be with us as well throughout the remainder of this book, especially as we consider one of Plato's most powerful conversation partners, Aristotle, a student of Plato and one of his greatest interpreters and critics. But before we get to Aristotle, we will be diving into two more Platonic dialogues. For those of you who have become curious about all the talk of "the soul" and "the Forms" in Plato, the next two chapters, on the *Phaedo* and the *Republic* respectively, will hopefully help to quench your intellectual thirst. Of course, in good Platonic fashion, they will do so not by giving you the answers, but by stimulating your own process of "recollection."

Chapter 3:

PLATO'S *PHAEDO*

AND THE

IMMORTALITY OF THE SOUL

HISTORICAL CONTEXT

For the present chapter and the one to come, we are continuing to dwell with Socrates and Plato, so we aren't moving around very much as far as the historical timeline goes. As we begin our discussion of Plato's *Phaedo*, however, we do need to dip back into the past a bit to understand some of the context of where his concerns in this dialogue are coming from. If you recall the brief discussion of Parmenides's concept of Being in Chapter One, you will find that you possess one of the keys to understanding Plato's Theory of the Forms, a theory that is very active in the *Phaedo*. For Parmenides, that which is real (Being) had to be perfectly stable, not admitting of non-being in any way. Furthermore, according to Parmenides, only such entities could be known; for this reason he concluded

45

Pythagoras, c. 570–c. 495 BCE

that the way of Being and the way of Truth were one and the same. Each of the Forms (at least in Plato's view of them in the middle dialogues) shares the key features of Parmenides's view of Being: each Form is highly unified, unchanging, eternal, and perfect.

Another Presocratic thinker who profoundly influenced Plato's views—a philosopher I did not describe earlier—is **Pythagoras**. You've probably at least heard his name before since the Pythagorean theorem is named after him. A figure surrounded by myths and legends, and even claimed by some to have been semi-divine, possessing a golden thigh, Pythagoras was born in Samos and lived roughly between 570 and 495 BCE. Pythagoras was perhaps more of a mathematician or a mystic and religious thinker than a philosopher, yet his views had a major impact on many of the philosophers who came after him, not least of all on Plato. Pythagoras, along with the members of the **Pythagorean school** he founded in southern Italy, believed that reality is fundamentally numerical, or that "all things are numbers." Plato later insisted, in the *Republic* 522c–528b for example, that before studying philosophy, a person should be instructed in mathematics. Among the views of Pythagoras most relevant to our present discussion is his belief in the transmigration of souls, that is, that souls are reincarnated and thus capable of living beyond the present life. Pythagoras was also an early proponent of vegetarianism—after all, he reasoned, you don't want to end up eating a reincarnated form of one of your old friends or family members!

INTRODUCTORY BIG QUESTION: WHAT IS A SOUL?

If we want to believe, as the Pythagoreans and Plato did, that we have souls capable of surviving beyond death, then we need to ask what these souls are like. What do you think of when you hear the word "soul"? Do you believe you have one? The broader question concerns the nature of the human person in general. What is it to be a person, or a "self"? Are we identical with our bodies, or is there some aspect of ourselves that is distinct from our bodies? Historically the two main competitors for answering this question are **materialism**, which holds that persons just are material bodies, and **dualism**, which holds that a human being is a composite of a body and some other element—something the ancients referred to as a "soul." Plato is standardly seen as the first systematic proponent of dualism, though as we have seen, Pythagoras and his followers clearly held views about this before Plato came on the scene. The debate on this subject continues to rage today in the discipline called Philosophy of Mind. There are by now myriad different positions a person can hold on the relation of the mind to the body, or of mental states to brain states. There are many ways of being a materialist, and many ways of being a dualist, and several interesting attempts to find something in the middle. Still, the basic distinction between materialism and dualism is a helpful place to start.

Whether or not you yourself believe that souls exist, it is worth asking why someone might hold such a belief. Early Greek thinkers felt there was an important difference between things that are alive and things that are not alive. Their way of expressing this difference was to say that living things have souls, while non-living things do not. (Part of the reason why Thales thought magnets had souls was that they were capable of moving things, which is one feature that distinguishes living from non-living things.) The Greek word for soul is *psuche*, from which the words "psychology" and "psychosis" derive. The *psuche* was understood to be the principle of the life of a living being. As thinkers in the fifth century BCE developed the notion of the soul further, it also came to represent that part of the human being that could initiate movement and control the life-functions of the organism, such as digestion, growth, and tissue repair. By the time of Socrates and Plato, the word *psuche* had come to refer to the subject of emotional and mental states, of pleasure and desire, and also of moral qualities like courage and temperance—what we called "virtues" in the last chapter. The soul was regarded as the part of the human being responsible for thinking, planning, and decision-making. This gets us much closer to the idea of a mind, or personal "self."

When you refer to yourself, using the personal pronouns "I" or "me," what are you referring to? Or what about your personality type (I myself am an INTJ or "mastermind")? What part of you *has* or *is* your personality? What part of you thinks the thoughts you are having, or desires the cheeseburger or the vegetarian alternative? When we speak of people being morally good or bad, guilty or innocent, what aspect of them possesses these features? It seems to strain language to say that my body is innocent, or that my brain decided to grab a tofu and chickpea salad for lunch. We think instead that it is I myself who does these things. I naturally think that I have, or better, I *am*, a unified self, and I think that other people with whom I have relationships also have, or are, selves. But if we do have selves (or are them), what are these, and what is their relation to our bodies? Further, do we have any reason to hope that these "selves" will continue to exist beyond the death of our bodies? If these questions strike you as important, or at least interesting, then you should try to think carefully about what comes next, since the Socrates of the *Phaedo* provides us with several arguments for the claim that we have immortal souls. After an overview of the dialogue itself, I will elaborate on and critique the main arguments.

1. THE STRUCTURE AND CONTENT OF PLATO'S *PHAEDO*

Scholars commonly understand the *Phaedo* to belong squarely to the "middle period" of Plato's writings. It retains the form of a dialogue, and Socrates investigates questions along with a few conversation partners (mainly Simmias and Cebes), spending some time refuting positions they raise. But unlike the early dialogues, the Socrates of the *Phaedo* argues very positively for conclusions he asserts—for example, that the nature of philosophy is the practice of dying, and that the soul is immortal. And the dialogue seems to state its conclusion as a more-or-less settled matter: The soul is indeed immortal, and thus the good soul does not need to fear death.

The opening sections 57a to about 60b of the dialogue take place in a setting distinct from that of the main part of the dialogue. In these sections, Phaedo relates to his friend Echecrates the discussion that took place between Socrates and some of his friends and followers in the hours just before his death. Because it was a holy season, there was a delay in executing Socrates, giving Socrates ample time for conversation with friends in prison. Plato's *Crito* contains another death-bed conversation in which Socrates resists his friends' offer to get him out of prison,

The Death of Socrates, by Jacques-Louis David (1787)

claiming that a just person must obey the laws of his or her city. Phaedo says that Plato was ill and unable to be present (59b). Xanthippe (Socrates's wife) and their child are led out, and Socrates's friends enter to find Socrates writing poetry—a hymn honouring the god Apollo—in obedience to a dream he had had.

a) Philosophy as the Pursuit of Death

Socrates then asks his friends to send a message to the poet Evenus, telling him to follow Socrates as soon as possible (by dying, presumably). When questioned about this cryptic advice, Socrates replies that any man who has the spirit of philosophy will be willing to die, though he will not take his own life. Socrates cites Philolaus, a Pythagorean philosopher contemporary with himself, who claimed that suicide is wrong even when death seems better than life, because our lives belong to the gods and not to ourselves. Cebes asks whether it would not be inconsistent to desire death, since death would involve leaving the care of our masters (the gods). In his initial response, Socrates tells his friends he believes that through death he will in fact be going to other gods who are wise and good, and also to departed human beings who are better than the ones he will leave behind.

Simmias asks for more explanation of this, and Socrates sets out to show that philosophy is a sort of pursuit of death. In order to substantiate his claim that the true philosopher not only should not be afraid of but should even welcome death, Socrates gives the following argument:

1. Death is the separation of the soul from the body.
2. The philosopher seeks to sever the soul from the body.

So,

3. Bodily death is the attainment of the goal of philosophy.

Therefore,

4. The true philosopher welcomes death.

Plato's argument, in the mouth of Socrates, seeks to show that philosophy, when practiced properly, involves precisely the same sort of thing that dying involves. The argument turns on premise (2), the claim that the philosopher's goal is to sever the soul from the body. But why think that premise (2) is correct? Plato supports this point with a number of considerations that centre on viewing the body as a hindrance to thinking. The body, with its diseases and its desires for food, sex, and clothing, constantly distracts us. These bodily desires lead to greed, which is the source of conflict and wars between groups of people. Furthermore, the body's senses are known to be unreliable, capable of deceiving us by giving us false information. Anyone who has experienced sensory tricks in a psychology experiment can attest to this. By contrast, the true objects of knowledge, the Forms, cannot be apprehended by the senses but only by the intellect, and this happens when the mind turns itself away from the bodily senses and looks into itself. As Plato says, "if we are ever to have pure knowledge, we must escape from the body and observe things in themselves with the soul by itself" (66d–e). Since philosophy is the pursuit of knowledge, and knowledge can only be attained when the soul separates itself from the body, it follows that philosophy seeks the separation of the soul from the body. But that separation is just what premise (1) defined as death.

The view of philosophy as a sort of purification process by which a person dissociates more and more from the body and identifies more and more with abstract intellectual thought derives from the Pythagoreans, or at least is heavily influenced by them. The idea that real being is to be located in abstract objects introduces us to an important aspect of Plato's Theory of the Forms, which we will be discussing at greater length in the next chapter. But because of the important role the Forms play in some of the arguments in the *Phaedo*, it is worth saying something here about what they are supposed to be. Plato asks Simmias, at 65d, "Do we say that there is such a thing as the Just itself, or not?" He also asks about the Beautiful and the Good, as well as "Size, Health, Strength and, in a word, the reality of all other things, that which each of them essentially is." The objects to which these abstract nouns refer are distinct from particular instances of beautiful or good things, or particular sizes (like 5 feet, 10 inches, which is my own height). They are the essences or common natures of all things that can be called by the same name.

To illustrate what motivates the Theory of the Forms, imagine you were visiting Waterloo (my hometown) from a distant country where there were no bunny rabbits, and that you had never seen a bunny before in your life. One summer night, you are out for a walk, and suddenly a small furry woodland mammal hops across your path. Your friend says, "There goes a bunny." You make a mental note that things of that sort are called bunnies. A few minutes later, your friend stops in her tracks and points out a small shape lurking in the shadows, its nose twitching as it nibbles the grass. "Look," she says, "another bunny." You think to yourself, "Okay, that first thing was a bunny, and now another thing, different from the first, is also called a bunny." You're almost home when out of nowhere a mass of creatures bursts away from where you are walking. "That was a whole family of bunnies—we didn't even know they were there," your friend says with a mild note of wonder in her voice. Each of the distinct, particular, material bunnies you observed is called by the same name, "bunny." There must be some reason for this! If Plato were to join you at that moment, he would surely say something like this: "There is indeed a reason. The reason is that there is an eternal, unchanging Form of Bunny-ness, and each of these particular bunnies participates, or has a share in, that Form. None of these particular bunnies is perfectly a bunny. Each of them undergoes various changes from moment to moment, eventually ceasing to be a bunny entirely upon death. But the Bunny Itself, the Form of Bunny-ness, never changes or ceases to be perfectly *Bunny*. And this is the reason for the bunny-ness of all these particular bunnies." Like bunnies, all particular sensible things are merely images or reflections of eternal Forms.

Of course, the Socrates of Plato's early dialogues—and to a great extent the Socrates of the middle period as well—was interested mainly in ethical concepts, rather than in objects like bunnies and cheeseburgers. But the idea of Forms, as the ideals or essences of things we experience within the sensible world, applies to all of these. Our experiences of particular just acts, virtuous people and beautiful bodies and souls, and our experiences of particular bunnies and cheeseburgers, all point, in Plato's view, to something much more real and stable than these ever-changing sensible realities. Plato believed the goal of philosophy was to contemplate and acquire understanding of the eternal Forms, and that this goal was constantly being frustrated by the intrusions and distractions of the body. For this reason, he thought, true philosophy was the art of dying, of learning to separate one's soul from one's body in order to approach more closely the ultimate and eternal realities.

b) Arguments for the Immortality of the Soul

Socrates's optimism about death and his hope to be in a better place after dying both require that he somehow be capable of continuing to exist after the death of his body, which at the time of the conversation being reported in the *Phaedo* was going to take place in just a couple of hours. But is it really the case that Socrates would still be around somewhere after his body has become a corpse? Cebes points out (at 70a) that not everyone agrees that this is the case:

> ... men find it very hard to believe what you said about the soul. They think that after it has left the body it no longer exists anywhere, but that it is destroyed and dissolved on the day the man dies, as soon as it leaves the body; and that, on leaving it, it is dispersed like breath or smoke, has flown away and gone and is no longer anything anywhere.

If you incline toward materialism, you probably think something along these lines, maybe without the details of the breath or smoke. If a human being is just a material body, then when the material body ceases to live, that's all there is to it. Cessation of brain activity means cessation of mental life. From the point of the death of your brain onward, materialism seems to imply, you will no longer have any experiences or be around anywhere. You'll just be *gone*—annihilated. Cebes continues: it will take "a good deal of faith and persuasive argument, to believe that the soul still exists after a man has died and that it still possesses some capability and intelligence" (70b). And a good deal of persuasive argument is exactly what Plato proceeds to give us throughout the remainder of the dialogue. We'll have to pay close attention to see whether his arguments are convincing or not.

ARGUMENT I: THE ARGUMENT FROM OPPOSITES

The first step in Socrates's first argument for the immortality of the soul consists in establishing the point that:

(1) All things come to be from their opposites.

Socrates does this by performing an induction: He enumerates a list of examples in order to move from those examples to the general point. The larger comes from the smaller, he says, and the weaker comes from the stronger, the swifter from the slower, the worse from the better, etc. So, Socrates urges, every opposite comes to be from its opposite. Furthermore, Socrates claims,

(2) Each pair of opposites is always accompanied by two processes of generation.

What he means by this is simply that for any two opposites, say the large and the small, there is one process by which large things become small (namely, the process of decreasing), and another process by which small things become large (the process of increasing). But we also have to admit that

(3) Being dead is the opposite of living.

Which, together with premises (1) and (2), entails that,

(4) Death comes from life (by the process of dying) and life comes from death (by the process of ... well, by some mysterious process anyway).

But if (4) is true, and life comes from death, then:

(5) Our souls must exist in the realm of the dead (what ancient Greeks called the Underworld) before birth.

And of course, if our souls exist before birth, then our souls are not limited to the body—they are capable of existing apart from the body. If the argument works, then it is at least a significant step toward showing that the soul is immortal.

But does the argument work? There are several places where one could poke holes. For one thing, the induction Socrates uses to establish (1) is not by any means comprehensive. All the examples Socrates uses are comparative terms that admit of a more and a less. Since something can be more or less strong, for instance, it makes sense to think that all stronger things come from something prior that was relatively weaker. But life and death do not seem to be comparative terms. There is no more or less dead; either you're alive or you're dead. So how can we be confident that a generalization from comparative examples will apply also to the case of life and death? We can think of other cases of opposites that are not comparative, where it does not seem to be the case that one always has to come from the other. Black and white are opposites, for instance, but it simply isn't true that all black things must come to be from white things or that white things have to come to be from black things. A white thing could come from a green thing instead, as happened in my own experience, when I painted the green banister in my home white. So we need a reason to think that life and death are more like the comparative cases than the noncomparative ones if we are going to use premise (1) to help establish (4). And even with comparative notions, it does not seem true that one thing must come from its opposite. Lead is a heavier element, but it does not come from lighter elements. Smarter people might have parents who are less smart, or smarter, than they are.

A second problem with the argument lies in the move from the sub-conclusion (4) to the argument's main conclusion, (5). Let's grant for the moment that Socrates has established that life must come from death, since life and death are opposites and all opposites come from each other. The question now arises, what does it mean for life to come from death? Socrates interprets this, in (5), to require a *place* (the realm of the dead) where souls already *exist* somehow prior to birth, in order that they may then come from that place to be born. But that is not the only way of spelling out what could be involved in life coming from death. We could instead think of "death" as inorganic matter, and imagine living organisms being generated from inorganic matter. In that case, souls that previously did not exist as such would come to exist due to the combining in certain ways of inorganic matter. I won't say anything more about this here, however, since the idea comes up later on in the dialogue. Instead, I will conclude discussion of this first argument by noting how instructive it is that Socrates uses the opposites of sleeping and waking as a comparison to being dead and being alive. When you think about it, death does seem very similar to sleeping. In each case, you enter, at least for some period of time, into a state where your consciousness ceases to function. In light of this, the fact that we dive into this state every night is a little odd. Do you ever say to yourself, just before going to sleep at night, "I'm about to plunge into the annihilation of my conscious self"? Well, it's probably best that you don't say that to yourself: you do need your sleep after all, and there's no point scaring yourself unnecessarily—or is there? Before you fall asleep reading this, allow me to move on to the next argument.

ARGUMENT 2: THE ARGUMENT FROM RECOLLECTION

After hearing the first argument, Cebes pipes up and exclaims that the same conclusion (that the soul exists prior to conception and birth) follows from the doctrine of Recollection. You will recollect, from the previous chapter, that according to this doctrine, all learning involves remembering things that were known in a more direct way at some prior point. The way Socrates presented this teaching in the *Meno*, the soul at birth already contains in itself the knowledge of all things, but this knowledge needs to be brought out by a process of Socratic questioning and examination. And how could the soul come to have such knowledge, unless it acquired it prior to birth? Therefore the soul exists before its present incarnation.

At this point, Socrates goes over a proof of the thesis that all learning is recollection. His argument goes like this:

1. A person can recollect something, X, from an experience of something similar to X or from an experience of something dissimilar to X. [Note that to recollect something here means to call or bring it to conscious cognition or awareness.]

2. Even when we recollect X by experiencing something, Y, that is similar to X, Y is never *perfectly* like X, but is always deficient. For example, we recollect the Equal itself (the Form of Equality) from the experience of things that appear to be equal, but in fact are not perfectly equal, e.g., two roughly equal sticks.

3. It is not possible to acquire knowledge of X on the basis of experiencing something else that is deficient in regards to X.

So,

4. The fact that we can recollect something perfect (X) on the basis of experiencing things that are not truly perfect (Y) shows that we must have prior knowledge of perfect things (X).

But,

5. We have no experience of perfect things in the present life.

So from all this we have to conclude that,

6. We acquired knowledge of all Forms (the Beautiful, Equal, Good, Just, Pious, etc.) by direct experience of these perfect things at some point prior to the present life.

But that entails that,

7. Our soul pre-existed our present embodied state and possessed intelligence, and is therefore immortal.

This snappy proof of the doctrine of Recollection, and of the immortality of the soul on its basis, is very helpful in understanding part of the motivation behind Plato's Theory of the Forms. Premise (3), the claim that it is impossible to acquire knowledge of some X based on experience of some Y that is deficient in similarity to X, does much of the work in this argument. Plato is urging us to see that nothing in our sense experience is capable of explaining our possession of various abstract concepts. Take, for instance, the concept of a circle. A circle is, by definition, an extended, round plane figure on whose circumference every point is exactly equidistant from its centre. Notice, now, that you have never encountered such a thing in your sense experience. Every time you've seen a circle drawn on a board or in a textbook, the points have never been perfectly equidistant from the centre. Even a computer-generated circle printed with extremely high resolution would still fall short of the level of precision involved in the concept of a circle which we possess. But if that is the case, and we have never experienced a perfect circle before, how is it that we now possess the concept of a perfect circle? How could we have acquired this concept in response to the presentation, in our experience, of a series of imperfect circles?

Plato's answer is that when we experience imperfect circles, this leads us to recollect the perfect circle that we knew directly, prior to our present embodied state. We knew the Circle itself, the eternal form of Circularity, before we were born, in the place where our soul dwelt at that time. What was this place like? I imagine it as a sort of immaterial museum, full of exhibits which disembodied souls could wander through at will. On one level you would have your exhibits of mathematical entities, such as the perfect Circle, the number Seven (Seven itself), and Equality itself. Elsewhere your disembodied soul could explore the Forms of living things, such as the Bunny itself, the Groundhog itself, and the Form of Ladybug. The important Platonic idea—one that many philosophers have accepted—is that our sense-experiences are insufficient for establishing general concepts of ideal entities. Plato's story of the soul's pre-existence and disembodied

The Spirit of Plato, by William Blake (1816–20)

cognition of the Forms of all things probably strikes you as quite strange. But notice that if you deny this explanation of how we are capable of reaching the general and ideal concepts we in fact possess, then the onus is on you to provide an alternative explanation. How do we come to have such knowledge? As we will see a few chapters down the road, Aristotle seeks to give an alternative account. But how would you explain this? And if you can't explain it, does that mean you have a reason to become a Platonist and accept that the soul really is immortal? I'll leave you to ponder that while I move on to the next argument.

ARGUMENT 3: THE ARGUMENT FROM SIMILARITY TO THE FORMS

Simmias astutely points out that this last argument shows only that the soul pre-exists the body, but not that it exists *after* the death of the body. "What," he asks, "is to prevent the soul ... existing before it enters a human body and then, having done so and departed from it, itself dying and being destroyed?" (77b). Socrates replies that the proof of this further point lies in the combination of the two arguments we've already considered: "If the soul exists before, it must, as it comes to life and birth, come from nowhere else than death and being dead, so how could it avoid existing after death since it must be born again?" (77c–d). Socrates's interlocutors feel that another proof is needed to establish more directly that the soul cannot be dissolved after the death of the body.

Socrates offers the third argument of the *Phaedo* to establish this point:

1. Only composite or compound things (things that have parts) can be dissolved.
2. Things that don't change are most likely non-composite and things that do change are likely to be composite.

Furthermore,

3. Things that are invisible tend to remain the same, while things that are visible tend to change.
4. The Forms are invisible and do not change, but sensible particulars (e.g., particular bunnies or cheeseburgers) are visible and change continually.

So,

5. The Forms are likely to be non-composite and indissoluble, while sensible particulars are composite and capable of being dissolved.

Additionally,

6. Whatever knows something must be like what it knows.

And,

7. The soul is invisible and capable of knowing the Forms.

Therefore,

8. The soul is more like the Forms than like sensible particulars, while the body is the opposite.

But this entails that,

9. "[T]he soul is most like the divine, deathless, intelligible, uniform, indissoluble, always the same as itself, whereas the body is most like that which is human, mortal, multiform, unintelligible, soluble, and never consistently the same" (80b).

Here we have a proof that the soul cannot perish after death, because of the sort of thing a soul is. The soul, Plato tells us, is a simple and indissoluble substance distinct from the body, which is a composite and dissoluble entity. One thing to note about this view of the soul as simple (without parts) is that it appears to conflict with accounts of the soul which Plato provides elsewhere. In the *Republic*, the subject of the next chapter, Plato will argue for a soul that consists of at least three distinct parts. But we'll explore this potential contradiction when we get there.

Plato thinks that a key reason to believe our souls really are partless, immaterial, and immortal is because of our ability to cognize eternal abstract immaterial

Forms. You can try this for yourself. Think about your favourite number. If you don't have a favourite, think about the number seven. Or think of a circle, as defined earlier—a round plane figure whose circumference consists of points each of which is equidistant from its centre. Now, you probably start by getting a mental image of something with a shape like "7" or of a group of seven things (dwarfs?) or of something vaguely resembling a circle. But try to penetrate beyond the images to the purely mathematical or geometrical features of these concepts. If you're doing this, and you can isolate one of these concepts just for a moment, you will be having the sort of experience that Plato is talking about. Plato thinks that when we genuinely contemplate the Forms, our soul is standing in relation to an eternal entity. Here's how he describes it: "But when the soul investigates by itself it passes into the realm of what is pure, ever existing, immortal and unchanging, and being akin to this, it always stays with it whenever it is by itself and can do so; it ceases to stray and remains in the same state as it is in touch with things of the same kind, and its experience then is what is called wisdom" (79d). How, Plato asks, could we experience such cognitive states if we ourselves (or at least something about us) were not very similar to the things we're relating to? If the soul were not itself simple, immaterial, and immortal, how would it be capable of interacting with simple, immaterial, and immortal things?

With this in mind, we can also better understand Socrates's conception of the afterlife. Since we are able to experience such cognitive states in this life, and since we do so when our soul removes itself as much as it can from reliance on the body with its senses, it stands to reason that when the soul has finally been severed completely from the body, it will exist in an even more perfect cognitive condition. The soul, once detached from the body for good, will be free to wander the immaterial museum of the Forms forever, delighting in pure abstract cognition, completely unhindered by the chains of the body. The conviction that life after death would be like this made Socrates not only peaceful in the face of death, but even excited. If there was one place the Platonic Socrates wanted to be, it was hanging around with the eternal Forms.

An obvious problem with the present argument is that it requires that we believe in the Forms. As we are seeing, Plato thought he had several reasons to postulate the existence of these eternal Forms. But can we really believe in such entities? Where, we should naturally want to ask, are such items located? I have somewhat fancifully suggested that they exist in a giant immaterial museum. But can we coherently conceive of disembodied souls wandering through such a museum, or of how the museum in question might exist? This is not to say that it couldn't exist, but only that it is hard to imagine it. Plato might respond to these sorts of questions by saying that this is precisely his point. As long as you're trying to imagine it, you're still letting yourself be tied too closely to your body. Instead you need to go deeper and deeper into the realm of the purely intelligible. Allow yourself to dwell there in contemplation long enough, and you'll start to understand for yourself what such an existence is like.

Before Plato gets to the fourth and final argument for the soul's immortality, several things happen. First, he has Socrates explain how reincarnation works and why people sometimes see ghosts. The philosophical person purifies her soul from the pollution of the body and "joins the company of the gods," but the soul that refuses the philosophical path ends up being dragged back down to the visible region after death, and eventually is re-imprisoned in a new body (81e). Before entering new bodies, these souls may be seen wandering about in misery as ghosts. Those who lived virtuous lives stand a chance to be reincarnated as gentle or social animals, like bees, ants, or human beings, but those who lived viciously come back as donkeys (for the drunkards and gluttons) or wolves or hawks (for those who love injustice), etc.

TWO OBJECTIONS

Socrates's final argument comes in response to the objections which Simmias and Cebes raise against the conclusions established by the first three arguments. So to set us up for the last argument, it will be worth trying to understanding the thrust of these objections.

[Objection 1: The Soul as a Harmony] Simmias goes first, and directs his objection primarily at the third argument we looked at. His main point is that the soul may indeed be invisible, immaterial, beautiful, and divine, and yet fail to be immortal. He seeks to establish this by comparing the soul to something else that possesses the traits just mentioned, and which we acknowledge to be incapable of existence independent of a material body. Simmias argues that the soul can be thought of as the "harmony of the body." A harmony produced by a musical instrument, such as a lyre, seems to be invisible, immaterial, beautiful, and divine, and yet no one would think it could exist apart from the physical instrument that produces it. In fact, the parts of a broken lyre last *longer* than any harmony it could produce. In the same way, the soul, as a "harmony" of the physical elements that compose the body, perishes long before the bodily remains of a human corpse. What Simmias has given us in this description can be seen as a more sophisticated or subtle version of materialism similar to positions from more recent philosophy of mind, such as "epiphenomenalism" and "supervenience emergentism." Simmias admits that it is meaningful to speak of a soul, and to attribute various properties to it, but in the end this soul is completely dependent on its body, can in no way exist apart from its body, and plays no causal role in relation to the body.

[Objection 2: The Weaver Objection] Cebes then presents his own argument from analogy, this time comparing the soul to a weaver who weaves many coats (bodies) to wear and so lasts longer than many of the bodies she inhabits, but nevertheless eventually wears out herself. Why, Cebes asks, may the soul not eventually wear out and perish even though it survives through many bodies and rebirths before its eventual destruction? Cebes, unlike Simmias, accepts Socrates's assumption of dualism and his claim that the soul is much more unified or integrated, and much less soluble, than any given body with which it might be associated. Nevertheless, he thinks the ability of the soul to last longer than many bodies does not show that it *never* disintegrates.

After a pep talk in which Socrates encourages his interlocutors not to give up the chase because of the apparently devastating critiques offered by Simmias and Cebes, Socrates proceeds to deal with the objections. His first reply to the harmony objection is that thinking of the body as a harmony is inconsistent with the doctrine of recollection, since the soul can't pre-exist the body if it depends on the body in the way a harmony depends on a lyre. Given the choice between recollection and harmony, Simmias says he would choose the former as something established and reject the latter as a mere unproven hypothesis. But Socrates has more to say. The soul can't be like a harmony because it differs from a harmony in various ways. The soul, he says, directs the body—it causes the body to do things and even opposes the desires of the body. But a harmony has no causal influence on the lyre. Further, something can be more or less a harmony, but a soul cannot be more or less a soul. And finally, if the soul was relevantly like a harmony, it would be incapable of being morally evil or wicked, since wickedness is a kind of disharmony, and it is incoherent for something that is completely a harmony to participate in disharmony. But we know that, unfortunately, souls *do* participate in wickedness.

Socrates spends significantly more time in responding to Cebes's weaver objection. He begins by stating that an answer to the problem Cebes has raised "requires a thorough investigation of the causes of generation and destruction" (96a). Socrates then launches into an autobiographical account of his own search for understanding of the causes of things. At first he thought natural science could offer him what he was looking for, but trying to explain things by appeal to purely natural causes only left him in great confusion about even the most obvious truths. For instance, I think you will agree that hardly anything could be more obvious than that one plus one equals two. But Socrates says that using only natural science, "I will not even allow myself to say that where one is added to one either the one to which it is added or the one that is added becomes two, or that the one added and the one to which it is added become two because of the addition of the one to the other" (96e–97a). In the case of addition, he says, separate ones mysteriously become two by being brought together, but in another case two results from exactly the opposite process, namely the division of one thing into two parts. Socrates's point here is that a purely physical approach to mathematics only leads to confusion.

Socrates thought he had found a better method for understanding the causes of things when he came upon a book by Anaxagoras, a Presocratic thinker who lived in Athens. Anaxagoras taught that "it is Mind that directs and is the cause of everything" (97c). Hearing this, Socrates got excited, thinking that if that was true, then in order to understand the causes of things "one had [only] to find what was the best way for it to be, or to be acted upon, or to act." So for instance, if a person wanted to know whether the earth was round or flat, she would simply figure out which was the best way for it to be, and would be assured that that is the way it is because, Mind being in charge, everything would be directed and arranged in the best possible way. After explaining everything in this way, Socrates expected Anaxagoras "to explain the common good for all," as the pinnacle of explanation, resulting in supreme knowledge and wisdom. But he was disappointed because Anaxagoras did no such thing in spite of his initial claims, but instead fell back on material causes. Part of Socrates's complaint is that in order to fully understand the universe, or at least significant parts of it, we have to speak of intention, purpose, and reasons for things. But a purely materialistic framework lacks the ability to do this adequately. When trying to explain why Socrates was sitting on his bed, a materialistic account could only speak of the relations between his bones, sinews, flesh, and skin. But to truly understand why he was there (or human action in general), Socrates argues, you have to grasp intentions and motives, in this case Socrates's judgement that it was best and more right for him "to remain and to endure whatever penalty [the Athenians] ordered" (98e). Socrates next leads up to his fourth argument for the immortality of the soul.

ARGUMENT 4: THE ARGUMENT FROM THE FORMS

Finding himself unable to acquire the sort of method he had hoped to get from Anaxagoras, Socrates turned to another method of explanation, a method he refers to here as a "second best" and "hypothetical" approach. Interestingly enough, what Socrates is referring to here is his use of the Forms as explanatory posits. In the discussion that follows, Socrates develops *two levels* at which the Forms can be deployed to explain things. The *first level* involves a straightforward refusal to allow that anything but Forms operate as causes. So if one were to ask why something, Katy Perry for instance, is beautiful, the only answer that could be given, at this level, would be to say that she is beautiful by the Form of Beauty itself, not because of anything to do with her shape or colour, but simply because she somehow participates in the Beautiful. It must be said that this does not give very practical advice on how to become more beautiful. I'm sure that *Cosmo* would never ask Plato to write an article on beauty tips.

Plato himself admits, in the words of Socrates, that this method is safe, naïve, perhaps foolish (100d) and ignorant (105c). And he goes on to present a somewhat more sophisticated account of how Forms can play a role in explanations of phenomena. This *second level* of deployment of the Forms starts by pointing out the difference between a Form and something that participates essentially in a Form. We have the Odd itself, the Form of Oddness, Plato says, but we also have odd numbers, such as the number three or five. Although the number three is not the Odd itself, it nevertheless always possesses the character of oddness, and indeed it would be impossible for there even to be a number three without it being odd. The suggestion that certain particular things have essential qualities, or possess the same character as a Form as long as they exist, makes room for a way of explaining phenomena—such as the generation and destruction of things—that provides a better grasp of how the relevant causation works. Instead of saying merely that a body becomes hot because of the Form of Heat, we can state, more subtly, that a body becomes hot because of the physical element of fire, which makes the relevant body hot because it is part of the nature of fire to be hot. The element of fire participates essentially in the Form of the Hot, and so fire brings the character of the Hot with it whenever it is present (105c).

In this way, the physical presence of fire itself does the work in the causal explanation of why bodies become hot, rather than simply suggesting that bodies become hot by means of the Form of the Hot itself. Indeed, it is hard to clearly grasp how the Hot itself could ever heat anything, since it is an ideal, immaterial object. Using this more subtle mode of explanation, we can say, for example, why snow can never become hot. Snow participates essentially in the Form of the Cold, so at the approach of something hot, like fire, snow can only retreat away (melt) or be destroyed. Because of the character snow possesses, it can never be hot.

The fourth argument for the soul's immortality makes use of the second level of explanation by Forms we have just been considering, especially in the key premise (2). The argument can be formalized as follows:

1. No Form can admit its opposite Form.
2. Nothing that participates essentially in a Form can admit the Form opposite to that in which it participates essentially.
3. What is present in a body that always makes it living is a soul.

Thus,

4. The soul participates essentially in life.

And moreover,

5. The opposite of life is death.
6. The soul cannot admit the opposite of what it participates in essentially.

So,

7. The soul cannot admit death or be dead, or, in other words, possess the character of Death.

We must say then that,

8. The soul is deathless, or immortal.

Furthermore,

9. The deathless (immortal) is indestructible.

Therefore,

10. The soul cannot be destroyed by the approach of death.

Let's take a minute or so to assess the fourth argument itself, before I make some final remarks about the *Phaedo* and its subject matter. As in some of the earlier arguments, everything falls apart if you don't believe in something like Plato's Theory of the Forms. So the success of the argument will depend on the prior credibility of some version of that theory. But granting Plato the Forms for the sake of argument, what else can we say about the cogency of the reasoning he presents here? Premise (3), and the justification Plato gives for it, are questionable. Today we think of the life of a physical organism in mostly mechanical terms. Roughly, we think the reason an organism is alive is because of the physical structures or organs exercising their functions—the heart pumping blood, the lungs taking in oxygen, the nerves transmitting electrical impulses, etc. All of these can be described in terms of bio-chemical or bio-physical processes, without needing to bring in some additional entity called a soul to do the work. So we don't tend to think of the difference between a living and a non-living being as equivalent to the difference between possessing and lacking an immaterial soul. Not having access to the highly developed body of scientific theories about the physical world that we enjoy in our own day, Plato clearly could only make the best of a crude theory of the physical elements in attempting to characterize the natures of particular things like snow or fire. We tend to see his forays into natural science as rather outdated.

I have represented premise (4) as following from premise (3), so that Plato's reason for concluding that the soul participates essentially in life is that the soul always brings life to the body it inhabits. But could we reach (4) independently of (3)? If we think of a soul more along the lines of a mind, do we have more reason to think that it is essentially alive than we would have on the view that the soul is simply a principle of life for a body? In other words, does it make sense to think that the mind is somehow essentially (always) active? An immediate response would be to point to unconscious states like deep sleep or a coma to show that minds are sometimes inactive. A later thinker like Gottfried Wilhelm Leibniz (1646–1716) would disagree, claiming that the mind is always conscious, even if the conscious states exist at higher and lower levels. Leibniz thought that unless the mind were aware of its surroundings, at least in some minimal way, we would not be able to explain how a person can be awakened even from a deep sleep by sufficiently loud noises. But even if you have a modified version of (3) along the lines we have just been describing, it remains unclear how we can move from saying the mind is always active *whenever we observe it*, to the claim that the mind is essentially alive in the sense that it is impossible for it not to be alive. If there is room for thinking something such as a mind might always be in a certain state whenever we observe it yet not be in that state as a matter of necessity because of the sort of thing it is, then there is a gap between (3) and (4).

So there are a few places to raise objections at the early stages of the *Phaedo*'s last argument for the soul's immortality. Once you have premises (1)–(4) in place, I take it that the rest of the argument follows fairly straightforwardly. If the soul really does participate in life essentially, in the sense that it can never lack life, it does seem pretty clear that the soul could never die or be destroyed.

So whether or not you accept the argument will depend mainly on what you think about Plato's view of the Forms and their relation to particulars, and of Plato's suggestion that we have souls (or at least minds), and that these souls are essentially alive. What do you think? Has Plato convinced you of these things at all? We will be giving him one final chance, in the next chapter, to persuade us that there might really be Forms after all. And the topic of the soul is by no means absent from the next Platonic dialogue we'll be considering, the *Republic*.

THE CONCLUDING MYTH

Having concluded that the soul cannot be destroyed by the death of the body, and so must continue to exist after bodily death, Socrates goes on to draw out several of the implications of this claim: "[W]hen death comes to man, the mortal part of him dies, it seems, but his deathless part goes away safe and indestructible, yielding the place to death" (106e). The deathless part is of course the soul, and where it goes, Socrates says, is "to dwell in the underworld." Since this is the case, it becomes urgent that we realize that we have to care for our souls, not only for the present life, but also for "all time," since our souls will be around for all time. This gives a different meaning to long-term planning; we aren't just talking about retirement anymore. Now, Socrates says, "there is no escape from evil or salvation for [the soul] except by becoming as good and wise as possible, for the soul goes to the underworld possessing nothing but its education and upbringing, which are said to bring the greatest benefit or harm to the dead right at the beginning of the journey yonder" (107d). The choices we make in this life, especially those choices that impact our moral and intellectual formation, have significant ramifications for the life that comes after bodily death. The immortality of the soul raises the stakes enormously for the path we choose to take—whether to follow philosophy and become educated or not.

In developing his concluding myth about the afterlife, Plato embarks on some interesting speculations about the nature of the underworld and its relation to the earth and the heavens (109a–113c). He tells of people who live at the edge of the earth's atmosphere and look up to the ether (in a kind of parallel to the way we live at the edge of the sea on earth and look up to the body of air surrounding the earth). These people have far superior vision, intelligence, and communication with the gods than we do. According to Plato's mythical account, human souls who have committed crimes or evil actions in life wander alone for long periods of time after death, until they come to the Acherusian lake in the underworld. There, if they have lived an average life, they are purified from their evil deeds and rewarded for their good deeds before being sent back to birth again in some form of reincarnation. Those who are thoroughly wicked are cast into the deep pit of Tartarus, where they remain forever. Those whose crimes are heinous but who are capable of being cured must continually return from Tartarus to plead for forgiveness from those they wronged; they can only be released if they reach reconciliation. Pure and moderate souls, on the other hand, quickly acquire companions and guides who lead them to a suitable dwelling place. The very pious come to dwell in new bodies in the high and pure regions near the earth's atmosphere, while those who have been sufficiently purified by philosophy go on to live, in a bodiless form, in still higher and indescribably beautiful places.

Socrates concludes that because of these things, "one must make every effort to share in virtue and wisdom in one's life, for the reward is beautiful and the hope is great" (114c). He does not insist on all the details of his account, but argues that since we know we possess immortal souls, we should "risk the belief" that something along these lines is true and seek to live accordingly. Further, a person should repeat such stories about the afterlife "as if it were an incantation," in order to keep up the motivation to be devoted to education and a morally upright life (114d–e). This sort of argument bears some similarity to Blaise Pascal's famous wager argument. According to Pascal (1623–62), if there is even a remote possibility of an afterlife in which we will be judged by God and either rewarded or punished for the way we have lived, we should (if we are rational) live in such a way as to secure the reward and avoid the punishment. Since the reward is so great, and the punishment involves such a significant potential loss, even without certainty about the afterlife, a rational person should bet on it being real. Whether or not we will continue to exist in some form after the death of our bodies is certainly a question that has profound practical implications. Plato's *Phaedo* concludes with the details of Socrates's last moments and his death, followed by Phaedo's concluding remark, "Such was the end of our comrade ... a man who, we would say, was of all those we have known the best, and also the wisest and the most upright" (118a). Plato's portrait of his teacher depicts Socrates as a man who lived according to what he believed and taught all the way to the end, and who now serves as an example for the rest of us, thanks in part to Plato's memorial tribute in this dialogue and elsewhere.

2. THE SOUL IN ARISTOTLE AND IN LATER THINKERS

Plato's thinking on the soul, like so much else he wrote about, has had an enormous impact on later philosophical theorizing. Although we will not be covering Aristotle's work entitled *Peri Psuches* (*On the Soul*) in this book, we will have some opportunity to think about his view of the soul in the context of two of his other works, the *Physics* and the *Metaphysics*. But it is worth pausing here to note the way Aristotle's views in some ways challenge and in other ways continue Plato's own thinking on the nature of the soul. For Aristotle, the soul is the form of the living body, the principle that structures the matter out of which the body is composed into an organism of a certain type, capable of exercising its various vital functions. This aspect of the view Aristotle presents in his *On the Soul* lends itself rather easily to a sort of materialism or naturalism about the soul. Although the soul is conceptually distinct from the matter out of which the body is formed, it nevertheless exists only as the form *of a body*. As such, Aristotle's general conception of the soul was not of something that could be separated from a body in order to descend into Hades or ascend into the blessed intelligible realm that Socrates hoped he would reach.

When it comes to Aristotle's view of the mind (*nous* in Greek), things are different. Aristotle seems to have believed that the highest component of the human being, our active intellectual faculty, was in fact immortal, and could exist in separation from the body (see *On the Soul*, iii.5, 430a23). What exactly Aristotle meant by the active intellect is a much-debated topic. But it does hold out the possibility that Aristotle was in some respects consistent with his teacher Plato, despite the differences posed by his own generally naturalistic approach to the soul.

Plotinus, the founder of Neoplatonism who taught and wrote in the second century CE, held to a more obviously Platonic conception of the soul, which could properly be called mystical, if not religious, in character. And through Plotinus, Platonic thinking about the soul profoundly influenced the philosophers of the Medieval period, beginning with Augustine. It is interesting to compare Plato's conception of the soul, and his corresponding dualistic understanding of the human being, to the view of the human person the Christian West inherited from the Hebrew Scriptural tradition. One of the major early heresies which the Christian church fought against is called Gnosticism, a view that understood matter to be inherently evil and the source of evil. The Jewish Scriptural account of the human person is much more earthy, and the importance of the material creation is attested to in the Christian doctrine of the resurrection of the body. Rather than seeing the soul as something capable of floating off from the body into an immaterial museum, the writers of what we call the New Testament understood life after death to involve a distinctly bodily existence, albeit a re-created body that is importantly different from the one we now possess—a "spiritual body" in the words of Paul from 1 Corinthians 15:44.

In the early Modern period, Descartes famously championed the cause of mind-body dualism. For Descartes the soul or mind was an immaterial, thinking substance, and the body was a purely material, mechanical substance. As such, the soul and the body were radically distinct in their natures, and this led to the famous mind–body problem, namely the problem of explaining how two completely different substances could possibly interact with and relate to one another. Thinkers contemporary with Descartes, and in the centuries following, spent a good deal of effort trying to solve this problem, and many ingenious solutions were proposed, but none of them has resulted in any generally agreed-upon solution. As I noted earlier, the mind-body problem is still with us today, as evidenced in current debates on the nature of mental states and conscious experiences and their relation to the neurobiological activity of the brain.

This state of affairs speaks to a broader, fundamental philosophical problem that underlies many of the particular debates contemporary philosophers still engage in today. The problem, expressed generally, is how to account for the existence of personal selves (as we experience ourselves to be) within the mechanical, naturalistic, and largely deterministic view of the universe we have inherited from the Scientific Revolution (roughly, 1550–1700). What place do conscious, moral agents, who act with free will, have in a mechanistic and materialistic universe? Is the way we naturally think of ourselves as free moral actors merely some sort of illusion? And what does all this imply about the meaningfulness of life, or the lack thereof? These are only a few of the many questions linked to the *Phaedo*'s central topic of the nature of the soul and its immortality.

3. CONCLUSION

So, did Plato convince you that you have a soul? More than that, did he manage to persuade you that the soul likely exists after the death of the body? If you think about it, the stakes are high on this issue, so that if there is even a remote possibility that we can survive bodily death, this would change everything. In Socrates's own words, "if what I say is true, it is a fine thing to be convinced ..." (91b). For this reason, it is unsurprising that many of the great thinkers since Plato's day have been concerned with the issue of the possibility of life after death. Even the great Enlightenment thinker Immanuel Kant (1724–1804), who did not believe it was possible to *prove* that there is life after death, held that existence beyond our present condition was something we had to postulate in order to uphold morality. Without life after death, and the divine judgement of human beings that goes along with it, Kant thought, there would be no assurance of the proper proportioning of moral goodness with happiness, and of moral evil with punishment. But since morality demands this proportioning, there must also be an afterlife in which it takes place.

Today, some empirically-minded philosophers of religion point to near-death experiences (NDEs) as another sort of evidence that life after death is possible, and perhaps even a reality. We can also approach the topic of life after death from a pragmatic approach, like that argued for by Leo Tolstoy (1828–1910) in his short work "A Confession." Tolstoy argues that if death is truly inevitable, then life cannot be ultimately meaningful, since all of our goals and projects will in the end be rendered null and void. One could argue pragmatically from these grounds that we should believe in life after death even if we don't know whether it exists or not, since without it there is no ultimate ground for human hope. But hope is arguably a necessity of life, without which human beings tend to descend into despair. This sort of argument would not justify a person on purely truth-oriented grounds in believing in life after death. But it would offer instead practical reasons for doing so.

Hopefully this consideration of Plato's *Phaedo* and some of the key questions it raises has been helpful to you as a way of sorting through what you yourself believe about these things. Why not take some time now to reflect a little further: Do you believe that human beings have immortal souls? If so, what considerations seem to support this? And if not, what considerations weigh against the possibility of our possession of immortal souls? Finally, do you think these questions are important? What difference might they make in a person's understanding of life?

Chapter 4

JUSTICE
AND THE
GOOD IN PLATO'S
REPUBLIC

HISTORICAL CONTEXT

In order to appreciate some of the context and motivation behind Plato's *Republic*, written around 375 BCE, we have to understand Plato's personal relationship to politics. Born into a noble Athenian family, it would have been natural for Plato to enter the world of politics. But he grew up in a period of Athenian history that involved intense turmoil and conflict, both with other city-states and within itself. In addition to the horrors of the war with Sparta, there were also significant crimes being committed at home. Plato saw Athens swing back and forth between republican and democratic forms of government multiple times. But each new form of government that arose seemed just as capable of corruption and atrocious behaviour as the others. The thing that probably disgusted Plato most about the Athenian politicians of his day was the fact that, in 399 BCE, they executed his friend and teacher Socrates, whom Plato regarded as the most virtuous and noble person alive. If Athens was a just state, how could its political and legal system have allowed it to commit this monstrous injustice?

From Socrates's death onwards, Plato sought a solution to the problem of justice and the state, a problem that he treats in several of his works, and which he also pursued in society. After the death of Socrates, he left Athens and travelled for a while before returning to found his school, the Academy, around 386 BCE. During his travels, Plato encountered Dionysius I, the tyrant ruler of Syracuse in Sicily, and became good friends with his brother-in-law Dion. In 367 Dion invited Plato to come and train his nephew Dionysius II as a philosopher ruler. The experiment was a flop: apparently Dionysius had a hard time with mathematics. But Plato tried again later in Asia Minor with Hermias of Atarnaeus, who was more open to his influence, and to that of other philosophers. The Academy, to which Plato devoted most of his time and energy for the rest of his life, was an institution designed to train and educate future rulers. All of this goes to show that Plato took pretty seriously his own theory of the ideal state expressed in the *Republic*, and took practical steps to try to realize his ideals.

INTRODUCTORY BIG QUESTION:
IS THERE AN OBJECTIVE MORAL STANDARD?

One of the big questions we will be encountering in Plato's *Republic* is whether or not there is an objective moral standard. From one perspective this is the central question of the dialogue—Plato develops his account of the ideal state at least in part as a response to the claim that justice, or morality, is merely subjective and arbitrary. (Keep in mind that the Greek word *dikaiosune* is broader than the English word "justice," and could be translated instead as "moral goodness" in general.) We've already touched on the question of a moral standard in our earlier discussion of the subjective relativism proposed by the sophist Protagoras, who argued that human beings are the measure of all things. And the *Euthyphro* raised the related issue of whether morality is grounded on the will of the gods.

Moral relativism is the view that moral claims are true or false only relative to a standpoint—the subjective viewpoint of a particular individual or shared by a particular society; and, further, that no standpoint is right or wrong. This means that there are no objective universal moral truths, but that it's up to each individual (or society) to decide what to hold right or wrong. So, for example, because slavery is morally condemned by our society but held perfectly morally acceptable in ancient Greece, then we can't say that ancient Greek society was morally defective; slavery is wrong according to us, but okay according to them, and that's the end of the story. It's like finding something delicious or not: I think Kalamata olives are delicious, and you hate them, but there's no overall truth of the matter.

A thoroughgoing moral relativist ends up having to say that the reason it's wrong to slaughter innocent children as a hobby is that people believe that it's wrong. If things changed so that people believed instead that it was right to slaughter innocent children, then, if moral relativism is true, *it would be morally right to do so.*

There are many problems with moral relativism, not least of which is how deeply counterintuitive it feels to say that enslaving other people could ever be the right thing to do. The moral relativist is also faced with an apparently fatal dilemma concerning the truth conditions of her own claim. Is the statement *"All moral truths are relative"* objectively true, or is its truth only relative? If the moral relativist says it's objectively true, she has admitted that at least one truth about morality is not relative, which seems to contradict her position that all moral truths are relative. If, on the other hand, the moral relativist says that the claim is *relative*, then she is forced to accept that if someone else were to assert the contrary claim, "Moral relativism is incorrect," that person would also be correct, because whether or not a claim about morality is correct depends only on what people believe to be correct. But if both her own claim and its opposite are equally correct, then what is the point of asserting moral relativism in the first place?

Possibly the biggest worry for moral relativism is that it seems to undermine morality altogether. If, according to moral relativism, one person or group of people are correct in thinking that (for instance) cannibalism is a good practice, while another person or group of people are equally correct in thinking that cannibalism is a bad idea, then moral relativism fails to give us any real *moral* guidance about cannibalism at all. We wanted to know whether or not cannibalism was morally right. But all moral relativism can tell us is that some people think it's right, and others think it's wrong, and that's all we can really say. In other words, moral relativism replaces a **normative** perspective of morality with a purely **descriptive** understanding. Normativity concerns the way things *should* be, or the way things *ought* to be, while descriptions only tell us how things in fact are. And if there is anything we want to know when we ask properly moral questions, it's whether something *ought* to be the way it is or not. *Should* there be such a large gap between the wealthy and the poor? *Should* people be discriminated against because of their race, gender, religion, or sexual orientation? A purely descriptive account that only tells us what people believe about these questions arguably fails to answer the moral questions in any meaningful way.

Of course, people have some good reasons for wanting to be moral relativists. For one thing, questions of morality are often difficult to answer, and we want to be respectful of the different ways people answer them. In a liberal, multicultural democracy like Canada, we value tolerance and pluralism, and we also tend to bristle at someone else telling us how we should live. But tolerance and humility do not require a person to subscribe to relativism. A **moral objectivist** believes that the facts about what is right and wrong, or good and bad, are not primarily facts about what people happen to believe about these things. According to the moral objectivist, moral truths are claims about *reality*, so that normativity is somehow part of reality itself. An objectivist moral theory is an attempt to locate the normative aspect or aspects of reality. **Utilitarianism**, for example, is a moral theory developed by Jeremy Bentham and John Stuart Mill in the nineteenth century; it identifies the moral goodness of an action with the consequences it produces. Roughly, according to the utilitarian theory, the morally right action is the action that produces the greatest net utility, that is, the greatest total benefit or happiness, for all people concerned.

Now it seems clear that a person can believe that there *is* an objective moral standard, and yet wonder about *what* it is. She might humbly think that she does not know what it is, or that other people have a better grasp of what it is than she does. Just because I believe that there is an objective moral right and wrong does not mean that I have to force my views about it on anyone else. Plato and Socrates (at least as Plato presents him) are without a doubt moral objectivists. Whether they are of the humble variety I'm describing, I'll let you decide for yourselves. Unsurprisingly, for Plato, and for the figure of Socrates who speaks for him in the dialogue, the objective moral standard has something to do with *virtue*, a notion that was central to ethical thought for both of these thinkers. And as will become apparent in our examination of the *Republic*, Plato is also after an *ultimate* moral standard, which he identifies as The Good, or the Form of Goodness itself. The search for an objective moral standard is another motivation for Plato's Theory of the Forms—if we are going to have genuine moral standards, we will want them to have the enduring, precise, and absolute features that belong to Forms, as opposed to sensible objects which are always changing and never perfect. So, as we will see, Plato's account of the nature of justice in the state and in the individual leads him to unfold further dimensions of the Theory of the Forms.

If you wanted to study this sort of issue in greater depth, you would be entering the area of **metaethics**, a branch of philosophy concerned with the general nature of morality (e.g., is it objective or subjective?) and the meaning of moral concepts (e.g., what do words like "good," "evil," "right," and "wrong" actually mean?). Before diving into the *Republic* itself, let me leave you with some questions to ponder: *Do you believe that there is an objective moral standard? If you think morality is relative, how would you respond to the objections I raised to that view? And if you think there is an objective standard concerning what is morally good and evil, what do you think that standard consists in?* Take a moment to think about how you would answer these questions before you go on to consider what Plato thinks.

1. *REPUBLIC* I & II: IS JUSTICE SOCIALLY CONSTRUCTED?

The first book of Plato's *Republic* reads like a typical Socratic dialogue focused on the question, "What is justice?" This contrasts with the rest of the work, in which Socrates elaborates a lengthy theory about the ideal political state. Plato thinks the task of identifying the ideal state is essential as a step toward understanding the nature of justice.

a) Problems with the Conventional View of Justice

The conversation begins with some light back-and-forth between Socrates and the elderly Cephalus, who is replaced by his son Polemarchus at 331e. The target of this part of the dialogue is the conventional view that [definition #1:] *justice is to give to each person what is due to them.* Socrates dismantles this view fairly quickly. His first point is that it would not always be right, or just, to give people what you owe them. For instance, if you borrowed an axe from a friend, and afterward your friend went insane and was foaming at the mouth and uttering threats against his neighbours, you should not return the axe to your friend even though it is due to her (since it is her property). This leads Polemarchus to spell out the initial definition more fully: [definition #2:] *Justice is to benefit one's friends and harm one's enemies.* Socrates's questions lead Polemarchus to agree to some absurd conclusions. But what ends up defeating the revised definition of justice is Socrates's argument that it is never just to harm anyone. To harm a person, the two agree, is to make that person worse, by the standards of human excellence (335c). But that would mean making that person unjust, so that a just and good person, by exercising their justice and goodness, ends up making others unjust and bad, which seems absurd. This is not a particularly strong line of reasoning, since we can harm people in various ways without making them morally worse off. But let's leave that to one side, in the interest of staying focused on the main flow of the dialogue.

b) Thrasymachus and Justice as Oppression

At this point Thrasymachus, a sophist who happened to be present, is unable to control himself any longer and bursts onto the stage with his own definition of justice. According to Thrasymachus, [definition #3:] *justice is the advantage or interest of the stronger party* (338b–c). It is important to understand the implications of this statement. Thrasymachus is asserting that justice, or morality, is a matter of whoever is in political control making up laws to suit their own purposes. We call it "just" to obey the laws that are in place in the state we live in. But these laws are simply reflections of the arbitrary will of those in power, who have made up these laws to keep the population under control, enabling the rulers to maintain their position and privilege. Part of what this entails is that justice is a matter of convention—those in power make it up as they please. It also follows from Thrasymachus's definition that, generally speaking, it is not in a person's interest to be just. Why follow the laws if you can get away with not doing so, especially if those laws are only the invention of rulers trying to control you? Thrasymachus has, in effect, defined justice as the oppression of the weak by the strong.

Socrates notes an immediate flaw in Thrasymachus's first definition by pointing out that rulers can be mistaken about what is in their interest. If so, they could create laws that actually end up working *against* their interest. In this case, it would be just to do what is *not* in the interest of the stronger party, since justice is the weak obeying the laws created by the strong. Not wanting to give up easily, Thrasymachus adds to his definition the somewhat *ad hoc* point that a ruler never makes a mistake while acting as a ruler, so that no ruler acting as a ruler could ever make a law that was not in her own interest. But Socrates dismisses Thrasymachus's revised proposal by generalizing from examples to the statement that *no science or art or skill aims at its own interest; all aim, rather, at the interest of their subjects.* The doctor acts in the interest of her patients; the horse-trainer seeks to improve horses, etc. To be consistent, we have to say that a true ruler acts in the interest of her subjects, not in her own interest, as Thrasymachus had maintained.

Thrasymachus counters with his own examples: shepherds and herdsmen tend to their flocks in the knowledge that they will make a profit from the sale of wool and be able to use the meat. So he restates his position that a political ruler does her job not for the good of the people ruled or governed, but for what she can get out of it for herself. He also asserts that being "unjust" (by which he means acting in one's own self-interest in disregard of moral constraints) is always better than being "just" (acting according to moral requirements). Note that the inversion of the meanings of "just" and "unjust" in this part of the argument stems from the fact that Thrasymachus is now critiquing Socrates's understanding of the terms.

Socrates's refutation of Thrasymachus's restated position involves drawing a distinction between the skill of profit-making and the skill of ruling or governing. His point is that making money is something additional and incidental to ruling. While a ruler may seek money for herself, she does not do this *as a ruler*, but as a wage-earner, an art she practices on the side or in addition to her task of ruling. Socrates also counters Thrasymachus's additional point about the relatively greater benefits of injustice over justice by a somewhat convoluted argument. Thrasymachus's claim rests on counting injustice as typical of a wise and excellent person, and justice as typical of an ignorant and bad person. The gist of Socrates's refutation consists in showing that these linkages fail. Based on the behaviour typical of a good and wise person, and on that of a bad and ignorant person, Socrates shows that the former is like the just person and the latter like the unjust, not the other way around, as Thrasymachus wanted it. As two final nails in the coffin, Socrates shows that (a) in order to be successful in crime, even thieves have to be just, at least toward one another, and that (b) being just is the very function or purpose of a human being. So justice turns out to be far better and more necessary than injustice after all.

c) A More Subtle Variation on the Theme

Thrasymachus leaves in an angry huff, but two of those listening are unsatisfied with Socrates's treatment of his position, and they propose, in Book II of the *Republic*, to present a stronger version of the view expressed by Thrasymachus. The two interlocutors in question are Glaucon and Adeimantus, the brothers of Plato, who act as Socrates's main conversation partners for the remainder of the work. Let's consider their reformulation of Thrasymachus's position.

Glaucon goes first, and he argues for three claims. He begins by portraying [claim #1] a sort of **social contract theory** of justice similar to the one Thomas Hobbes would later describe in his famous work *Leviathan*, published in 1651. According to the view Glaucon presents, people are basically motivated by self-interest—they try to get as much for themselves as they can. "Justice" emerges when people recognize that if they try to follow their own self-interest, taking what they want at the expense of others, they most likely won't be able to get away with it. Since any given individual is more likely to be harmed by others than to get away with harming them, people agree to a second-best situation and create laws protecting them from each other. So justice is something constructed by people.

This being the case, [claim #2] people only follow the laws against their will, because they know they can't do what they really want to do, namely, to get whatever they want without being caught. Glaucon seeks to prove this second point by a thought experiment. Imagine two people, Jane the Just and Tom the Unjust. Jane and Tom both come across a ring with the power to make them invisible. Tom, being unjust, sees this as the opportunity he has been waiting for, and promptly begins to use the ring of invisibility to steal things, sneak into people's homes and have sex with them, and generally do whatever he feels like, knowing that no one will be able to catch or stop him. Jane, unlike Tom, has lived a just life, following the laws and living according to moral principles. So you would expect that when Jane discovers her newfound powers, she would use the ring for good, or at least would not use the ring to do unjust things. But, Glaucon argues, no one who acquired such a ring would stick to her principles. Sooner or later Jane would go ahead and start taking what she wanted. And if she didn't everyone would laugh at her and think she was an idiot for not fulfilling her self-interest to the full measure when she had the chance to do so.

The third point [claim #3] is that the truly unjust person will always do better than the truly just person. In order to contrast these two types of people, Glaucon says we have to consider the extreme cases where the unjust person gets away with everything and even has a reputation for being a wonderful person, while the just person gets a reputation for being evil. The truly just person sticks to her moral principles even when she loses many things because of it. People misunderstand her, mistreat her, and finally torture and crucify her, but she refuses to compromise. These considerations show, Glaucon thinks, that a person is obviously better off who *appears* to be just rather than really *being* just.

Adeimantus adds to Glaucon's argument the further point that people never praise justice or the just life for its own sake, but rather for the sake of other things. Fathers encourage their children to be just because it will lead to favour with the gods and with other people. A just person will have a good reputation and will thereby gain access to all sorts of social and religious benefits. If a person reflects on these things, she will realize that the thing to do is not to actually *be* a just person, but to get people to *think* you are just. If you work at it, you can get people to think you're a good person, and all the while you are getting rich by taking all sorts of goods unjustly. The gods will know what you're up to, but if we are to believe what the religious poets Homer and Hesiod tell us, then we can simply pray and make offerings to restore their favour to us. By living unjustly, you'll have so much money that it will be easy to perform the necessary sacrifices to the gods, and still have a lot left over.

The two brothers conclude their speeches by urging Socrates to prove to them that justice really is good in itself, for its own sake, apart from the reputation and other benefits it can bring with it. They want him to show them the effect that each of justice and injustice "has because of itself on the person who has it—the one for good and the other for bad—whether it remains hidden from gods and human beings or not" (367e). In order to do this, Socrates will have to describe the nature of justice and injustice. Socrates admits this is a very tall order, but true to character he is willing to do his best.

d) The Significance of the Issue

Before turning to the way Socrates answers the challenge of the two brothers, it would be good to pause for a moment to make ourselves aware of what is at stake in the question they are posing. We could express the issue in various ways:

1. Is there any reason to be a morally good person when I could get away with being bad?
2. Is it likely that I will be somehow better off if I refuse to compromise my beliefs about what is right and wrong?
3. Is being morally good a reward *in itself*, or do I really only benefit from having a reputation for being good?

We could also pose the question in terms of moral relativism and objectivism:

4. Is moral goodness or badness an objective matter, or only a matter of what people think or believe about it?

However you understand the basic issue this dialogue is dealing with, it is worth noting that it speaks to our own lives in a particularly deep way. What kind of life are you choosing to live? Are you living the life of a morally upright (just) person, or are you living in a way that shows you don't care all that much about moral goodness? At the end of your life, would you be happy with the sort of life you have chosen to live, or would you regret it?

Most of us think of ourselves as more or less good people. At the very least, we get upset when other people say we are bad, or criticize our character in some way. But when we become upset by such criticism, are we concerned about whether or not we truly are good, or are we more concerned about what people think of us? Are you the sort of person who would stick to your moral principles no matter what, or would you compromise and do what you know to be wrong as long as the reward was high enough? Ask yourself what you would do if you yourself came across a ring of invisibility. If you could walk into a bank and take as much money as you wanted to without being detected, would you resist doing so simply because it is the wrong thing to do? You could hitch rides on planes anywhere you wanted to go for free, enjoy the finest life in palaces and resorts of your choice, and generally have whatever you wanted. Would you really avoid taking advantage of the situation because it would be unjust? If you would, then you are a person of integrity and a true companion of Socrates, at least as he is depicted by Plato. If not, then you rank alongside Thrasymachus and those who hold the views described by Glaucon and Adeimantus. Either way, if you care about truth, you should be willing to question and examine your beliefs about these things. In what follows, we will see Socrates arguing that it is always better for us to live as morally good or just people, as people of integrity. In fact, Socrates will try to show us how justice, or moral goodness, is inseparable from human well-being or happiness, and how the unjust person can never truly be happy.

2. JUSTICE IN THE STATE AND IN THE INDIVIDUAL

Socrates makes an important move early on in his answer when he reasons that in order to discover the nature and effects of justice in the individual, one must first discern justice in the political state. He claims that seeing justice in the state will be like finding a message written in large letters that can be read more easily than the same message written in small letters (justice in the individual). Socrates's assumption that we can expect there to be sufficient similarity between justice in the state and in the individual to warrant transferring what we learn about one to the other could certainly be questioned. Why might someone think that justice as an attribute of the state, which is an impersonal entity composed of many individual citizens, will be much like justice as a virtue of an individual person's character? It is certainly *possible* to think of a state on the model of a person. We speak of a state deceiving or oppressing its subjects, which can be understood using the analogy of an individual person lying or bullying others. But it is worth asking how far we can go in making such connections.

What Plato says to justify this move is that both individuals and states can be legitimately called just (368e). But we might reasonably point out that a single word can often be used in different ways when applied to different things. For instance, both my waist and my patience can be called "thin." I can say, "I lost ten pounds and my waist grew thinner," and I can also say, "That person was annoying me and my patience was growing thinner." But the thinness of my waist is a very different sort of thing from the thinness of my patience, even though there is some overlap in meaning, having to do with "becoming less." Because of this difference, I would not want to transfer conclusions about my waist to conclusions about my patience or vice versa. How can I know, in the case of the state and the individual, that there is enough of a link between the two to warrant my thinking that I can learn about justice in the latter from observations about justice in the former? Plato may have thought it was obvious that the two were similar since a state is, after all, made up of individual people. But he doesn't really prove this. This is important because, as we will see, Socrates's answer to the challenge posed earlier by Glaucon and Adeimantus depends on the move from justice in the state to justice in the individual citizen which he has not argued for.

Lady Justice, or Justitia, the Roman goddess who personifies justice

a) Characterizing the Just State

Socrates begins his account of the ideal political state by locating the origin of the city-state in human need. Because of our needs, and our inability to provide for all of our needs by ourselves, we band together with other people who have different natural aptitudes. Considering only our most basic needs, we require at least a farmer, a weaver of clothes, a builder of houses, a shoemaker, and a doctor to make up our minimal city. And for the city to run *efficiently*, each of these people would have to focus exclusively on his or her own task, doing a single job well rather than trying to do many different jobs and doing them all poorly. This principle, that in the good city each member will focus on his or her own task, plays an important part in later stages of Socrates's argument. It leads immediately to an expansion of the minimal city because the different workers will require tools, which means there need to be other people in the city who are skilled at producing tools of different kinds. Further, the workers will need animals to assist with the labour, so there will have to be herdsmen to care for the animals. And since the needs of the citizens will likely require some imports, there will be merchants, markets, and general labourers to make this expanded city run.

Up to this point, Socrates has described what he regards as a "healthy" city. Glaucon suggests that people will want more than just the minimal provisions—they will want various luxuries, delicacies, and desserts, fancy decorations and entertainment of many kinds. Socrates calls the city in which people pursue unlimited material possessions a sick or "feverish" city, and shows how this desire for more than the necessities of life is the origin of war (373e). To produce all these luxuries, the population of the city will have to be greatly increased, which will in turn require more land, leading to war with neighbouring cities. The city in fever will need an army and a soldier class dedicated to the art of fighting. Socrates calls the group of citizens dedicated to the protection of the city the guardians, and much of what follows in the rest of the *Republic* concerns the sort of education the guardians will need to do their job effectively. The guardians will have to be gentle toward their fellow-citizens yet harsh toward the enemies of the state. As such, Plato writes, they will have to possess high spirits, speed, strength, and a philosophical disposition (376c).

Leaving aside for now the portions of Books II and III that deal with the early stage of education, we pick up the argument again at 412b, where Plato divides the guardian class into two: (1) the guardians proper or the **rulers** of the city, and (2) the **auxiliaries** of the guardians who act to support and enforce the convictions of the rulers. In addition to these two classes in the ideal city-state there is a third class, (3) the **producers**, composed of the farmers and craftsmen. Plato thinks we need to tell the citizens of this ideal state a "noble lie" or myth to enforce the class distinctions. In brief, the myth states that although all the citizens are brothers, "the god who made [them] mixed some gold into those who are adequately equipped to rule, because they are most valuable. He put silver in those who are auxiliaries and iron and bronze in the farmers and other craftsmen" (415a). We could comment on many things about what Plato is doing here, but I want to keep in focus Socrates's answer to the challenge of showing that it's always better to be just than to be unjust. The main thing to observe in this context is the way Plato traces each of the four main virtues—wisdom, courage, moderation, and justice—to different aspects of his ideal state. These four virtues have traditionally been called *the cardinal virtues*, and classical thought understood all of morality to hinge on these four character traits or dispositions of the soul. Plato thinks that since the state we're looking at is acknowledged to be ideally good, it must possess each of these virtues. But where can each of them be found? In order to isolate justice, Socrates reasons, we must first locate the three other virtues and can then expect to find justice as what is left over.

Wisdom, according to Socrates, belongs to the first class, the rulers of the ideal state, who are charged with creating the laws, and must do so according to knowledge about the city as a whole and its "relations, both internally and with other cities" (428c–d). We find **Courage** in the auxiliaries, who must be able to overcome fear and act boldly in enforcing the laws laid down by the rulers. **Moderation**, or self-control, concerns agreement between the different parts of the state about who should rule and who should be ruled. Although Plato says moderation is a kind of harmony involving all the parts of the state, it can nevertheless be observed most clearly in the producing class, who show their agreement by submitting to the laws made by the rulers and executed by the auxiliaries. Socrates then discovers that **Justice** resides in the very principle he had used to ensure effective

The Cardinal Virtues, from left to right: Fortitude (Courage), Temperance (Moderation), Justice, Prudence (Wisdom). From Sandro Botticelli and Piero del Pollaiolo's 1471 painting of the theological and cardinal virtues.

functioning in the state throughout his whole discourse, namely the principle that each member or part must stick to its own task. Socrates argues for this view of justice in three ways. First, it is the power of preserving the state that remains after the other three virtues have been dealt with. Second, in courts of law the judges would judge based on the principle "that no citizen should have what belongs to another or be deprived of what is his own," which is another way of saying that each member should stick to his or her own thing. And thirdly, the greatest harm and ruin that could come to the city would classify as injustice. But the surest way to ruin and destroy the city would be to have one of the other classes besides the rulers attempt to usurp control of the state. Since injustice arises when one class tries to do the job of another class, it stands to reason that justice must be each part sticking to its own task.

b) Justice in the Individual Soul

After delineating the way justice and the other virtues arise within the state, Plato turns to the related appearance of the virtues in the individual human soul. According to the picture of the soul Plato presents here, the soul has three parts or faculties, and each part corresponds to one of the classes in the ideal state. The **faculty of reason**, or the intellectual power of the soul, corresponds to the ruling class in the state, and just as wisdom belonged to the rulers, so Plato wants us to associate the virtue of **wisdom** in the individual human soul with the faculty of reason. For Plato, if a human person is good, her reason will be in charge. As the rulers make the laws to govern the operation of the state, so an individual person's reason should provide her with the principles and rules of conduct that govern her life and activity. So it is crucial for the reason of a good human being to possess the character of wisdom. The part of the individual soul that corresponds to the state's auxiliary class, Plato calls the "spirit," or the "**spirited part**" of the soul. From the way Plato describes this part of the soul, we can understand it as something like the heart or the will, the seat of emotions (e.g., anger) and of our ability to carry out the choices we make. To the spirit belongs the virtue of the auxiliary class in the state, namely **courage**. As the auxiliaries had to enforce the laws of the rulers on the population as a whole, and especially on the large and "unruly" producing class, so the spirit has the job of ensuring that the principles laid down by the individual person's reason are followed by that person.

To illustrate this, consider a practical situation you may have encountered in your own experience: It is the night before a big test in one of your courses. Your reason has laid down the principle, "I will always study and have a good night's sleep before an important test." But your friends call you up and ask you to join them at the campus bar for drinks followed by a party back at someone's house. You realize that if you listen to your friends, you may have a good time in the moment, but will probably end up doing much worse on your test as a result. As

Plato sees it, if your spirit is working properly, it would oppose your friends and your own appetites and desires, even with anger if necessary, since they are seeking to turn you away from the law of your reason. The appetites (or the "**appetitive part**" of the soul) constitute the third part of the individual human soul, which corresponds to the producing class in the state. Here we are to think of our basic human drives, such as the drive for food and water or the drive for sex. In the ideal state, the virtue of **moderation** or self-control could be seen most clearly in the submission of the producing class to the rulers, a submission enforced by the auxiliaries if necessary. The same idea appears in the context of the individual soul; a person has the virtue of moderation when all the parts of her soul agree that reason should be in charge, not the appetites or the spirit. In particular, moderation involves the soul's regulation of its appetites in accord with the higher elements of reason and (rationally moderated) spirit.

If you've been following these chapters attentively, you may have realized that in Plato's description of the soul in the *Republic* we have a view that is in tension with the view of the soul he presented in the *Phaedo*. In the *Phaedo*, Plato described the soul as simple, immaterial, and partless, and seemed to identify it with what he now calls the intellectual part in the *Republic*. The soul's most distinctive activity, in the *Phaedo*, was cognizing the Forms. There, Plato described the appetites as belonging to the body rather than to the soul. In the *Republic*, by contrast, Plato explicitly argues for a tripartite (three-part) view of the soul based on the different functions the soul seems to exercise. The fact that Plato gives two different and apparently contradictory views of the soul in these two dialogues leads us to wonder whether he preferred one view over the other, or whether there is some way to reconcile the different perspectives so that they do not really contradict each other. Whatever we might say about Plato's considered view of the nature of the soul, our main goal at present is to understand how he uses the model of the soul he gives in the *Republic* to show how it's always best to be just rather than unjust. To that demonstration we will now turn.

c) *To Be Just Is Always Best*

According to Plato's account, **justice** in the individual soul is the same sort of thing it was in the state. In the state, justice involved each class sticking to its own task and not interfering with the tasks of the other classes. In this way the harmonious and effective running of the state could be assured. Similarly, in the individual, when each of the three parts of the soul stays focused on doing its own proper job, the whole soul can function in a maximally well-ordered and efficient way. If the appetites were ever to become too strong and begin to take over and control the individual's life, that individual would be in a condition similar to civil war, and would eventually be destroyed by this inner disorder or injustice.

Putting the whole picture together, we can see from the following table how Plato understands the analogy between the ideal state and the morally good individual soul to work, as far as the four cardinal virtues are concerned:

Table 2

VIRTUE	IN THE STATE	IN THE INDIVIDUAL SOUL
Wisdom	Rulers	Reason or Intellect
Courage	Auxiliaries	"Spirit"
Moderation	Producers	Appetites
Justice	Each part doing its own task	Each part doing its own task

You might be asking yourself, "What does all this have to do with the questions raised earlier by Thrasymachus, and then reformulated by Plato's two brothers?" Recall that Socrates is trying to show that justice is always better than injustice for an individual person. After working through the argument, he has concluded that justice is simply the well-orderedness, unity, or wholeness of the soul. He goes so far, in fact, to state that (paraphrasing): *justice is the health of the soul, and injustice is the condition of a soul that is diseased or sick* (444d–e). No one would think it would be better for herself to be sick than to be healthy. If given the choice, who would prefer to have brain cancer rather than not to have it? Or to have heart disease or kidney failure instead of a properly functioning circulatory and renal system? In the same way, Plato urges, no one in their right mind would choose to be unjust rather than just, because no one in their right mind would choose to have a disordered and dysfunctional soul rather than one that is working properly. If justice is the health of the soul and injustice its sickness, it follows fairly straightforwardly that it is always better to be just than unjust, and that justice has immediate benefits for the one who has it just because of what it is, apart from what else may be gained by being, or appearing to be just.

"Justice is the health of the soul, and injustice is the condition of a soul that is diseased or sick." (*Republic*, Book IV, 444d–e)

---

d) Critiquing Plato's Account

Plato himself acknowledges (see 504b–c) that the answer he has given up to the end of Book IV is incomplete, and needs to be filled out in greater detail, and indeed much of the later sections of the *Republic* involve the sort of filling out he thinks is needed. So it would be somewhat unfair to criticize his explanation of the superiority of justice over injustice for its lack of completeness. Still, although his position is powerful, it is worth being aware of the ways in which it falls short of what we might want. In a complete account, we would want a justification of the claim that moral goodness consists in the four cardinal virtues. Why should we think these virtues are the most important, or that they together make up the entirety of what it is to be morally good? Part of Plato's strategy for isolating justice was to subtract the other three virtues from the ideal state and look at what would be left over. But if more than four virtues are central to moral goodness, then this method can't ensure that we've located justice. If two or more aspects of moral goodness remain after having dealt with wisdom, courage, and moderation, then perhaps we've located something else and justice is still waiting to be found. In more general terms, modern readers like ourselves should want to know why we should accept the framework of Virtue Ethics instead of some other approach to ethics, like (for instance) Deontology or Utilitarianism and their alternative accounts of justice. Of course, Plato was not writing in a modern context, so we can't expect that he would have refuted these alternative approaches to ethics. But his insistence on the four cardinal virtues still feels somewhat arbitrary for someone not already committed to that mode of ethical thinking.

A deeper problem with Plato's account up to this point is that it arguably fails to provide us with any properly *moral* content. To explain what I mean here, consider a person who is *wise* in the sense that she has knowledge of the way things really are and of how to successfully achieve her goals. Furthermore, she is *courageous* in her ability to control her fears and not give in to temptation to turn aside from her goals, and *self-controlled* in that her appetites do not fight against what her reason and spirit command, but reliably submit to them. Imagine that this person is also *just* in Plato's sense; her reason, spirit, and appetites all do their own proper jobs without interfering with one another, so that her soul acts in a unified and efficient way in all that she does. Now, why couldn't this person live as an expert thief, an exquisitely skilled liar, or even a calculating murderer? Why could she not make use of the finely tuned faculties of her soul to commit terrible and devastating crimes? Plato has not told us anything to make us believe that his virtuous person will reliably act in ways we normally think of as morally good. The best *criminals* will be those who are really smart, really brave, and really self-controlled, and their souls will act effectively as unified wholes to accomplish their purposes. But for all that, they won't be morally good, but just the opposite. If, as I'm arguing, Plato's account of justice remains disconnected from our ordinary views of what it means to be morally good, then we have to ask whether he's really accomplished what he set out to do. He said he was going to tell us why it's always better to be just, and we thought that was going to include sticking to your principles, being honest, and not stealing or harming others to your own advantage. Instead, we seem to have an account of justice that can equally well be present in a person who lives in ways we would usually think of as *unjust*.

If Plato has an answer to the objection I've just raised, I believe it lies in his conception of wisdom. The morally good person, for Plato, must be wise. Indeed, the whole morality of the person, as Plato conceives of it, depends on the faculty of Reason laying down its principles for conduct based on its wise apprehension of reality. And there is more to being wise, Plato can argue, than just being very smart and knowing how to get the things you want, though that is also part of what it means to be wise. Being wise involves, crucially, possession of knowledge of *the Good*. As we'll see in the final part of this chapter, the Form of the Good is the key to everything for Plato.

3. THE PHILOSOPHER KINGS AND THEIR EDUCATION

Plato makes a pivotal claim in Book V, concerning the simplest alteration that would have to be made to currently existing states in order to move them toward the ideal political state Plato has been describing:

> The society we have described can never grow into a reality or see the light of day, and there will be no end to the troubles of states, or indeed ... of humanity itself, till philosophers become kings in this world, or till those we now call kings and rulers really and truly become philosophers, and political power and philosophy thus come into the same hands. (473d)

Now as a professional philosopher myself, I am naturally inclined to think Plato is right here. The philosophers should be made kings—how true! If any of you see my name listed on a ballot for a provincial or federal election, be sure to remember your lessons from the *Republic* and vote for me! In all seriousness though, Plato was well aware of how crazy what he was saying would sound to his hearers. After all, not too many years earlier the Athenians had executed Socrates, the paradigmatic philosopher, out of fear of the sort of influence he was having on the Athenian youth. What could be less likely than that these same people would now hand over power to Socrates's followers?

But Plato was dead serious about this suggestion. The fact that he took it seriously can be seen from two of the historical situations I mentioned in the introductory section of this chapter. The first is his political experiments in other city-states like Syracuse, and the second is his foundation of the Academy as a philosophical training school for future rulers and statesmen. If we can get over the apparent absurdity of the idea that your current philosophy professors would make great politicians, we can begin to appreciate the rationale of Plato's recommendation that political power be entrusted to the philosophers. Who are the philosophers, in Plato's view? The true philosophers are those people who are completely dedicated to the pursuit of wisdom and truth. As a result, they are the citizens most likely to actually be wise. If you ask yourself, "Would I rather have decisions made about public policies in my city by someone who is wise and understanding, or by someone who is relatively foolish and ignorant?," the answer seems obvious. The wise person is the one likeliest to understand how human beings and their societies function, how they can function *well*, and how to realize the condition of ideal functioning. As a result, it only makes sense to let the wise person be in charge and make the rules, doesn't it?

Maybe you're still not convinced. That's okay. But for the sake of following the reasoning that comes next, try to accept it at least for the sake of argument, and see what follows. If we are really going to take some philosophers and put them in charge of our cities, then we're going to want to make sure they really are wise. And how, as crafters of an ideal state, do we make sure that our citizens turn out to be wise? A big part of the story is going to involve the sort of education we provide for them. Plato's concerns with education appear in various places in the *Republic*, and the following sections outline the main moves that he makes.

a) Basic Training

In Books II and III, and again in Book X, Plato critiques the Greek education system of his day and offers a program of educational reform. While the big picture of what he is up to concerns primarily the education appropriate for the guardians, many of the implications would affect the education of citizens more generally. After accepting the traditional division of education into physical training (for the body) and poetry and music (for the soul), Plato takes Homer and Hesiod to task for the false conceptions of the gods they portray in their poetry. Keep in mind that the stories recounted in such poems functioned as the basic sources for ideas about religion and morality for the Greeks of Plato's day, beginning from the earliest days of their childhood. Plato's Socrates argues that many of these stories are simply false; that is, they are inaccurate accounts of the nature of God or the gods. Firstly, Socrates gets his interlocutor, Adeimantus, to agree that a god must be good, and thus not the cause of anything harmful but only of what is beneficial (379b). As a result, the accounts of the shocking moral behaviour of the gods, and of Zeus doling out good fates to some and bad fates to others, need to be expunged. A god would only cause harm in order to benefit someone by a just punishment, and the stories the young learn about the gods should portray them in this way. Secondly, Socrates secures agreement that the nature of the gods does not permit their changing form or deceiving people by appearing in illusory ways (381c–383a). Just as the gods themselves (being good and true) must hate falsehoods, so should we; and we must especially hate and reject falsehoods about the most important subjects (theology and morality). But if so, then once again the accounts of the gods offered by Homer and Hesiod are in many places seriously flawed. Socrates and Adeimantus agree that the laws of the ideal state should include laws that prohibit any such accounts from the education of young citizens. The goal is to ensure that the future guardians "will be as god-fearing and godlike as human beings can be" (383c).

Plato's Socrates lays down these further requirements about the content of education (and the corresponding censorship and reform of the current education system) in the ideal state (386a–392c):

1. Stories heard by children should lead them to praise, rather than to fear, life in Hades, so that warriors will not be afraid to die in battle if necessary;
2. Lamentations and pitiful speeches of famous men and gods should be erased, to bolster the future guardian in bearing misfortune calmly;
3. Gods and admirable people must not be represented as being overcome by laughter;
4. Moral examples of people who submit to their rulers and who possess control over their appetites will be presented, while examples of those who do the opposite are deleted;
5. Stories of gods and heroes who love money, are willing to be bribed, or are arrogant and cruel, should be expunged from the curriculum.

Having considered aspects of the *content* of the stories suitable for the education of the young, Plato next considers what *style* these stories should or should not have (392c–398b). His point is that in reciting poetry that involves imitation of base characters or things that are beneath the virtue of the good citizen, that citizen debases him or herself. This is because good or bad character is formed by acting in good or bad ways. Plato's ideal state, then, will allow only simple narrative (non-imitative) poetry, or poetry that involves imitation of the thoughts and words of virtuous people. Later on, in Book X, Plato's critique of poetry goes even further, to the point that he wants to banish poets altogether from the ideal state. He raises three charges against poetry there: First, poetry consists of copies of copies of real things (Forms), so that the things it presents are twice or three times removed from reality. Plato uses the example of a bed: the artist who depicts a bed (whether visually or with words) represents only a certain appearance of a physical bed, which is itself only a pale imitation of the Form or nature of bed-in-itself (598b). Secondly, poets lack any firm knowledge—or even correct opinion—of the things they depict. Those who make or manufacture objects have correct belief about the merits and defects of their products, which they acquire from those who actually use the products. Those who have the skill to use the products have something closer to knowledge of their goodness and badness. But the poet is not acquainted with things in either of these ways (602a). Thirdly, poetry stimulates the lower, instinctive part of our souls, urging us to give free reign to our feelings rather than reason. The result, Plato says, is that pleasure and pain become our masters rather than the laws and principles laid down by reason

(605b). For these reasons, Plato concludes that the only sorts of poetry acceptable in the ideal state are "hymns to the gods or paeans in praise of good men" (607a).

Following his discussion (in Book III) of poems that present stories, Plato turns to songs, advising that the only songs to be allowed in the ideal state are those whose lyrics spring from a virtuous soul, and whose harmonic mode and rhythm are adapted to suit the words. A young person trained by poetry and music of the sort described here will be attracted to, and will easily recognize, the things that are beautiful and good. And precisely this, Plato tells us, is the goal of the education of the soul (403c). Plato's initial discussion of physical education is relatively brief, emphasizing an avoidance of unnecessary pleasures that can overcome a person's self-control. Plato assumes that if the soul has been properly trained, the training of the body will follow. He also asserts that physical training is only for the sake of the body accidentally; like training in poetry and music, physical education is also primarily for the health of the soul.

b) Advanced Education

Book VIII lays out a program of further education for those guardians who will become rulers in the ideal state. The basic education described above (together with two years of compulsory military training between ages eighteen to twenty) is a preparatory stage for the higher education Plato now describes; basic education gives the rulers-to-be habits that make their souls (and bodies) harmonious with what is good and beautiful, but it does not yet impart *knowledge* of these things to their minds. For this, the rulers-to-be must be trained for ten years in the five mathematical sciences, after which they will move on to an additional five years in pure philosophy, which culminates in a vision of the Good (as we will see in the next section). Plato discusses the way arithmetic, plane geometry, solid geometry, astronomy, and harmonics have the effect of drawing the mind away from the world of becoming (the ever-changing, sensible world) toward reality (525c) by compelling it to use pure thought to attain the truth (526b). The objects of plane geometry are two-dimensional (triangles, circles, etc.) and the objects of solid geometry are three-dimensional (pyramids, spheres), but in each case they are, Plato says, "eternal." Geometry considers shapes and bodies in the abstract, while astronomy (in Plato's sense) makes use of the heavenly bodies—the most perfect among visible things—to lead the mind on to contemplation of "the true relative velocities, in pure numbers and perfect figures, of the orbits and what they carry in them, which are perceptible to thought and reason but not visible to the eye" (529d).[1] As astronomy leads the mind to numerical relationships and proportions starting from the sense of sight, harmonics performs the same function in mathematical education, but beginning from the sense of hearing.

---

1   I have used Desmond Lee's translation here: *Plato: The Republic*, 2nd ed. (New York: Penguin Books, 2003), pp. 260–61.

The study of mathematics is itself only a preparation for a still higher form of thinking, which Plato calls dialectic. Dialectic is philosophy, properly speaking, and it alone can take the mind to the pinnacle of the intellectual realm, where it grasps the Good in itself. Mathematics is always hypothetical in that it proceeds from starting points (assumptions; e.g., axioms) that it leaves unquestioned. Dialectic, Plato tells us, "destroys" or "does away with" the hypotheses in order to reach the first principle itself, and so to attain a secure base for knowledge (533c–d). It involves a systematic attempt to grasp the very being of each thing in itself (533b), and results in the ability to give an account of the being of each thing (534b).

The rulers of the ideal city will be chosen from those who successfully complete each course of study. After their education in dialectic is complete, the rulers-to-be will then be sent into the political sphere for fifteen years of practical training in political offices. Then, at the age of fifty, those who have proved themselves at all the prior stages must now use their knowledge of the Good as a pattern to put the city, as well as themselves and their fellow citizens, in order (540a–b). These roles would be open to women as well as to men, so long as they possessed the required nature and could succeed at the relevant training (540c). Plato implemented something like this educational curriculum in his Academy, which has been called the first Western university. Although his approach to education was quite revolutionary for a culture that regarded Homer and Hesiod as the functional equivalent of the Bible, it exercised a profound influence in shaping the schools that would develop over the following centuries.

c) The Analogies of the Sun and the Divided Line

Book VI and the earlier part of Book VII fill out the account of education described above, explaining in greater depth what true wisdom consists in, and who the true philosophers really are. This part of the *Republic* also ties Plato's program of education to his middle-period epistemological and metaphysical doctrines, which centred on the Theory of the Forms. In Book VI Socrates says that the thing a wise ruler needs to know most of all is the Form of the Good, since "it's by their relation to it [their participation in Goodness Itself] that just things and the others become useful and beneficial" (505a). Without adequate knowledge of the Good, the knowledge of many other things will not be truly helpful. The only problem is, Socrates says, we don't have adequate knowledge of what the Good is. And in spite of the persistent requests of his interlocutors, Socrates says he can't explain the nature of the Good to them since he does not know it. He does, however, offer to describe what he calls "an offspring of the good," and to let the offspring function as an analogy for its father. The offspring Socrates refers to is **The Sun**. The sun illuminates all visible things, and as a result is the cause of our ability to see. The sun also plays a causal role in the existence of visible things—at least in the case of living things, the sun provides "growth and nourishment" which enables living things to exist (509b). Thinking of the Form of the Good on the model of the sun, we must understand it to accomplish two things: First, it illuminates all the intelligible things, and is thereby the cause of our ability to know them and of their being known, and second, it causes the very *being* itself of the objects of knowledge, namely the Forms. The Good, according to Plato, is the cause of all knowledge, truth, and being, but is itself somehow beyond them. He says at 509b, "not only do the objects of knowledge owe their being known to the Good, but their being is also due to it, although the good is not being, but superior to it in rank and power."

I'm guessing that for many of you, the idea of a Good which is beyond being, truth and knowledge is not the sort of thing you ordinarily think about or discuss with family and friends. The Form of the Good, superior to being itself in rank and power, receives further treatment by Plato in a second analogy, what is usually called **The Divided Line**. The divided line image is a way of delineating the different cognitive conditions a human soul can be in. Here is how the line looks, when drawn in the way Socrates describes it.

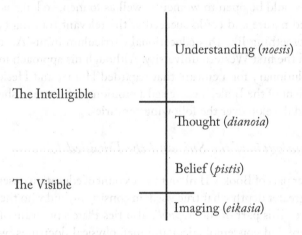

Diagram 4: Plato's Divided Line

Following Socrates's instructions, the lower section of the line represents the visible realm. Plato sees the two cognitive states that operate in us with regard to the sensible world (namely imaging and belief or opinion) as deficient relative to the higher states that deal with the intelligible realm. Neither the images or impressions we receive in sensation, nor the opinions we form without using properly dialectical methods, are truly stable cognitive states. Plato describes the two cognitive states of the soul placed *above* the divided line—the two that deal with intelligible objects rather than merely sensible ones—in terms of hypothetical or non-hypothetical reason. Hypothetical reasoning (labelled "Thought" in the diagram) begins with principles or definitions and makes use of them to follow their implications, much in the way you start out in geometry with definitions of a line, a point, etc., and make use of them to reason to further conclusions, but you don't question these definitions themselves. They are mere *hypotheses*—suppositions. Moreover, hypothetical reasoning makes use of images (for instance, a drawing of a circle), even if it's only to bring to mind the intelligible things represented by the images (for instance, circularity itself). Plato thinks there is a higher cognitive state, located at the top of the divided line (and labelled "Understanding" in the diagram). This state occurs when a person reaches "the non-hypothetical first principle of everything," that is, the Form of the Good, and then comes down from it to conclusions "without making use of anything visible at all, but only of forms themselves, moving on from forms to forms, and ending in forms" (511b–c). As becomes clearer in later parts of the *Republic*, Plato identifies this highest level with the exercise of true philosophy.

d) The Allegory of the Cave

Book VII continues the exposition with still another analogy, and this one may be the most famous analogy in all Western philosophical literature: **Plato's Cave**. Plato sets out by asking us to "compare the effect of education and of the lack of it on our nature to an experience like this ..." (514a). He proceeds to describe prisoners chained in a cave staring at a wall on which shadows are being projected. They've been this way from birth, so that they've never experienced anything but shadows, and they think that's all there is to reality. But one prisoner escapes, and this prisoner's ascent through the cave to the outside world represents the process of a soul becoming educated. The escaped prisoner first sees a fire and statues of things being paraded in front of it; she understands that these statues and the fire providing light

A seventeenth-century portrayal of Plato's cave. The figures at the top are projected onto the wall on the right. From Jan Saendredam's 1604 print of Cornelis van Haarlem's painting, *Antrum Platonicum*

are the cause of the shadows she had been observing all her life. The shadows on the wall correspond to the lowest level of the divided line, where the soul considers only images of sensible or visible things. The fire and the statues represent the next level, visible things themselves and the physical sun that makes them visible. The cave as a whole represents the entire visible or sensible realm. Pretty much all of us start out our intellectual lives in the cave, inundated by images and information, beliefs and opinions, that have no reliable grounding in reality.

But there's more! For Plato, you'll remember, there is an entire intelligible realm (the world outside the cave), separate and distinct from the visible realm. The escaped prisoner eventually leaves the cave altogether and begins to see the things themselves of which the statues in the cave were only images: real living animals, plants, and humans, etc. As the statues were more real than the shadows produced by them, she now sees that the statues themselves were only copies of these things that are still more real. This stage represents the third level of the divided line, labelled "Thought" in the figure above. Finally, her eyes become strong enough to look at the sun itself, and she understands that the sun is the cause of the entire world of visible things, making them visible and also giving them existence. Bringing the various images of the Line, the Cave and the Sun together, I have represented Plato's perspective in the following table:

Table 3

THE CAVE	THEORY OF FORMS	THE LINE
The sun	The Form of the Good	Understanding
Things in the world outside the cave	The world of the Forms	Thinking
The fire in the cave	The physical sun	Belief/Opinion
The shadows on the wall	The world of sensible things	Imaging

Leaving the cave behind and entering the outer world represents the beginning of the mind's real education. But once a person has learned to concentrate on the intelligible objects (Forms) rather than the sensible world, she still has a long way to go before she can ascend to the pinnacle of all learning, education, and knowledge. Plato calls the Form of the Good the "non-hypothetical first principle of all that exists." It is the ultimate basis and reason for everything else that is. As we've already discussed, the forms represent ideal principles in the sense that the particular empirical examples we see around us (e.g., visible horses or cheeseburgers) are only imperfect approximations to the ideal form (e.g., the Form of Horseness or the Cheeseburger itself). For these reasons, the Forms are "higher" and "better" than the sensible particular things that participate in them.

Given this normative asymmetry between particulars and Forms, Plato owes us an account of how it is established. His answer is that there is a normative Form (the Good) that "radiates" directly upon all the other Forms, but only indirectly upon the empirical copies, through the Forms themselves. We can also recall the older Socratic idea that formulation of proper definitions (corresponding to forms, for Plato) is epistemologically superior to the delineation of particular examples. The normative asymmetry we see represented in the *Republic* thus relates to the cognitive asymmetry anticipated in the earlier Socratic dialogues.

In Plato's view, once you come to gaze intellectually on the Form of the Good, you no longer need any assumptions or hypotheses, since you've made contact with the very heart of reality itself. This is the cognitive condition of the true philosophers whom Plato believes should be in charge of the state, so that the state, and the individual citizens in it, might be truly good. To look upon the Form of the Good, and then to "descend" back down and see everything else in its light, is a stage of education only a few people reach, and those who do reach it do so only with great difficulty. But without such knowledge, Plato believed, no one could possibly direct her own life, let alone an entire state, in a way that would lead to true happiness and flourishing. It follows that the power to make decisions about the governance of human life ought to be entrusted to those few who possess this vision, namely the true philosophers.

4. CONCLUSION

I have presented Plato's *Republic* mainly from the point of view of its argument for an objective standard for morality. I have not gone into the explicitly political side of the work, about which much could also be said, but have sought to emphasize aspects of Plato's profound ethical and meta-ethical explorations in the *Republic* that have to do with his understanding of ultimate reality and knowledge. The whole picture of education that sets apart the true philosophers from others rests on the claim that there exists an intelligible world, and that this intelligible world is both more real than the sensible world around us and somehow causally related to the sensible world. Plato's intelligible world also involves an ultimate principle or source of intelligibility and being, the Mother of all Forms and all reality, namely the Form of the Good. One of the biggest problems this approach faces, then, is that it remains unclear how this intelligible realm is supposed to exist. In the chapter on the *Phaedo* I referred to the realm of the Forms somewhat jokingly as a kind of immaterial, unchanging museum through which disembodied souls might wander. Joking aside, however, we might ask, "Seriously though, Plato, where is this supposed other world, and what is its manner of existence?" Keep this question in mind as you work through the coming chapters. We will find Aristotle critiquing Plato's Theory of the Forms along somewhat similar lines. Later thinkers like Plotinus and Augustine after him devised an innovative answer to this question that would have a profound impact on philosophy for centuries in the West: they placed the eternal Forms (Ideas) in the mind of God.

As our discussion of the *Republic* comes to a close, we also conclude our examination of Plato's work. Nevertheless, the spirit of Plato will continue to be with us throughout this text. Our next great philosopher, second only to Plato in terms of his influence on the course of Western thought, is Aristotle, who was a student of Plato in the Academy and who developed most of his own views in dialogue with his master. Plato's metaphysical and epistemological views, and in particular his theory of an intelligible world of Forms governed by the ultimate principle of the Good, would provide the materials for Neo-Platonism, a later movement that would embed Platonic themes deeply in the history of Western thought, where they would continue to inspire and evolve all the way through the Medieval period and even up to the present day. Though we've completed our tour of Plato, I hope some of the themes we've covered will stay with you, provoking you to self-examination and challenging you to find your way to a life of greater virtue and wisdom.

Chapter 5:

LOGIC AND SCIENCE IN ARISTOTLE

HISTORICAL CONTEXT

Like Plato, Aristotle exercised an enormous influence over the history of Western thought. He wrote over 200 treatises, covering pretty much every topic you can think about, and pioneered many of the disciplines or sciences that still exist and are studied today—from biology to psychology to physics and astronomy, to literature, rhetoric, political science, and many other fields, in addition to the various parts of philosophy, including ethics, metaphysics, aesthetics, and logic. Aristotle wrote so much, and with such profound insight, that some of the later Islamic commentators on his work wondered whether Aristotle was really a human being or rather an angel sent by God to show humanity what is possible with human reason and intellect.

Born in 384 BCE in Stagira, a city in Macedonia, Aristotle came to Athens and joined Plato's Academy as a young man, about the age when a person would begin his or her undergraduate studies today. He stayed with the Academy until he left Athens after Plato's death in 347 BCE. At the Academy, Aristotle engaged in

The School of Athens (1511) by the Renaissance Italian painter Raphael. At the centre are Plato (left) and Aristotle (right), surrounded by other Greek philosophers.

discussion and debate with Plato and other great minds of the day, and began to develop his own approach to philosophy. Whether or not Aristotle was a committed Platonist (a follower of Plato) is a question that people are still debating today. In Raphael's famous painting *The School of Athens*, Plato and Aristotle take centre stage, with Plato pointing upwards—presumably toward the realm of the Forms—and Aristotle pointing downward, toward concrete earthly realities. This highlights some of the profound disagreements that seem to exist between the two great philosophers. Yet the later Platonic tradition understood Aristotle's philosophy as an *interpretation* of Plato's, rather than as a series of contradictions of the master. As we will see, there is truth to both of these perspectives on their relationship.

Alexander the Great (356–323 BCE)

After Plato's death, Aristotle continued to carry out philosophical and scientific research, and was probably helped in this by his association with Alexander the Great, who, if we believe the stories about him, used to bring back strange biological specimens for Aristotle from his military expeditions. Aristotle was Alexander's personal tutor for between two and eight years. Returning to Athens in 335, Aristotle founded there his own philosophical school, the Lyceum, which continued to function until it was destroyed in 86 BCE, and was active again in the second century CE. The philosophers in Aristotle's school were called "Peripatetics," after the *peripatos* (covered walkway) in the Lyceum, and maybe (as a later story has it) because they liked to walk around while discussing their thoughts. Aristotle wrote in and managed the Lyceum until he left Athens again in 323, fearing for his life because of the anti-Macedonian attitude that arose from time to time in Athenian society. Famously, Aristotle claimed he left the city so that Athens would not sin a second time against philosophy—a reference, of course, to the execution of Socrates in 399 BCE. Aristotle died in 322 BCE.

INTRODUCTORY BIG QUESTION:
PHILOSOPHY AS OBSESSION WITH ORDER

Some people are more organized than others. We need organization in many areas of our lives, whether it's keeping your room clean and tidy, or managing time in your schedule, or planning out a diet and exercise regimen for yourself. Personally, I'm the sort of person who has a great *desire* for order and organization, but I often struggle to realize this desire in my practical daily life. In my undergraduate days, once or twice a term I would set aside a couple of days to do nothing but clean my room. It would take me hours to do this, because each piece of paper or miscellaneous object strewn across my desk and floor had its own proper place, and I would not be able to set it down until I could determine exactly where it belonged.

The desire to organize things also plays a role in some ways of philosophizing, and Aristotle was possibly one of the most obsessive philosophical organizers. At least that's how I like to think about Aristotle's *Categories*, and about his logical enterprise more generally. In the *Categories*, Aristotle presents the ten "highest kinds" of things that exist. He sees everything that exists as falling under one or another of these ten categories. One could draw an analogy to a filing cabinet with ten clearly delineated drawers, into which every item in the whole inventory of reality could be placed. Of course, each drawer would be internally divided into folders, and the folders further subdivided into subfolders as needed. Aristotle viewed his *Categories* as a kind of organizing strategy that made visible the basic joints of reality, reflecting the orderly structure of the world itself.

Logic is a key part of Aristotle's mental organizational effort, but science is just as important. Not only did Aristotle want to get his conceptual categories in order, but he also wanted to put in order the totality of the reasons or explanations for things. For Aristotle, "science" did not necessarily refer to hard empirical science, like physics or chemistry, which make use of the scientific method we are familiar with today. A science was simply an organized body of knowledge, which started from first principles (such as axioms in mathematics) and displayed the rational relationship between the other statements in the science and the principles by means of deductive argument forms. After discussing Aristotle's logic, epistemology, and physics, we will eventually get to metaphysics, the discipline that examines the basic starting points of all knowledge and reality. It is tempting to see Aristotelian philosophy as one massive system incorporating everything a person could possibly know. Of course, Aristotle couldn't quite pull that off—after all, even an angel of reason can only do so much in a limited lifespan!

Do you buy into Aristotle's idea that reality can be organized into a certain number of basic kinds? If *you* were to come up with a list of basic sorts of things that exist, what would your list include? Another question: Are you excited by the prospects of putting all of human knowledge into a structured system, showing how all truths can be derived from basic principles? If these are the sorts of thing that get you going, then you'll love the readings associated with this chapter. As we go through them, ask yourself whether you think Aristotle is on the right track, and if not, how his organizational strategy could be improved, or what other methods could be employed in the pursuit of knowledge and truth about all aspects of reality.

1. LOGIC AND REALITY IN THE *CATEGORIES*

Aristotle's *Categories* is the first of his logical treatises. And yet, as we will see, the *Categories* also covers some significant metaphysical themes. If we understand the way Aristotle thinks about the relation of language and reality, his apparent blurring of logic and metaphysics should not surprise us. For Aristotle, human thought and extra-mental reality are bound much more tightly than they are for many philosophers after Immanuel Kant. Kant, like Aristotle, presented a scheme of "categories." But Kant thought of the categories as belonging strictly to our mind, and he called them "categories of the understanding." For all we know, thought Kant, our conceptual categories may have no relation to reality as it is in itself. Aristotle, by contrast, thought of the categories as categories *of being*, which are open to be grasped by our minds. For Aristotle, the world was thoroughly intelligible, and our minds are capable of representing the intelligible structure of reality itself. In fact, Aristotle's understanding of the nature of knowledge involves our minds somehow *becoming* what we know, so that in cognition there is a profound identity between thought and thing. But before we get there, let's begin by orienting ourselves around some basic Aristotelian logical vocabulary.

a) Categories in Context: Aristotle's Organon

Aristotle's logical apparatus was such a powerful invention that up until the last two hundred and fifty years or so, when someone wanted to study logic, she would simply study Aristotle's logic. Aristotle's logical works include the following six treatises: *The Categories, On Interpretation, The Prior Analytics, The Posterior Analytics, Topics,* and *On Sophistical Refutations.* These works comprised the "organon," a Greek word meaning "tool" or "instrument." Logic, for Aristotle, is *reason's instrument* for exploring and discovering reality. In his view, since all scientific and philosophical progress depends on the logical inferences we make, it is crucial that the tool our reason uses in making those inferences be in top condition.

The basic idea holding together Aristotle's logical system is the **syllogism.** A syllogism is a deductive argument form that typically consists of two premises and a conclusion that follows necessarily from the premises. Here is an example of a syllogism:

1. All philosophy professors are amazing.
2. I am a philosophy professor.
Therefore,
3. I am amazing.

As you can see, given premises (1) and (2), the conclusion, (3), follows necessarily. In other words, there is no way that premises (1) and (2) could be true without the conclusion also being true. (Of course, the problem with this argument is that premise (1) isn't true.) Aristotle's ideal for developing the sciences is to lay out all our knowledge on each subject in a systematic way, and this means laying it out in terms of syllogisms. A syllogism displays the reason a given conclusion is true, or—to say the same thing in different words—the structure of the rational support for the conclusion. In reference to the syllogism under discussion, the reason I am amazing is because I am a philosophy professor, and all philosophy professors are amazing.

The building blocks of syllogisms are **statements,** or propositions. Each of the premises and the conclusion of any syllogism must be a statement. For Aristotle, every statement has, or is a variation on, the following basic form: "S is P," where "S" stands for the subject term (roughly, the thing you're talking about), and "P" stands for the predicate term (roughly, the thing you are saying about the subject). In premise (1) of the syllogism we were just discussing, "philosophy professors" serves as the subject term, and "amazing" serves as the predicate term. These two terms are joined together by the copula, which is some form of the verb "to be." Statements can *affirm* a predicate of a subject (as in "Cheeseburgers *are* wonderful") or *deny* a predicate of a subject (as in "Cheeseburgers *are not* repulsive").

As we have already seen, statements themselves break down into further components. Both the subject and the predicate are **terms**. So terms also have a place in

Aristotle's logic. And it is of the utmost importance to reach adequate definitions of your terms, since the whole logical apparatus depends on clarity about the terms that provide the basic building blocks of statements, out of which syllogisms are composed. Unfortunately, we'll have to leave aside further explorations of Aristotle's logic as a whole. But we do so only to dive into a detailed examination of one of his foundational logical works, the *Categories*.

b) Substances and Accidents: Aristotle's Ontology

Aristotle's ontology—that is, his view of what most basically comprises reality— can be called a "substance–accident ontology." The words "substance" and "accident," in the senses in which Aristotle used them, are fairly unfamiliar to us today, but you can get a working idea of what he's talking about by substituting the word "object" for "substance" and "property" for "accident." Our everyday world is a world of objects (substances), and objects have properties (accidents). For instance, I am now sitting on a chair (an object), and my chair has the properties of being black, curved, and capable of swivelling. Aristotle thought that at the most basic level, the world consisted of substances along with their accidents. This is a fairly intuitive view. When children begin to draw pictures, they usually focus on depicting substances—animals, trees, people, etc.—and their features or properties—the *brown* dog, the *tall* tree, the *happy, smiling* person. These are the things that populate the world around us. We can also speak of the basic material building blocks (for Aristotle this would include the elements fire, air, earth, and water) as substances that possess their own properties. Although Aristotle would not have liked this way of speaking, we can talk of atoms as substances. People who do ontology today often try to dispense with one or another of Aristotle's two basic items. Some believe, for example, that substances are unnecessary, and that we can understand the world as being composed completely of properties that hang together in collections or groups. Others try to explain what the world is basically like in terms of events or processes rather than substantial entities and their properties. But Aristotle's view captures some powerful ontological intuitions that continue to exert their influence on the thinking of many contemporary metaphysicians.

Part of what a substance–accident ontology enabled Aristotle to do was to explain how change is possible. It was especially important for an ancient philosopher to develop an account of change because of the paradoxical and strange views of Parmenides, who (you'll recall from the first chapter) claimed that change was an illusion, and Heraclitus, who (at least as some interpreted him) claimed that all things were in flux and had no stability. To have change, there had to be something that remains the same, along with something that ceases-to-be, and something that comes-to-be. Thinking of substances as underlying their properties enabled Aristotle to identify the elements in natural things that enabled change to occur. For instance, when I was a boy, I was short, and now I am (comparatively) tall. How can we account for this ontologically? We start by identifying the thing that remains the same—that would be me, a substance, and in particular a human being. We then ask what ceased to be, and identify the property of shortness (or to be more specific, two-foot-talledness), and what came to be, namely my present height, which is another property. This, I take it, is what Aristotle is discussing toward the end of chapter 5 of the *Categories*, where he says that all change involves "something numerically one that is able to receive contraries," and illustrates this by the example (4a10–23) of an individual human being going from being pale to being dark (perhaps after a visit to the tanning salon). For Aristotle, one of the benefits of a substance–accident ontology is that it gives us a framework for explaining how change takes place in nature.

c) The Four-Fold Division of the Things That Are

Aristotle's *Categories* divides the totality of things into ten categories (see the next section), but before doing that, it provides us with another division of the things that are (*ta onta* in Greek) into four groups. Aristotle uses two distinctions to generate the four groups: first, the distinction between *what is said of a subject* and *what is not said of a subject*, and second, the distinction between *what is in a subject* and *what is not in a subject*. What is he talking about here? Well, the easiest way to approach this is probably to do another translating move, similar to what we did with substances and objects earlier. To be "said of a subject" is to be a **universal**, and to be something "not said of a subject" is to be a **particular**. A universal is simply some one thing that can be said, or predicated, of many other things. I can predicate the term "cheeseburger" of many individual cheeseburgers. I call them all "cheeseburgers," indicating that they all share something in common (cheeseburgerness), and so the term "cheeseburger" is a universal term because it applies to many. But let's say I go to the drive-thru and order a particular cheeseburger. I open up the wrapper and am so enamoured with this particular cheeseburger that I give it a name, "Freeda." Now I cannot say "Freeda" of many different cheeseburgers—it is a term that refers to only one particular entity. In other words, there is no other Freeda; only this particular cheeseburger is Freeda. Since I can't predicate "Freeda" of any other subject, Freeda is a particular.

As for the second distinction, we can translate being "in a subject" as being an accident or property, and being "not in a subject" as being a substance. Being in a subject denotes the sort of existence that accidents or properties have. Socrates's baldness is *in* Socrates—this is simply another way of saying that Socrates possesses the property of being bald. And substances are never in a subject in the way that properties are. Nothing *has* a human being or a bird; instead things just *are* human beings or birds. It would not be far from Aristotle's meaning to say that you *just are* a human being—"human being" is not something *in* you. But you *are not* your properties; instead, you *have* them; or, in other words, they are *in* you. The four-fold division of the "things that are" comes from chapter 2 of the *Categories*, 1a20–1b5 in the Bekker numbers. I have represented this scheme in Table 4, using

Socrates and Disco the talking parakeet as examples of substances, along with some of their accidents.

Table 4: Aristotle's Four-Fold Ontology

	IN A SUBJECT	NOT IN A SUBJECT
Said of a Subject	*Universal Accident* e.g., Baldness, Blueness	*Universal Substance* e.g., Human Being, Bird
Not Said of a Subject	*Particular Accident* e.g., Socrates's baldness, the blue of Disco's feathers	*Particular Substance* e.g., Socrates, Disco the parakeet

In *Categories* chapter 5, Aristotle argues that "[w]hat is called substance most fully, primarily, and most of all, is what is neither said of any subject nor in any subject—e.g., an individual man or horse" (2a12–14). He goes on, in the same chapter, to show how these particular substances are the ontological foundation of everything else that exists (2a35–36). In other words, if we were to ask, "What is most basically real, for Aristotle?" the answer would be "concrete, particular substances," such as individual human beings and individual birds and trees. The idea that particular substances are most real stands in direct contradiction to Plato's claim that the really real things are the eternal, unchanging Forms. For Plato, Forms are precisely the universal essences of things, in which all the concrete particular sensible realities participate, and which they reflect in a shadowy sort of way. Aristotle, by contrast, urges us to look to the sensible realities as the "subjects for all the other things" that exist since "all the other things are predicated of them or are in them" (2b15–18). In other words, particular substances are the ontological ground or basis for universals themselves.

In explaining how Aristotle sees this working out, I'm going to be bringing in some ideas from elsewhere in his writings, but in a way that is fully compatible with what he is saying here in the *Categories*. Universal substances, represented in the upper right quadrant of Table 4, are derived from particular substances by a process of **abstraction**. In abstraction, the mind draws out the common nature of a given sort of thing from sensory experience of particulars of that sort. For example, you might acquire experience of a number of different trees by observing them with your senses—you walk through a forest and carefully examine first a pine tree, then a maple, then a birch. Aristotle believes our minds have an ability to somehow "pull out" from the totality of those experiences a universal concept that captures something of the essence that all the individual trees share in common. So from your impressions of the different particular trees, your mind generates the universal concept of "tree." We will return to this inductive mental process of abstraction in our discussion of the *Posterior Analytics* in the next part of this chapter. The point to notice here is that particular substances are more basic than universal substances, since we only know universal substances by a process of abstraction from particular substances.

What about the two quadrants on the left side of Table 4, namely universal accidents and particular accidents? Particular accidents are grounded in particular substances since particular accidents are *in*, or are had by, particular substances. I'll try to spell out what this means in another way. Accidents are (ontologically) dependent on substances, but substances are not dependent on accidents. What this means is that, if you were to take away a particular substance, you would immediately take away all of its accidents as well. As soon as Socrates is gone, his baldness, intelligence, friendliness, etc. go along with him. But the same is not true if you reverse things and start by taking away the accidents. You can take away Socrates's baldness (by giving him a miracle hair-growth treatment) without thereby taking away Socrates himself. Socrates does not depend on any of his particular accidents for his existence, but all of his particular accidents depend on him for their existence. So there is an asymmetrical relation of dependence between substances and accidents that indicates that substances are more ontologically basic than accidents. So much for particular accidents. What about the last quadrant in Table 4, the universal accidents? These are derived from particular accidents in much the same way as we explained the abstraction of universal substances from particular substances. Observation of multiple particular instances of a given type of accident enables the mind to draw out (to "abstract") the universal concept that expresses the common nature of all accidents of that sort. From my experience of many instances of the colour blue (a blue car, a blue chair, a blue parakeet ...) I draw out the common feature of blueness shared by all the instances, which gives me my notion of the universal accident, blueness. Since we derive universal accidents from particular accidents, which in turn depend on particular substances, we can trace universal accidents back to the particular substances as well.

The moral of Aristotle's four-fold division of the "things that are" is that particular substances are the most basic realities, and everything else that exists depends on them. As should be clear from this discussion, Aristotle's emphasis on concrete particular substances, and his appeal to sense experience as the basis of universal concepts, stand in marked contrast to the vision of reality and knowledge we found in Plato.

d) The Ten Categories

After showing how reality divides into substances and accidents, each of which can be conceived as universal or particular, with particular substances as the foundation for everything else, Aristotle goes on in *Categories* chapter 4 to discuss the ten highest kinds of things, or the ten categories. Here we are dealing with logical terms, "things said without combination" (1b25), as opposed to statements (things said involving combination of terms) or syllogisms. In providing his list of the ten categories, Aristotle lists substance as the first category, followed by nine basic types of accidents or properties. I list them here together with the examples Aristotle provides of each in brackets: (1) substance (man, horse); (2) quantity (two feet long, three feet long); (3) quality (white, grammatical); (4) relative (double, half, larger); (5) where (in the Lyceum, in the marketplace); (6) when (yesterday, last year); (7) being-in-a-position (is lying, is sitting); (8) having (has shoes on, has armour on); (9) acting on (cutting, burning); (10) being affected (being cut, being burnt). These ten categories make up the "drawers" in the "filing cabinet" of reality, and Aristotle apparently believed that any item you could find in the cosmos would belong to one and only one of these categories. This could provide the basis for an interesting game that you might try playing with your friends or family: You would start by having someone randomly think of an item, and then everyone would try to sort out which category that item belonged in, and whoever got it first wins that round. (Okay, that probably doesn't sound like a particularly fun or exciting game—unless you're Aristotle.)

The scheme of the *Categories* plays a useful role in locating the definitions of terms. The first step in coming up with a definition is to discern which of the categories the thing being defined belongs to. That gives you its highest logical *genus* or kind. Next you have to figure out which of the "sub-folders," or lower genera, it belongs in within its category. You repeat this process until you reach the genus that specifies most closely the sort of thing you're dealing with, and then you combine that with the specific difference or *differentia* (the essential feature that separates what you're talking about from everything else within the kind), and that combination gives you your definition. This scheme for thinking through the definition process was called "Porphyry's tree" (after the third-century CE philosopher who suggested it). For example, let's say you want to define the term "cactus." A cactus belongs in the category of substance, but substance divides into corporeal (bodily) and incorporeal substances (such as angels or gods); clearly, a cactus is corporeal. Corporeal substances can be subdivided into animate (living) or inanimate (non-living), and a cactus belongs in the living folder. But living corporeal substances can be sensible (having sense perception) or insensible (not having sensation), and it appears that all plants belong in the *in*sensible side of that division, so that's where we'll put our cactus.

At this point you're going to need a more detailed understanding of salient differences between kinds of plants than I possess, but I think you get the idea. You've reached a definition of the term "cactus" once you've located the kind clos-est to the essence of a cactus that is still general—maybe "succulent plant"?—and have stated what it is that separates cacti from other species within that kind. The classification schemes used in contemporary plant biology are much more detailed than Aristotle could have imagined, which is only natural, given that he pretty much invented the discipline of biology. And the logical notions of "genus" and "species" do not map on in any direct way to the current biological scheme of kingdom, phylum, division, class, order, family, etc. But the basic idea of sorting

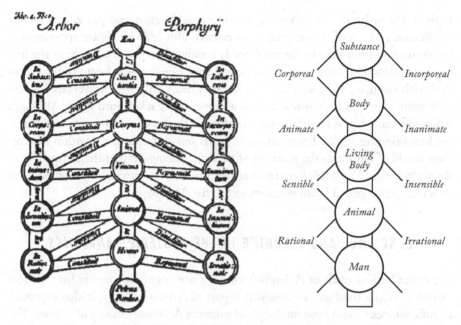

Porphyry's Tree, from Edmond Pourchot's *Institutiones Philosophicae* (1730), along with a modern translation

out different items into their proper place in an overall ordering system does stem from Aristotle, which is not to say that he didn't pick up the idea from Plato, who also had a method of division he employed to come up with definitions. We can follow Aristotle in giving a more complete situating of a term in logical space by defining "human being." A human being, for Aristotle is, of course, a living, corporeal substance. To be more specific, a human being is a rational animal, where "animal" provides the genus, and "rational" provides the specific difference that sets the human being off from every other sort of animal. "Rational animal," Aristotle thinks, gives us the definition of the term "human being."

One last point about the categories and definition. The ten highest kinds themselves cannot be defined; nor can particular substances. Why might this be the case? Well, if a definition involves taking a more general notion and combining it with a differentia that sets off your item from everything else in the genus, then there is no way to do this with the highest kinds, because there is no more general notion above them (that's what it means to say that they are the *highest* kinds). So the categories themselves—substance, quantity, quality, etc.—are indefinable. (Notice, however, that this did not stop Aristotle from performing an in-depth analysis of the nature of substance in the *Metaphysics*, which we will come to in the next chapter.) But why are particular substances indefinable? Particular substances, you'll remember, are individuals like Socrates, Disco the parakeet, or Freeda the cheeseburger. In Aristotle's view, individuals are not definable because you have to be in the realm of the universal, or "conceptual," before you can engage in the intellectual process of characterizing an essence. But individuals are apprehended by the senses rather than by the intellect. It is only when you reach at least the first level of abstraction—the level of the logical species—that you begin to be able to deal with essences. The claim that the intellect deals only with universals and not with particulars brings Aristotle at least a step or two back toward Plato. Although Aristotle went to great lengths to criticize Plato's Theory of the Forms, many people see him bringing Plato's Forms down to earth and situating them within the concrete world of nature, as the essences of particular beings, rather than disposing of them altogether. We'll think more about the similarities between the metaphysical views of Aristotle and Plato when we get to the *Metaphysics*.

2. SCIENCE AND LEARNING IN THE *POSTERIOR ANALYTICS*

The other logical work of Aristotle's that we are going to cover is his *Posterior Analytics*. While the *Posterior Analytics* is part of Aristotle's logic, it also expresses significant ideas about epistemology and presents Aristotle's theory of science. The central idea of this work is *episteme*. Although this word typically gets translated into English as "science," it can also be rendered "knowledge," though it denotes a particular kind of knowledge, namely demonstrative knowledge. To understand what Aristotle means by demonstrative knowledge, we have to return to the notion of deduction, which for Aristotle was equivalent to the idea of the syllogism, or syllogistic reasoning. As we noted earlier, every syllogism starts with premises and draws a conclusion from them. To refresh your memory, here's another example:

1. All donkeys are mammals.
2. No mammals are cold-blooded.
   Therefore,
3. No donkeys are cold-blooded.

In this example, the conclusion, (3), is derived or inferred from the premises, (1) and (2). In relation to the conclusion of a syllogism, the premises act as starting points, or what Aristotle calls "principles." This is what Aristotle is referring to when he says in the first line of the *Posterior Analytics*: "All teaching and all intellectual learning result from previous cognition" (71a3). In the case of demonstrations, the premises must be known prior (or previous) to the conclusion, because the premises are what produce knowledge of the conclusion. The syllogism just presented is clearly deductive, but is it a demonstration? That depends on whether the premises—the principles of the syllogism—are "true, primary, immediate, better known than, prior to, and explanatory of the conclusion" (71b21–22). Consider premise (1). Is the claim "All donkeys are mammals" true? Obviously. Does it explain the conclusion? Together with premise (2) it does apparently display the rational account that underlies the claim that no donkeys are cold-blooded. The facts that donkeys are mammals and that no mammals are cold-blooded secure knowledge of the fact that no donkeys are cold-blooded (How could they be? After all, they're mammals, and no mammals are cold-blooded!). So the premises seem to meet Aristotle's criterion of being explanatory of the conclusion. But the premises are not statements of logical necessity. We only know that donkeys are mammals and that no mammals are cold-blooded by means of observing the world around us. For this reason, the premises of the argument themselves need to be supported by some further rational argumentation. This point helps us to see how the dilemma concerning knowledge arises in chapter 2.

According to Aristotle, all learning results from prior cognition. For anyone who remembers reading chapter 2 of the present book, speaking of prior or "previous" cognition should bring to mind Plato's views on the subject. In the *Meno*, Plato introduced the doctrine of recollection—the view that all learning is recollection, and that our souls in some sense already know all things from birth—in order to counter what we called the debater's paradox. Aristotle describes this paradox at 71a29–30 as "the puzzle in the *Meno*, since we will turn out to learn either nothing or else nothing but what we [already] know." Plato's doctrine of recollection was a powerful answer to the question of how learning is possible, and it led to Plato postulating one kind of prior learning. But Aristotle has a different way of accounting for prior cognition, which will develop as we follow the flow of the argument of the *Posterior Analytics*. We can start with the question, "What does it mean to know something?" Aristotle says, "We think we know a thing without qualification ... whenever we think we recognize the explanation because of which the thing is [so], and recognize both that it is the explanation of that thing and that it does not admit of being otherwise" (71b9–12). In a demonstration, the premises provide the explanation for the truth of the conclusion. They do so by displaying the reason why the fact stated in the conclusion is the way it is and, ideally, they tell us why it could not be otherwise. For this reason, we need prior cognition of the premises in order to be able to use them to establish the conclusion. Aristotle will introduce some serious innovations vis-à-vis Plato in his account of how such prior cognition is possible.

a) The Dilemma of Prior Cognition

Any demonstration will have premises that act as principles in the syllogism that constitutes the demonstration. But what about the premises themselves? We must know them better than the conclusion, Aristotle thinks. But how do we know them? If we are using demonstration as our model for knowing, then each of the premises in the syllogism must itself be a conclusion of another syllogism. But then the same question arises for the premises of *those* syllogisms, and an infinite regress seems to be looming. I have illustrated what I mean by this in a Diagram 5.

Diagram 5

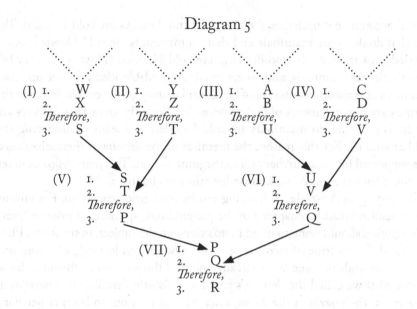

In Diagram 5, there are seven syllogisms arranged in hierarchical order and designated by bracketed Roman numerals. The premises of syllogism (VII), represented by the letters P and Q, are the conclusions of further syllogisms (V) and (VI), and the premises of those two syllogisms are themselves the conclusions of further syllogisms (I) and (II), and (III) and (IV) respectively. The dotted lines above the last four syllogisms represent the fact that this process of establishing premises by further demonstrations could go on forever. If in fact the process of demonstration goes on forever, so that any premise in a syllogism always requires another syllogism to establish it, then we have reached what Aristotle calls an "infinite regress." Any time you have a premise in a demonstration, it must either be immediate (having no other premises prior to it), or it must be proven, appearing as the conclusion of a further demonstration. This situation gives rise to a dilemma about knowledge, which drives the rest of what Aristotle is concerned about in the part of the *Posterior Analytics* we are looking at.

Aristotle presents two attempted solutions to the dilemma, neither of which has things quite right, as we will see. We'll imagine that the first is offered by a group of philosophers that we'll arbitrarily call the Waterloo Warriors; and the second, the Laurier Golden Hawks. The Waterloo Warriors believe that we must conclude that we do not possess any knowledge of anything, because we don't know "primary things," or first principles. In the context of what we've been saying so far, first principles would be premises in demonstrations that are immediate, in the sense that they are known without requiring any further demonstration to establish them. In fact, according to the Warriors, we *can't possibly* know primary things, because our only way of coming to know anything is by demonstration. But primary things are things known without demonstration. Under the assumption that all knowledge is demonstrative, the only other possibility would be to posit an infinite regress, so that the process of demonstration never ends. But saying that the process never ends is just another way of saying that there are no primary things. However you look at it, say the Warriors, we can never reach knowledge, because knowledge of anything would require knowledge of the primary things, and we don't know any primary things.

The Laurier Golden Hawks, on the other hand, agree with the Warriors that all knowledge results from a process of demonstration, but they conclude that we do in fact know all sorts of things. They justify this claim by postulating "circular and reciprocal demonstration" (72b18). The Golden Hawks envision knowledge as an interconnected system of demonstrations, where each premise in a given syllogism is demonstrated by other premises from within the system. For instance, premise R may be demonstrated by a syllogism with premises U and V. V in turn might be demonstrated by a syllogism involving premises C and D, and C by a syllogism involving S and T. Following the chain of demonstration far enough along, one would eventually discover that premise S is itself demonstrated by a syllogism involving R as one of its premises. In this case, demonstration would be circular, since R is ultimately involved in a demonstrative process that leads to R as a conclusion. I've illustrated this in Diagram 6:

Diagram 6

(I)
1. R
2. X
Therefore,   (II)
3. S   4. S
                             5. T
                             Therefore,   (III)
                             6. C   7. C
                                                     8. D
                                                     Therefore,   (IV)
                                                     9. V   10. V
                                                                             11. U
                                                                             Therefore,
                                                                             12. R

The Golden Hawks take it that *all* premises are ultimately demonstrated in the way R is demonstrated in Diagram 6, so that all demonstration is ultimately circular. By saying this, the Hawks are able to avoid an infinite regress and retain the legitimacy of knowledge, though they do so only by paying the price of circularity infecting all our knowledge. This, the Waterloo Warriors think, is unacceptably odd, but not untypical of the Golden Hawks, who have a reputation for being a little off the wall. The Golden Hawks in turn think the Warriors are just plain crazy to deny that we have any knowledge. So who should we believe? Should we accept that knowledge is impossible, or that knowledge is circular? To an impartial observer either horn of this dilemma will probably seem unacceptable.

b) Aristotle's Solution

Fortunately we have Aristotle with us to resolve the dispute and show how neither the Warriors nor the Golden Hawks have the whole story. He begins his own solution by dismantling the possibility of circular demonstration. A demonstration has to move from what is prior and better known to what is posterior and less well known, but a circular demonstration would involve us in the claim that some statement, P, is both prior and posterior to itself, since we concluded P on the basis of the premise P. Furthermore, if you accept it as a legitimate move to support an argument's conclusion by the same statement as the conclusion, then you make it possible to prove anything you want. If I want to claim that "I am the owner of everyone else's property," and to prove the point I am allowed to simply assert, "I am the owner of everyone else's property," I have made a valid argument (the conclusion P follows from the premise P), but in the process I have failed to provide any independent reason to believe the conclusion. And that is both too easy a way to win an argument, and ultimately an avoidance of argument altogether. For these reasons we can't accept the Golden Hawks' view that demonstration is circular.

But Aristotle will not accept the Warriors' view that we have no knowledge either. That would be the height of blasphemy for a man like Aristotle, for whom the very purpose of human life is to come to know as much as we can. But if he rejects the possibility of circular demonstration, and agrees with both the Warriors and the Golden Hawks that an infinite regress in demonstrations would undermine knowledge, how can he find a way out? Aristotle's key move is to reject an assumption made by both the Warriors and the Golden Hawks. Both groups took for granted that all knowledge is produced by demonstration. Aristotle's solution consists in showing that we can come to know certain things in another way, namely via a process he calls induction.

The way Aristotle describes induction links it primarily to coming to know the essences of things, which is what happens when we learn what a thing is and acquire a definition of it. (I take it that this is part of the take-home lesson of Aristotle's somewhat convoluted argumentation in chapters 8, 9, and 10 of the second book of the *Posterior Analytics*.) When we reach a definition of something, and put our knowledge of its essence into a verbal formula or account, we are dealing with terms. If you recall our earlier overview of Aristotelian logic, you'll remember that syllogisms are built out of statements, and statements in turn are composed of terms—a subject term and a predicate term combined via the copula (some form of the verb "to be"), as in the statement "S is P." An adequate definition of a given term arrived at by induction will provide us with a basic claim that can serve as a "primary thing" or a principle from which further scientific knowledge can be derived by deduction. According to chapter 10, when defining something immediate, we must give "an indemonstrable account of the what-it-is" or essence of the thing in question. How we might be able to do this is what Aristotle proceeds to explain in chapter 19.

c) Induction and Abstraction

Aristotle explicitly rejects Platonic recollection as a legitimate way of explaining how we acquire the basic principles of knowledge, or the immediate first principles of demonstration. "[H]ow," he asks at 99b4, "do we come to recognize the principles?" At 99b27 he says, obviously jabbing at his teacher Plato, "It would be absurd if we had the principles [innately]; for then we would possess cognition that is more exact than demonstration, but without noticing it." Instead of innate knowledge of the principles, Aristotle thinks, we need to identify some sort of mental capacity or potentiality to know, but this state must be less exact than the knowledge we acquire from it. To give us an idea of what he has in mind, Aristotle takes us through a quick survey of the sorts of cognition animals have. All animals, he says, have sense perception. But only some of them also have the capacity to remember what they perceive. The animals with memory "keep what they have perceived in their souls even after they have perceived" (100a1). We might contrast here a slug (or an even more rudimentary organism), which can sense things in its environment but likely does not have much use for remembering what it comes across, with more complex animals like cats and dogs, who clearly make use of their capacity for memory when they recognize their owners or perform tricks in order to receive treats.

The next stages in cognition, as Aristotle describes them, most likely belong to human knowers alone among the animals. "[F]rom repeated memory of the same thing experience arises; for a number of memories make up one experience. From experience, or [rather] from the whole universal that has settled in the soul— the one apart from the many, whatever is present as one and the same in all of them—arises a principle of craft (if it is about what comes to be) or of science (if it is about what is)" (100a4–9). What Aristotle here calls "experience" is a cognitive state that goes beyond mere perception and memory. Somehow, when various sense impressions of a given sort of thing (for instance, impressions of trees) are retained in memory, our minds are able to extract from those various impressions something common to all of them, and this results in a "whole universal" settling in the soul. To return to the example of abstraction I gave earlier in this chapter, a person might encounter in perception a variety of trees—an oak tree, a pine tree, a maple tree, etc.—resulting from her observation and study of trees. Retaining her impressions in memory, the person eventually comes to have a general concept of a tree.

Aristotle concludes, "Clearly, then, we must recognize the first things by induction; for that is also how perception produces the universal in us" (100b4–5). We already considered the process of induction and abstraction in our earlier discussion of the relation between universals and particulars in Aristotle's four-fold division of reality. It is now time for me to fulfill the promise I made then to discuss these processes in greater detail. The concept of a tree is a universal, in the sense that it is one thing that applies to many different things. It is also the expression of the essence or the "what-it-is-to-be" of a tree. A person who possesses a true concept of the kind I just described should be able to provide a definition (a universal formula expressing the essence) of the sort of thing in question. Such a person should also be able to identify other things she encounters as trees and explain how trees work. Knowing these things, she would be able to understand and express essential truths about trees, such as "All trees are woody perennial plants." The truths expressed in such statements could function as the first principles in a science of trees, which would trace all of its demonstrations back to some set of basic statements like these. The key thing to notice, in the context of what we've been looking at so far, is that this inductive process of acquiring certain truths is a way of coming to know that does not involve demonstration. And this allows Aristotle to say that knowledge is possible, that it is not infected with circularity, and that the regress of demonstration comes to an end at first principles and so is not infinite.

Aristotle does not elaborate much on the process by which the mind is capable of drawing out the universal from the collection of impressions retained in the memory. But combining what he does say here with his description of the active and passive intellect in his work *On the Soul*, we can say a little more about how Aristotle seems to think this works. For Aristotle, coming to know something involves somehow becoming one with the object of knowledge. But how might our minds become one with, say, a horse? Obviously, Aristotle is not imagining a horse crawling into your brain and taking up residence there. To understand this we have to consider that for Aristotle, a particular substance like Jimmy the horse or Socrates the human being consists of both matter and form. We will think about this in more detail in relation to Aristotle's *Physics* and *Metaphysics*, but for now it will suffice to say that particular substances have physical bodies comprised of material parts, but the matter that goes into any such body must be structured or organized in a certain way in order to count as a substance of a given sort. If by some unfortunate circumstance Jimmy the horse was hit by a train, the matter composing Jimmy's body (Jimmy's flesh and bones) would still be there, strewn around the train tracks and in the surrounding grass, but in spite of that, Jimmy the horse himself (the particular substantial organism) would no longer be there.

To make a horse like Jimmy, you need to have horse flesh and horse bones organized in a very particular sort of way—a way that is characteristic of the mode of being of a horse. Not being a specialist in mammal biology, I can't say very much about what an account of a horse's essence would include. But whatever structure (in Aristotle's terms, whatever *form*) it is necessary to have in order to be a horse, that structure can in principle be understood by our minds. Those who study biological science in depth will be in a position to acquire a much more adequate concept of an organism such as a horse. And when our minds understand the structure or form of a horse, what has taken place is that our minds have *become* the horse, in a formal sense.

If this still doesn't make a lot of sense to you, think of your mind as a lump of immaterial play dough. Just as physical play dough can be made into whatever shape you like, so our minds have the potential to take on the form (again, think "structure") of anything that exists. When we come to know what a given thing is, our active intellect abstracts the form from our collated impressions of that thing, and produces a concept of the thing. The result is that the form in our minds is identical with the form in the thing—the difference is that in the thing the form is realized in matter, while in our minds the form is realized in "immaterial play dough" (that is my term, not the way Aristotle puts it). Now, as we already know from the *Categories*, all of our concepts are universal—we have no intellectual cognition of particulars, which we can only know via our senses. This is why individuals cannot be defined—definition is always of the species or genus that marks out the kind to which individuals belong. In other words, we can have a *concept* of "horse" but not one of "Jimmy the horse." When we know the essence of Jimmy, we know the essence of horse in general, which Jimmy has in common with all other horses.

Are you starting to hear Plato again here? Even though Aristotle makes concrete particular substances the fundamental entities, and makes everything else (particular accidents as well as universal accidents and universal substances) depend on them, Aristotle also prioritizes the universal over the particular as far as knowledge is concerned. For Aristotle, the goal of philosophy, of science, and of human life is to attain abstract intellectual cognition of things. Of course, we get there, for Aristotle, by means of a process that starts with the senses. Insofar as he makes empirical observation and experience the basis of knowledge, Aristotle distinguishes himself from Plato, who regards the senses as completely inadequate means of acquiring knowledge. But this difference takes place within an overall project, one that Aristotle very much shares with Plato. As Aristotle will tell us in the *Metaphysics*, all human beings by nature desire to know, and we can never rest until our knowledge attains the highest heights of abstraction and reaches the ultimate principles which are separate from matter.

3. CONCLUSION

In this discussion of Aristotle's view of logic and science, I have tried to show how Aristotle sets out in some directions that are radically different from those taken by his teacher Plato. Plato tells us that what is really real are the Forms—abstract,

unchanging, immaterial patterns in which the changeable, unstable, particular entities that make up the physical world participate. Aristotle turns this perspective
on its head by claiming that the particular substances themselves are really real—
universal concepts are only abstractions from the particulars, without which there
would be no universals. When we turn to Aristotle's understanding of scientific
knowledge, however, we find that the character of such knowledge always deals
with the universal essences of things. Particulars are only needed as the inductive basis from which we draw our concepts, which we then combine into statements, which in turn enable us to construct demonstrative arguments. For Aristotle,
demonstrative knowledge is the gold standard as far as science goes. Demonstrations display the rational structure of reality by linking concepts together in a way
that indicates why things are necessarily the way they are. Aristotle wants science to
follow a model that reflects very closely the methods used in mathematics, in which
theorems are derived from fundamental axioms. When we take note of Aristotle's
emphasis on the essentialistic and universalistic character of scientific knowledge,
we have to admit that his apparent differences from Plato do not prevent him
from holding to a very Platonic view of knowledge, and even of reality. Aristotle
does take Plato's Forms down from Platonic heaven, and places them inside the
concrete realities surrounding us. But he does so only to let our intellect crack open
the particular shells in order to locate the universal nuggets inside.

In his approach to ontology, in his logic and in his theory of science, Aristotle
shows himself to be, among other things, a master organizer. Ideally all our
knowledge of terms, and all our scientific demonstrations, could be categorized
and ordered in such a way that we would have something like a mental map of
the intelligible structure of all of reality. If that gets you excited, you'll be glad
to know that as we go on to study more of Aristotle's works, we will be attempting to expand and deepen our understanding of the key themes and ideas introduced in this chapter. In the *Physics* and the *Metaphysics*, we will learn more about
Aristotle's analysis of particular substances, as he develops his theory of matter
and form and his conception of what it means to possess a nature. For Aristotle,
Metaphysics is the ultimate science, the science of all sciences, in the sense that it
deals with the most basic and with the ultimate principles of all reality.

Chapter 6:

NATURE AND
FIRST PHILOSOPHY

HISTORICAL CONTEXT

Aristotle's *Physics* represents his most general views about nature and natural beings. He also composed a number of more specific treatises on particular topics in natural philosophy, such as meteorology, sensation, memory, sleeping, dreams, respiration, and the history, generation, and parts of animals. Aristotle's work *On the Soul*, which I have already referred to but will not be discussing in detail, could also be classed as a treatise within the domain of natural philosophy, since it treats the soul or *psuche* as a natural entity, having its own place within nature as the principle of life.

Some readers might be wondering why a person would think of separating out "natural" philosophy as a distinct domain. After all, isn't everything that exists "natural"? There are a few ways of responding to this. We might distinguish the domain of the natural from the domain of the supernatural, and place anything divine—God, or the gods, and perhaps angels and demons—in the domain of the supernatural, as distinct from the natural. For a more directly Aristotelian answer to this question, we need to have in place a bit of Aristotle's cosmology. Aristotle's cosmological views drew on ideas found in the Presocratic natural philosophers and in Plato. He described his views most thoroughly in his work *On the Heavens*, and these remained the accepted view for Western science for nearly two millennia, right up until the time of Copernicus (1473–1543) and Galileo (1564–1642), and the scientific revolution.

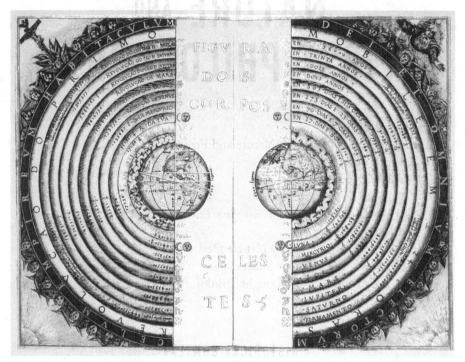

The Aristotelian/Ptolemaic conception of cosmology. Earth is at centre, with the heavenly bodies embedded within surrounding spheres. From the Portuguese cartographer Bartolomeu Velho (1568).

Aristotle understood the earth to be spherical in shape, and to be at rest in the centre of the cosmos. All the heavenly bodies (the moon, the sun, the planets, and the stars) were embedded in distinct heavenly "spheres," which revolved around the earth. This cosmology drew a distinction between things that took place beneath the moon (inside the sub-lunary sphere), and things that took place above it. The moon's orbit around the earth marked out a sphere inside of which things could undergo motion and change in the form of coming-to-be (generation) and ceasing-to-be (corruption). Examples of this abound: think of the first growth of a tomato on a tomato plant as the generation of a tomato; now think of the moldy tomato decaying inside of your refrigerator as an instance of corruption. Above the sphere marked out by the orbit of the moon, according to Aristotelian cosmology, things did not change in this way. The planets and the stars were eternal, |and although they could move, in the sense of revolving around the earth, they could not come-to-be or cease-to-be. All bodies beneath the moon were made up of the four elements of earth, air, fire, and water, while the heavenly spheres were composed of a fifth, incorruptible element, the *aether*.

According to Aristotle, we need another science or discipline besides natural philosophy to deal with the incorruptible heavenly bodies in the super-lunary spheres, and especially to treat of the spiritual intelligences that move the spheres. This science is what Aristotle calls Metaphysics, or First Philosophy (physics being designated as Second Philosophy relative to Metaphysics). We also need Metaphysics to treat of the hallowed Prime Mover, the completely perfect immaterial substance at the pinnacle of the cosmos (more about this later as well). *Physics* and *Metaphysics* go together as a package, since for Aristotle they both involve the search for the most fundamental account of what reality is like.

INTRODUCTORY BIG QUESTION: NATURE AND FREEDOM

As I have already indicated, Aristotle's *Physics* can be described as his "natural philosophy" or philosophy of nature. It would be good to pause for a moment to consider what the terms "natural" and "nature" might mean in the context of Aristotle's thought. What do you think of when you hear the word "nature"? For many Canadians, images of canoes gliding through the silky waters of quiet Northern lakes, the call of the loon, and the majestic figure of the mighty moose come to mind. We associate "nature" with the natural environment, which today is at such risk due to industrial practices of human beings. Environmental groups seek to lobby the government and protect our "natural heritage" by (among other activities) designating certain areas as nature reserves and protected parks. Or maybe the words "nature" and "natural" cause you to think about the organic food aisles in the more upscale grocery stores, or certain forms of alternative medicine. Aristotle, of course, did not use the word "nature," which is an English translation of the Greek word *phusis*. So what does *phusis* designate, and what is a philosophy of nature actually about?

One way to get at what Aristotle is thinking about here is to consider what people mean when they ask about *human* nature. It's *in our nature* to care about others, some say; others say human beings are selfish *by nature*. When Aristotle himself defined human beings as rational animals, he believed he was saying something particularly profound, expressing something completely basic about the sort of being a human being is. For Aristotle, the most salient fact about the nature of human beings was their intelligence, which he understood as an ability to read into the intelligible structure (e.g., the natural laws) of the world. In Aristotle's view, the reason we can do science is because human *nature* is fundamentally rational. The genus of the human being is "animal," which entails that we are embodied beings with sensation, capable of moving around in our environment and of reproduction, self-nourishment and growth. But the specific difference that sets us apart as unique among the animals is our rationality. Many of the great religious traditions have emphasized other features as expressive of human nature. People who belong to the monotheistic faiths, for instance, often speak of human beings as created in the image of God, so that it is in our nature somehow to reflect or reveal God. Those traditions also tend to depict God as possessing personal qualities, such as compassion and the desire for justice, for instance. So it is thought that human beings are by nature beings for whom justice is of great importance, and capable of a profound compassion for others. Through the Medieval period and well into the modern one, a concept of human nature as combining rationality and moral qualities of the kind I've described prevailed.

If we fast-forward into the twentieth century, we encounter thinkers like Jean-Paul Sartre, who, inspired by people like Friedrich Nietzsche, denies that human beings have any nature at all. According to Sartre, we have to create ourselves, and we do this in utter and complete freedom. Today you can hear many people talking of aspects of our lives as socially constructed—aspects which once were thought to be objective parts of our nature: race, gender, ethnicity, family, health, sexuality, intelligence, etc. In fact, one way to think of the shift from the premodern and modern periods to the post-modern (contemporary) era is to see the latter as replacing the concept of human *nature* with an emphasis on the will as capable of making things whatever it wants them to be. In our consumerist society, we want choice without constraints, and our freedom to choose is almost an absolute value. Some contemporary reactionary thinkers (like David Bentley Hart, for instance) criticize the idea of freedom at the core of contemporary Western culture by claiming that it leads to nihilism, the refusal to believe in anything as true, or to accept any values as having any basis at all.

We probably do not need to get quite that extreme. But there is something to the question of whether we have gone too far in the direction of freedom, without recognizing the continuing importance of nature, in the sense of objective features of our being as humans. Do you think that things in the world have natures, in the sense of essential features that they possess objectively, and that mark them off as belonging to natural kinds? Do you think, in particular, that human beings have an objective nature that we share in common with each other? If so, what features do you think would be definitive of being human? If not, why not?

1. ARISTOTLE'S *PHYSICS*

Let's begin with a very brief overview of what Aristotle is up to in the *Physics*. He is concerned, on the one hand, with explaining how "coming-to-be" and "ceasing-to-be" takes place, and on the other hand with the "principles" and "elements" that must be in place to account for these processes. Aristotle uses the term "motion" as more or less synonymous with "change," and change always involves coming-to-be and ceasing-to-be. Consequently, much of Aristotle's *Physics* consists in an analysis of motion. Given the paradoxical views about motion proposed by Parmenides, who claimed that there is no motion or change, and Heraclitus's supposed view that all things are in flux, Aristotle had his work cut out for him to provide a theory of motion that avoided these extremes. And this is clearly one of his main goals in writing his major treatise on physics. Central to his theory of motion or change is the concept of a nature, which we've already been discussing. Among other things, the notion of a nature provides us with the idea of something that remains stable through change (contra the Heraclitean flux doctrine), while allowing genuine change to take place (contra Parmenides). The student who has been paying attention will recall that one of the benefits Aristotle touted for his theory of concrete particular substances in the *Categories* was that it allows us to account for change.

That leads me to the related point that there is a close connection between the term *phusis* (nature) and some other key items in Aristotle's philosophical vocabulary with which we have already become familiar, such as "essence" and "substance" (both of which can serve as translations of the Greek word *ousia*) as well as "definition." Let's explore some of these links a bit further, to bring out the meaning of "a nature" in Aristotle's thought. On his view, the nature of a thing *just is* its essence (the what-it-is-to-be of that thing), and the definition of a thing is the rational formula that expresses its essence. Recalling our previous discussion of Aristotelian science: the definitions of things are the ground floor of science. We start with definitions of terms, like "mammal" or "warm-blooded" for instance, as the principles in our scientific knowledge, and we work to express the rational structure of reality by linking together terms in propositions or statements, for example, "All mammals are warm-blooded." These statements in turn are linked together into demonstrative arguments (syllogisms) that ideally lay bare the causal structure of our world, providing us with an understanding of the reasons why things happen. Since the natures of things are what our definitions define, natures are foundational to all scientific knowledge. For this reason, it makes sense to devote some sustained consideration to what can be said about the natures of things in general. Now let's get into the details of the theory as we have it in Aristotle's text.

a) What Is a Nature?

Aristotle opens Book II of the *Physics* by distinguishing things that are natural (things that have natures) from things that are not. Examples of natural things include "animals and their parts, plants, and the simple bodies, such as earth, fire, air and water." What makes things of these sorts natural, Aristotle says, is that "each of them has within itself a principle of motion and stability in place, in growth and decay, or in alteration" (192b10–15). You can see how two of the groups of things included in Aristotle's list, animals and plants, can be thought of as having these principles of motion built into them. But Aristotle interestingly includes also the parts of animals and "simple bodies" or elements, the basic building blocks of the bodies of all physical beings. This is all the more interesting in light of the fact that Aristotle identifies all natural things as substances (192b34). It would seem to mean, for instance, that my heart or my eye is a particular substance alongside myself as a whole.

Let's think a little about why Aristotle might categorize all these things together as "natural," according to his criterion for being naturally constituted. First, how exactly should we understand animals and plants as possessing "a principle of motion and stability in place, in growth and decay, or in alteration"? All living beings have an ability to maintain a certain organization of their parts, sometimes by adding matter to their bodies (as in eating and drinking), and sometimes by the growth and repair of their bodies. So, when a living being gets injured, its body works to repair itself as far as is possible (think of getting a cut, and the way the body restores skin to cover the wound). Matter enters our bodies on a regular basis, and matter exits our bodies regularly, as waste through excretion, for instance, or via the shedding of skin cells or hair. Yet throughout these processes, the same basic organization of parts remains constant. A horse keeps up its structure as a horse, a maple tree keeps up its structure as a maple, etc. And it is noteworthy that the work of maintaining an organism's "pattern" all takes place *from within*—that is, normally the body does all these things by itself without needing anyone to act on it from outside (except in more serious cases, like surgery).

Here Aristotle draws a contrast with non-natural things, or "artifacts," like a bed, or a cloak. Beds, socks, tables, and chairs—none of these is able to maintain its structure, as the kind of thing it is, from the inside. If you scratch the metal frame of a bed or tear the mattress, these entities are not going to repair themselves. Nothing internal to them is striving to retain the pattern which their makers gave to them. They can be repaired, but only by external agents acting on them (e.g., a person who sews up the tear in the mattress). In the context of this discussion, Aristotle cites the Greek rhetorician Antiphon, who pointed out that if you planted a wooden bed in the ground, and if a plant were to sprout from the buried wood, the plant would not grow into a bed, but into a tree of the same type as that from which the wood was originally taken to make the bed. For Aristotle, this difference is quite significant. Aristotle takes this to show that a bed is not substantial, but only a conventional arrangement of parts, which themselves are substances or composed of substances. Even a metallic bed would be composed of physical elements, and as we have seen, Aristotle understands these basic elements (earth, air, fire, and water) to be natural substances. Applying his criterion for being natural, then, these also must possess an internal principle of constancy and change. And within the view of the physical world that Aristotle was working with, these elements did indeed contain such internal principles. Something internal to fire, for example, is responsible for sustaining it as the type of element it is, and this "pattern" is what dictates the sort of interactions fire can have with other elements, and with the composite beings whose bodies are composed of these elements. The natures of the elements also determine their "natural place"—Aristotle understood the tendency of the heavier elements to move toward the centre of the earth, and of the lighter elements to move upwards to be a function of the sorts of things they are (their natures).[1]

That leaves the parts of animals, which Aristotle also thinks can reasonably be understood as natural substances. Although the organs of an animal cannot normally survive without being integrated into the organic life of the whole organism, we can nevertheless single them out as relatively independent entities that tend to maintain their own distinctive structural patterns, much like whole organisms do. A heart can suffer damage and repair itself, and it grows and maintains itself in existence, so that it too can be seen as possessing an internal principle of motion and rest. In our own time, the boundaries between the natural and artificial have become significantly more blurry than they were in Aristotle's day, mainly due to the exponential advances in technology made over the last century or so. From robotic insects to artificial hearts to vehicles capable of driving themselves, human beings have produced "artifacts" which seem to have come very close to possessing an "internal principle" of motion and stability. Science fiction novels and films have been exploring for some time now the lines between human and artificial intelligence in cyborg or android forms. The example that jumps to my mind most readily is the character Data from *Star Trek*, whose exploration of his own lack of emotions and other "human" traits was a major theme running through that TV series. The drive to produce life artificially is very much alive in our time as advances are made in the biological sciences, in genetic engineering, and research with embryos, for example.

b) Aristotle's Hylomorphism

In the *Categories*, Aristotle presented the view that particular substances are the ontologically basic entities in our universe. In the *Physics*, and also in the *Metaphysics*, Aristotle embarks on a more thorough analysis of what particular substances are like. We've already seen his identification of substances and natural entities. Aristotle next asks about "the nature and substance of a natural thing" (193a10). We need to unpack this use of language a bit. What does it mean for something to be the nature or substance *of* a natural thing? Aristotle is looking, here, for an explanation of what makes a natural thing to be natural—in other words, among the ingredients that go into a natural substance, which of them should we identify as the principle or source of motion and rest within the substance? Aristotle considers two possibilities: the nature of a natural thing may be its **matter**, or alternatively it may be its **form**. Matter and form are the two basic constituents of every substance, in Aristotle's view. This view, that all natural beings are composed of

---

1   See *Physics* IV, chapter 5 for more on this subject.

matter and form, is known as **hylomorphism**, a term that combines the Greek words for matter (*hyle*) and shape or form (*morphe*).

We can get an appreciation for the distinction between matter and form, and for the relationship of these two constituents within a given natural substance, by considering some examples. Although Aristotle did not think man-made objects counted as substances in the strict sense, he nevertheless often used them to illustrate ideas about substances. Take a house for instance. To have a house, we need materials like wood, cement, bricks, glass, etc. But we also know that those materials on their own do not give us a house. If someone were to dig a hole in a plot of land and throw a bunch of bricks and wood and glass into the hole, that would not yield something that could be put on the real estate market—at least not with any expectation of it selling. These materials provide the "matter" of a house, but unless they are organized according to a particular sort of structure or "form," we can't say that we have a house yet. To be more precise, the bricks, cement, wood, and glass have to be arranged in such a way that they provide an enclosed and liveable shelter from the weather. The arrangement which the material parts must be given is the form of the house. In the same way, for Aristotle, all substances have material "ingredients," but these ingredients must be organized in a certain way to produce a substance of a certain determinate kind. In the case of living organisms, we can generalize and say that the matter is the flesh and bones, and the form is the arrangement of the flesh and bones according to a pattern that enables a distinctive sort of organic life to operate. Each sort of animal and plant has its own characteristic way of being in the world—think of a giraffe, or a cactus—and in each case a pattern can (at least in principle) be identified according to which material parts of a certain kind must be organized in order to get an instance of the kind we call "giraffe" or "cactus." In contemporary science, we might be inclined to speak instead about the genetic code of a type of organism, carried in its DNA. If we understand a genetic code as a sort of program (a set of instructions) which tells how to build an organism of a certain type, then we can discern a meaningful overlap between the idea of a genetic code and Aristotle's notion of form.

When Aristotle asks the question, "What is the nature of a natural thing," he is asking whether the nature of such a thing should be identified with its matter or with its form. His answer is "both." The true student of nature, unlike the mathematician, must study forms as they exist in matter. Someone who studies geometry thinks about lines completely abstracted away from how they exist in the world, but the person who studies optics thinks about the shapes of actual physical surfaces, and how they interact with light. (This seems to be the point of Book II, ch 2.) But even though in physics we can and should speak of a thing's matter in addition to its form as key aspects of its nature, Aristotle argues that "the form is the nature *more than* the matter is" (193b6–7; my italics). Why does he think this? The reason he gives is as follows: "For what is only potentially flesh or bone does not have its nature, and is not naturally flesh or bone, until it acquires the form in accordance with the account by which we define flesh or bone and say what it is"

(193b1–3). The basic idea here is that the actual takes precedence over what is only potential, and something is only actual when it possesses its proper form. A pile of flesh and bones does not give you a donkey; you only have a donkey when the matter has been structured in the necessary way (according to the donkey-pattern). Aristotle seeks to give further support to this idea from the fact that only actual things can cause other things to happen. For example, you can only get a new human being from already existing (actual) human beings. And you can only get medical treatment from medical knowledge which already exists (is actual) in the mind of your physician. In general, Aristotle connects the idea of form with what is actual, and the idea of matter with what is only potential or in potency.

c) The Four Causes and Aristotle's Teleology

The discussion of matter and form just covered flows naturally into a consideration of Aristotle's four causes, located in Book II, chapter 3, since both the matter of a thing and its form enter into the causal explanation of the thing. Recall that when we are looking for a causal explanation for a thing, we are asking about the reason or reasons why the thing is the way it is and not otherwise. As Aristotle says, "we think we know something only when we find the reason why it is so, i.e., when we find its primary cause" (194b20). To know a thing, for Aristotle, is to be able to situate it within the nexus of causal relations between it and other things, whether these other things are components of itself (its parts), or things outside of itself.

In Aristotle's view, there are four, and only four, distinct kinds of cause that enter into the account or explanation of a thing. They are (1) the **material cause**, that from which a thing comes to be or that out of which it is made; (2) the **formal cause**, which Aristotle here describes as "the account ... of the essence ... and the parts that are in the account" (194b27–28); (3) the **efficient cause**, what produces a thing or initiates the change that brings it about; and (4) the **final cause**, which Aristotle calls "something's end—i.e., what it is for" (194b34). The first and the third of these causes should be more or less familiar to us. If you want to understand something, it makes good sense to ask what it is made of, and what causal mechanisms produced it. There is also some intuitive basis for the formal cause, in the sense of asking for a definition or categorization of the thing in question. However, from a modern-day perspective, we don't usually think of the form or essence of a thing as playing a *causal* role in making it what it is, unless, as I suggested earlier, the connection between a genetic code and the Aristotelian idea of form can be made.

It is difficult for modern people to think of final causation—i.e., purposes or ends—as making a real contribution to the causal explanation for why things are the way they are. We do see purpose in nature, insofar as human beings and other living beings can be understood as acting for the sake of achieving certain goals and purposes. In fact, we simply cannot understand certain things without appealing to some sort of purposiveness. For instance, we cannot understand the historical battle of Waterloo, where Napoleon was defeated by Wellington, without grasping the intentions and purposes of the different armies and their leaders. Why were Wellington's soldiers lined up along the ridge of Mont-Saint-Jean on the morning of June 18, 1815? You could try to explain this by speaking of the material parts of their bodies and the physical mechanisms that were at work in generating motion within their bodies; you could even bring in neural and cognitive mechanisms as an effort to say how the brain states of the soldiers affected their behavioural outputs. But if you wanted to understand the battle as a *battle*—a type of historical event—you would have to discuss the strategies being contemplated by the generals, their awareness of each other's positions, the state of the morale in the competing camps, etc. Similarly, it would be a fairly shallow explanation of the depression of a man who was abandoned by the woman he loved that only described the neuro-chemical state of his brain. The cause of the depression, we would naturally want to say, resides in the facts that he loved the woman and wanted to be with her, but now had to face the prospect of life without her.

The role of purposiveness just described in these examples makes sense to us because we understand ourselves as beings that have purposes. Furthermore, we understand what it means to ask what a car is for, or what a fork is for, because such things are made by human beings to serve *our* purposes. But now consider again what Aristotle means by "final cause." A thing's final cause is its end or purpose, and Aristotle thinks that final causes pertain not just to human actions and productions, *but to all natural things*. If we begin to ask what the purpose of a snail, or a waterfall, or the element of fire is, we are at a loss. What is a snail for? Or what is the purpose of a mosquito (other than to spoil our efforts to enjoy the outdoors in summer)? We tend to think that there is no answer to such questions. At least, within a naturalistic framework that assumes there are no supernatural beings such as divine minds, a snail would seem to have no objective purpose at all.

One of the main reasons people in our time tend to disregard the idea that nature contains any genuine purposiveness or "teleology" is our widespread adherence to an evolutionary biology and consequently to an anthropology inspired by **Charles Darwin** (1809–82). For centuries, the argument for the existence of a divine Intelligent Designer, based on the beautifully ordered and intricate purposiveness of organic structures and the organisms that house them, seemed to be irrefutable. How could it possibly be the case that all this vastly complex, carefully ordered beauty we observe around us originated by pure chance operating on completely mindless matter? Darwin's theory provides an account of just this, claiming, in principle at least, to explain the origin of all the different organic forms of life by means of the process of random genetic mutation and natural selection. Commonly seen as a major triumph for materialism and atheism, Darwinian evolutionary biology transformed the way the mainstream scientific community understands human life within the universe, without final causes. We are still trying to deal with the implications of this view for the meaning and value of human life today.

1. Geospiza magnirostris.
3. Geospiza parvula.
2. Geospiza fortis.
4. Certhidea olivasea.

Galapagos finches, varying from island to island as a result of natural selection. From John Gould's nineteenth-century drawings of Charles Darwin's records.

Given that the Darwinian shift took place in the not too distant past, it may come as a surprise that Aristotle discussed something very much like the theory of evolution in his *Physics*, which he wrote over two thousand years before Darwin gazed upon his first Galapagos finches. In fact, it was Empedocles (492–432 BCE), the Presocratic philosopher, who propounded the theory that Aristotle here criticizes. In chapter 8 of Book II, Aristotle describes Empedocles's view as follows:

> ... why not suppose that nature acts not for something or because it is better, but of necessity? Zeus's rain does not fall in order to make the grain grow, but of necessity.... Why not suppose, then, that the same is true of the parts of natural organisms? On this view, it is of necessity that, for example, the front teeth grow sharp and well adapted for biting, and the back ones broad and useful for chewing food; this [useful] result was coincidental, not what they were for. The same will be true of all the other parts that seem to be for something. On this view, then, whenever all the parts came about coincidentally as though they were for something, these animals survived, since their constitution made them suitable [for survival]. Other animals, however, were differently constituted and so were destroyed; indeed they are still being destroyed, as Empedocles says of the man-headed calves. (198b17–33)

The last two sentences of this passage express fairly clearly the basic mechanism we now call "natural selection." Aristotle spends the rest of chapter 8 explaining why this sort of view could not possibly be true. I will present the outline of his argument here, and will conclude this section by a short discussion of it.

1. The parts of animals come to be as they do either always or usually.
2. No result of luck or chance comes to be either always or usually.
3. The parts of animals are either coincidental (resulting from chance), or they are for something (purposive).

But,

4. The parts of animals cannot be coincidental. [*This follows from (1) and (2)*]

So,

5. The parts of animals must be for something. [*From (3) and (4)*]

Therefore,

6. There is teleology (final causation) in the natural world.

The nub of the argument is that purely random processes would be incapable of producing the kind of regularity and order in the production of biological life that takes place in the natural world. Aristotle's argument is fairly effective against the simplistic sort of evolutionary perspective offered by Empedocles, according to which the parts of animals were produced first, and stuck together in myriad haphazard forms, most of which died off because they could not survive. Against such a view, Aristotle's premise (2) holds. But contemporary Darwinian biology possesses a much more sophisticated account of how genetic mutations result in slow, incremental changes over time that eventually yield new species, and Aristotle would need to work substantially harder to be able to refute that view (assuming that he would want to). Intelligent Design theorists today still make efforts to argue for the presence of purposiveness in nature, against a view of nature as operating entirely according to non-purposive forces. It is indeed interesting to ask how certain biological species could have come into existence as they do by the gradual, step-wise process of random mutation and natural selection postulated by evolutionary biology. For instance, the gastric brooding frog gestates its offspring in its stomach. Its digestive enzymes shut down just for the period of time when its eggs are developing, and kick in again once it spews its offspring out of its mouth. The difficulty of imagining how such a reproductive system could have developed by small gradual mutations does not mean that it could not be explained within this framework. But it suggests that there are questions that still need to be answered. More generally, if we understand genetic information as instructions, in the ordinary sense of that word, then we seem to require some sort of being with intentions and purposes capable of *issuing* those instructions (the divine programmer or designer). In other words, understanding natural structures as the products of conscious intentional activity requires some sort of a (divine) mind responsible for designing and producing it. Contemporary science generally tends to reject appeals to intentionality and purposiveness in the natural world, and this is one place where the difference between Aristotelian and modern science comes to the fore.

Book VII, chapter 6, of the *Physics* contains Aristotle's argument that there must be a "prime" (or "first") mover. As we will soon discover, this prime mover is the *pièce de résistance* of Aristotle's theory of causation, the cause of all causes, and the ultimate answer to the question "why?" But because the prime mover also features prominently in Aristotle's *Metaphysics*, I'm going to discuss the arguments he gives in the context of that work instead of going into them here.

2. ARISTOTLE'S *METAPHYSICS*

The title of what we think of today as Aristotle's treatise on *Metaphysics* means "the things that come after physics," but this can be interpreted in a couple of ways. Some believe that it was called this because of the way an early editor arranged the works of Aristotle in order; this treatise was placed *after* the treatise on physics. Others see the reason lying in the fact that the subject matter of the *Metaphysics*—the basic principles of all that exists—should properly be dealt with after an understanding of the material dealt with in the *Physics*. The work was most likely not composed by Aristotle as a single treatise at all, but as a number of smaller treatises, or even as a set of lecture notes recorded by some of Aristotle's students, and compiled based on similar themes.

Within the work, Aristotle gives a few names or descriptions of the kind of science we're dealing with. He calls it "First Philosophy," since it deals with the primary, or most fundamental, elements and principles of being. Elsewhere, he refers to it simply as "Wisdom," since wisdom consists in knowing the ultimate causes or reasons why things are as they are. And this links up with a third designation he gives to the discipline, namely "Theology" or the "divine science," since this branch of study includes the highest causes of all, namely God or the gods. Finally, Aristotle calls metaphysics the science of "being as being," because, while every science examines being under a particular designation (e.g., physics studies being in motion; biology deals with being as living), metaphysics deals simply with being itself, or with the attributes common to everything that exists insofar as it exists.

This probably sounds fairly abstract—and it is! A professor of mine once compared reading the *Metaphysics* to descending, in a small submarine, into the deepest and darkest regions of the ocean. My hope is to highlight some of the main features and ideas of this work, linking them to what we've already been considering in our discussion of Aristotle, rather than attempting to give an exhaustive analysis of the work.

a) All Human Beings by Nature Desire to Know

In the opening line of the *Metaphysics*, Aristotle states, "All human beings by nature desire to know" (980a21). We have already discussed his view that a human being is essentially a rational animal, that is, the sort of living being capable of grasping the intelligible structure of reality. For Aristotle, this view about human nature had powerful resonances in his views on ethics. So, in his *Nicomachean Ethics* (another very important work which we will discuss at length in the next chapter), Aristotle asserts that happiness is the ultimate goal of each person's life, and this happiness consists in reaching the highest possible human excellence or fulfillment. What is the highest fulfillment of human existence for Aristotle? It is the joy-filled contemplation of reality, the act of the mind in grasping how everything in the cosmos fits together, as far as we possibly can, within the kind of life we must live as moral and social animals. Aristotle took it very seriously that the human being is made for wisdom—we cannot reach our full human potential without a cognitive openness to reality that allows us to progress toward becoming, intellectually, a microcosm of the whole cosmos.

It should not come as a surprise then that the first book of the *Metaphysics* concerns itself with the subject of wisdom, and contrasts this mode of knowing with others. Aristotle distinguishes between "experience" (*empeiria*) and "craft" (*techne*) by pointing out that a person who has only experiential knowledge of something knows *that* x is the case, while the person who possesses "craft" grasps the reason *why* x is the case, and as a result is in a cognitively superior state. For instance, a person who has learned to practice medicine by observation and experience, but has never *studied* the subject, will know *that* certain symptoms require a certain course of treatment. But without a more penetrating study of human physiology and the nature of pathology, she will not grasp *the causal connection* between the underlying condition and the patient's symptoms, and as such will not be capable of explaining *why* the treatment works to relieve those symptoms. The possession of craft, furthermore, involves an apprehension of the universal, which is attained by the exercise of reason, while experience comes to us from our senses and is as a result limited to the particular. Since science deals with the universal, craft is a higher mode of knowing, and the craftsmen are wiser than people of (mere) experience.

The distinction between experience and craft moves us toward Aristotle's description of the characteristics commonly attributed to the wise person, or the one who possesses what Aristotle calls "universal science" (982a23). (Note that this is yet another term for the discipline of metaphysics.) We think, Aristotle writes, that a wise person should

1. know about all things, as far as possible,
2. know about things that are difficult to know,
3. be able to teach the causes of things in an exact way,
4. know what is choiceworthy in itself,
5. possess the superior science (the science that orders other sciences).

The wise person knows the first causes or principles of all things, and knows these things in a universal way. Such a person knows not only what exists, but also what is good, since the good, or in other words the end or purpose (*telos*), Aristotle says, is one of the causes (982b10). The metaphysician, then, is seeking to know the ultimate reasons why things are the way they are, along with what the purpose or goal of all things is.

The discipline Aristotle describes here really is just what philosophy was classically understood to be. My own interest in philosophy came as a result of my desire to know everything that can be known, combined with the realization that to do so is impossible. The best I could do then, I thought, was to study philosophy, since that would allow me to think about everything at least in a very general way, because philosophy is the critical assessment of the most basic assumptions and principles of all knowledge and reality. Aristotle makes a similar point about the nature of first philosophy (metaphysics) by considering how human beings began to philosophize. Philosophy begins, he famously says, in *wonder*. People made observations about the world, about the moon, the sun, and the stars, and began to wonder how these things, and even the universe as a whole, came to be the way they are. But wonder implies ignorance—we experience wonder when we perceive a fact but do not know why it is the way it is. Aristotle draws the interesting conclusion that philosophy is useless, and he thinks this is a good thing! "[S]ince, then, they engaged in philosophy to escape ignorance," he writes, "they were evidently pursuing scientific knowledge [simply] for the sake of knowing, not for any further use" (982b20–22). This is also what makes philosophy "the only free science, since it is the only one that exists for its own sake" (982b28). Aristotle's point is that all other sciences are tied down to practical purposes of people or of the state, but philosophy is free to pursue whatever path it finds to the goal of knowledge for its own sake. Further, it is the most divine or godlike science, because it yields the sort of knowledge a god would have, and also because it includes the divine itself within the objects it seeks to know.

In Book I, chapters 3–9, Aristotle presents a brief overview of the history of speculation about the ultimate causes of things, which has the interesting feature of showing that everyone who came before Aristotle was more or less fumbling toward Aristotle's own view of things. The Presocratics limited themselves to material causes; Plato took the important step of adding formal causation, but unfortunately understood this in a deficient way. Of special note for our purposes is Aristotle's critique of Plato's Forms, especially as it appears in chapter 9. I offer here a short summary of the main objections Aristotle raises against "those who posited Ideas" (recall that "Ideas" is another name for the "Forms"):

1. Instead of explaining things, the Forms only multiply things needlessly.
2. The theory of Forms seems to imply the existence of Forms for things we think do not have Forms (e.g., negations, things that perish, mud, etc.).

3. The Third Man argument (mentioned at 990b18; developed at 991a2–8; considered in detail below).
4. The Forms don't "contribute to perceptible things" (that is, to their being, or to their being known).
5. Talk of Forms as "patterns" in which particulars "participate" is empty, merely "poetic metaphor."
6. Making Forms the substance-of particular things separates the substance-of the thing from the thing itself.

Some of the reasons Aristotle presents here are easier to follow than others. The basic thrust of his arguments is that the Forms are supposed to explain why particulars are the way they are, but they are incapable of doing so given that they are abstract entities with no clear causal relation to the actual things which we wanted to explain.

The Third Man argument (objection 3 above) goes something like this: Imagine you have two particulars, x and y, both of which exemplify some feature F. On the Theory of Forms, there must therefore be a Form of F. But the Form of F will itself exemplify the feature F (how could it not, since it is F-ness itself?). But this leads to a situation in which we now have three items which all share a common feature—x, y, and F. For instance, take two dogs. In order for them both to be dogs, there must be a third thing, the Form of Dogness, in which they both participate. But then, the Form of Dogness will itself be doggish (how could The Dog Itself not have the character of doggishness?), just like the particular dogs that participate in it. The Theory of Forms seems to entail that we thus need another Form (The Super-Dog) in which these three entities participate, to explain how they could have this feature in common. But we have to say that the Super-Dog Form is itself doggish, along with x, y, and the Form of Dogness. And so we need still another Form, Super-Duper-Dog, to cover those four entities.... This process appears as though it will go on forever, multiplying more and more entities in order to explain the two particulars we started off with. But it is absurd to have to postulate an infinite number of things in order to explain just two things.

Interestingly enough, the criticism Aristotle raises here appears in one of Plato's own late dialogues—the *Parmenides*, where Plato himself offers a number of arguments critiquing his own Theory of Ideas or Forms. Reading passages like these where Aristotle is critical of Plato, and then finding similar objections dealt with in Plato's own writings, helps us to understand what things would have been like in Plato's Academy. Far from being an institution where people were simply indoctrinated into Platonism, there was likely a very lively atmosphere of debate and discussion, where even the great master could be led to revise his views in response to incisive objections raised by bright students.

b) Revisiting Particular Substances

In Book I.9, Aristotle raises an important problem for the very possibility of metaphysics as a unified scientific enterprise. "[B]eings are spoken of in many ways," Aristotle tells us at 992b19. We've already seen how this is the case in the *Categories*, where he listed the ten highest kinds of beings. But given that these kinds represent very different modes of being, it seems unlikely that we can investigate the elements (or the basic causes) of all of being in a single science, since being comes in many different kinds that bear no obvious relation to one another. Furthermore, Aristotle says, we have to face a problem of "prior cognition" concerning the basic elements of being which metaphysics is supposed to be considering. How could we ever learn these elements, since they are the basic elements that we would need to presuppose in order to know anything else? We find Aristotle's answer to this challenge to the possibility of metaphysics in Book IV, to which we now turn.

Aristotle states his answer to the problem of the unity of metaphysics as a science at 1003a33–35: "Being is spoken of in many ways, but always with reference to one thing—i.e., to some one nature—and not homonymously." If we flip back to the opening lines of the *Categories*, we can recall Aristotle's distinction between words used homonymously (the same word refers to two distinct "accounts") and words used synonymously (the same word designates the same "account of the essence"). We know already that the word "being" does not mean precisely the same thing when applied to entities in different categories (substance, relation, quality, quantity, etc.). Since substance and relation, for instance, are distinct ontological kinds, they do not share the same account. So the word "being" cannot apply to different kinds of being synonymously (or "univocally"). But if the term "being" is used *homonymously* (or, in contemporary parlance, "equivocally") when applied to entities belonging to different categories, then there would be no common account that the *Metaphysics* could claim as its subject. Again, this would undermine the claim to the unity of metaphysics as a science.

What Aristotle needs, then, is an explanation of how the word "being" can be used in different ways when speaking of different kinds of being, while showing at the same time that all these different uses are meaningfully related to one another. To get at how this might work, Aristotle discusses the examples of "health" and "medical" (see 1003a35–b16). The primary meaning of "healthy" is the proper functioning of a biological organism, for instance, Fifi the chihuahua. But I can also use the word "healthy" to characterize Fifi's diet, Fifi's urine, and even Fifi's flesh, at least in the culinary products of some cultures. When I call Fifi's diet "healthy," I'm not using the word in the same way as I do when I say that Fifi himself is healthy. But the meaning is also not completely different. Indeed, Fifi's doggie kibble is properly called "healthy" because it contributes to Fifi's health in the primary sense of that word. Similarly, Fifi's urine is healthy in the sense that it provides a vet with a sign of Fifi's health, in the primary sense of the word. And if Fifi's flesh ever found its way into a stir-fry, it would be "healthy" by reference to my own health, understood again in the primary sense as the well-functioning of an organism.

So what is the primary sense or account of the word "being," to which all other uses of that word have reference? Unsurprisingly, given how much Aristotle likes substances, the primary sense of "being" just is "substance." All other beings, then (all the entities that fall under the other nine categories), are called *beings* because they relate somehow to substance, which is being in the primary sense. This accords with what we have learned already from Aristotle's prioritization of particular substances in the *Categories*: accidents (e.g., tall, purple, sitting ...) are always accidents *of* substances (a giraffe, a dragon, Socrates ...). But now Aristotle deepens his analysis of particular substance, embarking on a very in-depth analysis of the notion in *Metaphysics* Book VII. He approaches this topic by asking what is the *primary* substance, or in other words "the substance *of* a given thing." I understand Aristotle to be asking about what it is that makes particular substances to be substantial or real. Recalling Aristotle's teaching in the *Physics*, every particular substance is a composite of matter and form, in other words, a hylomorphic compound. Aristotle considers a few ways of answering the question of what it is about such hylomorphic compounds that makes them the basic realities. Maybe (1) the *matter* of a particular substance like Fifi the chihuahua is what brings about Fifi's substantiality. Or maybe (2) it is Fifi's *form* that plays that role. Or, finally, it could just be that (3) Fifi herself, the *compound* composed of both matter and form (1029a29–30), does this. To make a potentially long story short, Aristotle clearly rules out matter along with the compound, to conclude that it is the form or essence of a particular substance that is the substance-of that thing.

Without going into the details, suffice it to say that Aristotle's investigation of the formal aspect of the particular substance in the remainder of Book VII is complex and difficult. For the purposes of our overview of his thought, it may be enough to note that although Aristotle has taken pains to distinguish his approach from that of Plato, and has even openly criticized the Platonic Theory of Ideas or Forms, when he faces the question of what is really real about concrete particular substances, Aristotle himself concludes that it is *their forms* that endow them with actuality as the kind of thing they are. But since the form of a hylomorphic compound is so bound up with notions like "essence" and "definition," both of which seem to be understood only intellectually and therefore as universals, it is difficult to see how Aristotle can manage to avoid slipping back into some sort of Platonism. Indeed, many prominent thinkers in the late Classical and early Medieval periods depicted the teachings of Plato and Aristotle as very compatible, taking Aristotle as one of the greatest of all the Platonists.

c) The Prime Mover: Thought Thinking Itself

We have mentioned the "Prime Mover" already in the context of Aristotle's search for causal explanations in Book VIII of the *Physics*. This same mysterious entity is also the subject of the *Metaphysics*, Book XII, chapters 6 and 7. There we find

Aristotle intent on showing "that there must be an everlasting unmoved substance" (1071b3). Later philosophers, especially those working from within one of the monotheistic faith traditions (Judaism, Christianity, Islam), came to see Aristotle's proofs here as a proof of the existence of God, the Creator of heaven and earth. It is worth noticing that, while the being Aristotle speaks of here possesses a number of features that later theologians would attribute to God (everlasting, unmoved, uncaused, etc.), Aristotle's Unmoved Mover is not obviously identical with the personal God of Abraham, Isaac, and Jacob, the God who gave the Ten Commandments to Moses and promised to send the Messiah to save His people. Nevertheless, later on, many Medieval theologians would make much use of such Greek philosophical concepts and arguments concerning the divine reality.

What is Aristotle's argument for the necessity of an Unmoved Mover? Actually a few distinct arguments can be discerned here, but I will focus on what I take to be the main one (found at 1072a10–17):

1. Some things (motion, time, the succession of coming-to-be and ceasing-to-be) are everlasting.
2. Anything in motion requires a cause (a reason why it's in motion).
   So,
3. There is an everlasting substance capable of causing everlasting motion.

Though he does not explicitly state it here, the basic principle Aristotle is utilizing is the Principle of Sufficient Reason, according to which anything that exists contingently—that is, anything which is a certain way but could have been another way—requires an explanation as to why it is the way it is and not otherwise. Aristotle believes that since the cosmos consists of an everlasting succession of motion in time, there must be something capable of explaining why this succession is the way it is, and only an everlasting substance capable of causing everlasting motion would be capable of doing this. Much more could be said about this argument and its merits, and the way it appears again in the famous five ways of Thomas Aquinas in the late middle ages.[2] For now, let's conclude our discussion of Aristotle's *Metaphysics* by considering what Aristotle deduces about God's nature based on the argument given above. He explains,

1. Whatever has potentiality in its essence need not actualize it.
   And,
2. Unactualized potency could not produce everlasting continuous motion.
   So,
3. The essence of the substance that causes everlasting motion must be pure actuality.

---

2 In question 2, article 3 of the first part of the voluminous *Summa Theologiae*, Aquinas offers five demonstrations of the claim that God exists.

4.   A substance that completely lacked potency would be immaterial.
Therefore,
5.   The substance that causes everlasting motion in the cosmos must be
     immaterial.

Aristotle goes on to make further claims about what kind of being this ever-lasting, immaterial Unmoved Mover must be. Given that it is pure actuality of the highest kind, and the highest kind of actuality Aristotle knows of is the actuality of the mind in thinking, it follows that the Unmoved Mover must be a Mind capable of thought. And of what, we might ask, will this everlasting Mind be thinking about? Itself, of course! Since it is having the most perfect thought, the object of its thought must also be perfect. But anything less than itself would be imperfect. So, Aristotle concludes, the Unmoved Mover is a pure and perfect absolute Mind that spends all of eternity thinking about itself (1072b18–24).

But wasn't the Unmoved Mover supposed to explain why everything else in the cosmos is in motion? How would such an apparently self-centred and detached divinity be capable of exercising any causal power over the rest of the world, especially since it is unmoved and hence not itself in motion at all? To appreciate Aristotle's answer, I find it helpful to think of something with somewhat similar powers, namely, a cheeseburger. Imagine a cheeseburger, sitting on a plate on a table in the middle of a room. Without moving at all, the cheeseburger has the ability to move other beings in the room, for example, me, toward it. How does it do this? It moves me as an *object of my desire*. Since I love (or at least desire) cheese-burgers, I move (more or less slowly, depending on how hungry I am) toward the cheeseburger, seeking to become one with the cheeseburger, in a sense. Aristotle's Unmoved Mover moves the rest of the universe in a similar way. It "initiates motion by being an object of love" (1072b4). So, for Aristotle, it is literally true that love makes the world go around. All other things, including the heavenly spheres, the spiritual intelligences responsible for moving these spheres (this is where the gods fit in to Aristotle's cosmology) and every living creature on the earth, are ultimately moved by desire for this Unmoved Mover. All other things seek to be like the Unmoved Mover as much as they can, within the constraints of their own natures. This is why what Aristotle calls the second mover, the everlasting "first heaven," moves continuously in a circular motion (1072a23–24), since that sort of motion is the most perfect way something can imitate the life of the Unmoved Mover. Since the Unmoved Mover is the ultimate reason why all other things in the cosmos move, it is the ultimate final cause of all things.

3. CONCLUSION

First philosophy, as the highest of all the sciences, culminates, for Aristotle, in the contemplation of the highest of all realities—the pinnacle of substance and supreme final cause, Thought Thinking Itself, or more simply "the god." This being is the ultimate cause or reason why the cosmos is the way it is, and contemplation of it is in a sense the highest human activity, since human beings are made to know, and ultimate knowledge consists in understanding the highest cause, and everything else as related to, and hence unified by, it. Ending our discussion of Aristotle's natural philosophy and metaphysics on this note points us in the direction of the Medieval period, some of whose key thinkers, as I've already pointed out, found much to be excited about in Aristotle's philosophy. Reflecting on Aristotle's preoccupation with the Unmoved Mover, together with Plato's Form of the Good as the source of the being and intelligibility of all other realities, it is easy to understand how later religious philosophers and theologians found in these pagan philosophers a way of approaching by natural reason the insights which they held by faith on the basis of revelation. If you were to go on to study this period, you would find that the story of philosophy in the Middle Ages is in large part the story of how the greatest minds of that era combined the philosophy of Plato and Aristotle with the scriptural revelation of the Abrahamic faiths.

Chapter 7:

GOOD PEOPLE
AND GOOD CITIES:
ARISTOTLE'S
ETHICS AND *POLITICS*

HISTORICAL CONTEXT

Virtue Ethics, already touched on in our discussions of Plato's *Republic* and (to a lesser extent) the *Meno*, is the Western world's longest-standing ethical tradition.

Textbooks on ethics usually give virtue ethics a place alongside Utilitarianism and Deontology (or Kantian ethics) as one of the three major approaches to ethics. Utilitarianism emphasizes acting in ways that lead to good consequences, and Deontology urges us to act according to our duty. Virtue ethics, by contrast, is more concerned about what kind of person you are than about how you should act. In other words, virtue ethics is primarily concerned with the cultivation of good *character*, where character is understood as the settled qualities or traits that make up the kind of person you are, morally speaking. People will be good or bad depending on whether their character is virtuous (exemplifying the virtues) or vicious (exemplifying the vices). Virtue ethics was the standard approach to ethics in the Western intellectual tradition until the Enlightenment period (i.e., the period beginning around 1650 or 1700). The image in chapter 4 depicts the four "cardinal" or "hinge" virtues—prudence (practical wisdom), courage, justice, and temperance—emphasized by the Greeks as the basis of good moral character. Medieval ethical thought (most notably in the work of Augustine and Aquinas) built on these classical foundations, adding the "infused" virtues of faith, hope, and charity (divine love), which were understood to be given to believers by the direct work of the Holy Spirit. The eighteenth century witnessed a shift away from the virtues toward utilitarian and deontological approaches, views that remain central to contemporary ethical analysis. But the mid-twentieth century brought a resurgence of virtue-oriented ethics sparked in part by an influential 1958 paper by Elizabeth Anscombe entitled "Modern Moral Theory," and this trend has continued to the present day. Some of the now classic twentieth-century texts on virtue ethics include Alisdair MacIntyre's *After Virtue* (1981) and Philippa Foot's *Virtues and Vices* (1978). While the overlap between contemporary virtue ethics and Aristotle's pioneering work is sometimes overstated, most ethicists working in the virtue tradition today continue to take the core ideas of virtue, practical wisdom, and happiness as foundational. This further attests to the lasting influence of Aristotle.

Although the concepts of virtue and vice were discussed before him—not least by Socrates and Plato—Aristotle was the first to give virtue ethics a systematic presentation. He did so in the work we call the *Nicomachean Ethics*, one of his two major ethical treatises, the other being the *Eudemian Ethics*. Since these two works overlap significantly, many scholars believe that the *Nicomachean Ethics* is a revision and expansion of the *Eudemian Ethics*, and it is common practice to take the *Nicomachean Ethics* as the definitive statement of Aristotle's ethical thinking. As in the *Physics* and *Metaphysics*, in the *Nicomachean Ethics* we find Aristotle once again critically engaging with Plato's philosophy. It is worth comparing Aristotle's ethics with the ethical views Plato expresses in the *Republic*, and especially with Plato's ideas about the necessity of a vision of the Form of the Good, which Aristotle directly attacks in Book I, chapter 6. We find the same critical engagement again when we turn to Aristotle's *Politics*, which includes an extended critique of Plato's theory of the ideal state developed in the *Republic*. In this chapter we will be examining some of the main concepts and arguments from Aristotle's

Nicomachean Ethics and *Politics*. Ethics and politics are both practical sciences, the former focusing on the individual, the latter on the state. We will observe the overlap between the two, as well as the connections with Platonic ethical and political theory as we move through this material.

INTRODUCTORY BIG QUESTION:
DOES LIFE HAVE A MEANING?

No question we can ask is more obviously philosophical than the question about the meaning of life. Occasionally things happen that jolt us out of the routine of everyday life, with its mundane tasks of studying, work, groceries, laundry, video games, and social events. Often these disturbances are tragic: we get hit with an unexpected sickness, an important relationship breaks up, or someone close to us dies. At such times we often end up asking ourselves questions like, "What is this all about anyway?" or "What am I here for?" Do our lives have a meaning, a purpose, or a point? Or is life absurd and meaningless? Twentieth-century existentialist philosopher Albert Camus famously claimed that our lives are comparable to the mythical figure Sisyphus, who was condemned by the gods to an eternity of pushing a rock up a hill, only to watch it roll back to the bottom again. Camus urged us to embrace the absurdity of life and to accept its meaningless activity as our own. In this act of defiance, he claimed, we could exercise our freedom and find our human dignity.

Historically, many have rejected Camus's premise that life is absurd, claiming that human life does have an objective purpose. However, they have located this purpose in different places. Some hold that the purpose of life is to love our Creator and do God's will. To others, life acquires meaning and purpose through helping relieve suffering, or raising a family, or contributing to society through the arts or through creative innovations. Some people find engaging in vibrant, passionate activities—for instance in athletics or playing music—to be meaningful in themselves. This diversity of views raises further questions:

Sisyphus Pushing the Rock Up the Hill, from the Austrian painter Matthäus Loder's *Sisyphus* (nineteenth century)

If human lives *do* have some ultimate purpose, do they all have the *same* purpose, or does purpose differ for different people? Is life's purpose something each individual must invent for herself? Or is there some overarching purpose we all have in common, based on the fact that we share the same human nature? Furthermore, is purpose something that individual lives possess, or are social groups the true bearers of purpose—families, cities, nations, or even the human species as a whole? According to at least one prominent modern way of thinking, human purpose (insofar as there can be said to be one) is just the survival of our species. Can we infer from this that individual lives only have purpose insofar as they help prolong our species in existence?

Aristotle thinks each human life has an identifiable meaning, and a meaning we more or less share as human beings. Knowing what this purpose is, he thinks, will help us fit the pieces of our lives together into a coherent whole in a way that will lead to happiness. Happiness (*eudaimonia* in Greek), for Aristotle, is the foundational ethical idea, and it connects with other key concepts—purpose (*télos*), virtue (*areté*), and character (*éthé*)—to form the basic framework of his approach to ethics. If we remain ignorant of our purpose, claims Aristotle, we will be like archers shooting arrows randomly into the air: unlikely to hit the target (happiness). So what does happiness consist in, for human beings? What can we say in general about what a good human life looks like? As we dive into Aristotle's ethical and political views, I invite you to pay attention to his arguments about what human purpose and happiness consists in. Try to use this investigation of Aristotle's views as a way to help you explore your own thoughts and convictions about the meaning and purpose of life.

1. PRACTICAL PHILOSOPHY

According to Aristotle, the sciences divide into three types: (1) the theoretical sciences, (2) the practical sciences, and (3) the productive sciences, or what he calls the crafts. Theoretical sciences, like physics or metaphysics, aim at knowledge for its own sake, and the productive sciences aim at making things that are useful for human life, like toothbrushes or smart phones. Ethics and political science fall into the second category, the practical sciences, which focus on what is good and bad concerning human life and action. In Aristotle's view, ethics stands in a very close relationship to politics, so much so that ethics can be viewed as a part of political science. Like politics, ethics seeks to establish what is good for human beings. But ethics does this with a focus on the good of an individual human being, while politics more broadly construed attempts to reach the good of an entire nation or city-state, which encompasses the goods of the individuals that compose the state. Hence, Aristotle reasons, political science is the finer and more godlike science (1094b8–9). Political science (understood as including ethics) aims at the highest of goods achievable by action (1095a15).

The goodness or badness of human action depends in part on the circumstances in which that action is performed, and these circumstances can be complex. To take one example, cutting another person's stomach open with a knife would usually be morally wrong, but when a doctor does this while performing an operation, it can be a very good act indeed. And in general, the things we call good can often turn out to be bad, as for instance, when suffering from certain sicknesses (like dropsy, or edema) it can be harmful for us to drink water, which would ordinarily be a very good thing to do. In the *Ethics*, Aristotle frequently points out that for an act to be morally good, it is not enough that we do what is, in general, "the right thing." The act must also be done in the right way, at the right time, involving the right people, etc. The complexity of real life makes it impossible to say in detail what the right action will be in every situation. Aristotle urges us, in view of reasons like these, not to expect the practical sciences to be able to reach the same level of precision in its conclusions as, say, mathematical proofs. "We must be content, then," he writes, "to indicate the truth roughly and in outline, and in speaking about things which are only for the most part true and with premises of the same kind to reach conclusions that are no better" (1094b19–23). Despite the relative imprecision of ethics and political science, these disciplines remain, for Aristotle, legitimate sciences in his sense of that word—organized bodies of knowledge in which truth can be attained.

For Aristotle, ethics is a practical science consisting in the knowledge of the human good. It is *practical* in the sense that it is ordered toward action, toward what human beings ought to *do*. It is a *science* in the sense that it involves first principles and conclusions derived from them. And the first-principles or starting-points of this practical body of knowledge involve knowing what is truly good for human beings, that is, what a good human life and good human character amount to. For this reason, Aristotle devotes a lot of attention, in the *Ethics*, to describing in detail the various virtues (moral excellences or good character traits) that human beings may possess, and the related vices (bad character traits) that we end up with if we fail to cultivate the virtues. Before we get into those details, we will set the stage by examining some of Aristotle's foundational ethical doctrines concerning happiness, the nature of virtue in general, and human action.

2. KEY TEACHINGS AND ARGUMENTS FROM THE *NICOMACHEAN ETHICS*

a) Happiness and the Good Life

Let's start by making a distinction about the way things can be good. The opening lines of the first book of the *Nicomachean Ethics* state that "Every craft and every method of inquiry and likewise every action and deliberate choice seem to seek some good. That is why they correctly declare that the good is 'that which all seek'" (1094a1–2). Here, Aristotle makes the general point that we do everything that we do for the sake of something we regard as good. The good, we can say, is the object of desire. The next thing to notice is that we desire and value some things for their own sake (these are called *ends*), while we value other things only because they help us to obtain the things we consider to be good in themselves, as a *means* to attain some other end or goal. Maybe you strongly dislike the taste of some medicine, but you are willing to take it because you believe it will help you to become healthy. In this case, the medicine is valued only as a means to your goal of being healthy—you don't want it for its own sake, but only for the sake of health. The medicine, then, is only *instrumentally* good. Health, on the other hand, is something you desire for its own sake. As such, it is *intrinsically* good. Now some things might be valued *both* for their own sake, and also for the sake of something else. For instance, you might go out to see a movie with some friends, and you may regard the experience of watching the film as valuable in itself, but you may also value it because it provides you with an opportunity to spend time with friends. In this case, the movie is both an end in itself, and a means to another end (the enjoyment of your friends' company).

"Every craft and every method of inquiry and likewise every action and deliberate choice seem to seek some good. That is why they correctly declare that the good is 'that which all seek'."
(*Nicomachean Ethics*, 1094a1–2)

THE ARGUMENT FOR HAPPINESS AS THE GOOD

With the understanding of "good" as the object of desire or value, and the distinction between intrinsic and instrumental goods behind us, we can now move on to observe Aristotle's next move. He presents a very important, but very condensed argument that is worth spending some time unpacking, since it plays a central role in the project he is engaged in:

> If, then, there is some end of the things we do, which we desire for its own sake (everything else being desired for the sake of this), and if we do not choose everything for the sake of something else (for at that rate the process would go on to infinity, so that our desire would be empty and vain), clearly this must be the good and the chief good. (1094a17–21)

Aristotle is attempting to focus our eyes on the target or goal of ethics, which he takes to be the goal of human life as well. This goal, he thinks, will have the character of being desired for its own sake, but will not itself be desired for the sake of anything else. In other words, it will be the end-point of the process of human desiring and pursuing, and for this reason it will be the highest good. Everything else we desire will be for the sake of this ultimate good. Aristotle is also arguing here that there *must* be such an end-point of our desire, because otherwise there would be no point in desiring anything at all. If we want everything we want for the sake of something else, then that is the same as saying that we don't really want anything. In order to avoid the conclusion that all our desires are ultimately pointless, Aristotle thinks we have to conclude that there is some single good thing that we want for itself, and that whenever we want anything else, we want it also for the sake of this further good thing.

Someone could object to Aristotle's argument by pointing out that a person could desire a number of things for their own sake, without having to also desire them for the sake of some further single thing. Why couldn't I desire good friends, good music, good food and meaningful employment, for instance, without also wanting all of these things for the sake of something else? While this objection does make some sense, I think Aristotle would say that it doesn't map on to the psychology of human desire. Most people, if pushed far enough, would admit that they do in fact want the things they want because, in addition to simply being valued for their own sake, those things also contribute to a happy human life. It makes sense to ask a person *why* they desire good friends or good music. And it makes sense for that person to respond, "Because they make my life happier." But it doesn't make sense to then ask, "And why do you want to be happy?" At that point, the appropriate response is probably something like, "Shut up and stop asking stupid questions." Arguably, pretty much everyone thinks there is some condition of life that deserves to be called "happiness," and whatever this condition involves, it is indeed the thing we ultimately want, and everything else we desire, we also desire because we think it will contribute to making us happy. If this is so, Aristotle says, then knowing what happiness is will be one of the most important things we can know. For then in our actions we will be like archers with our eyes on the target, instead of shooting arrows aimlessly here and there in some vague hope of finding the good life.

THE NATURE OF HAPPINESS

If we agree with Aristotle that we do in fact want to be happy, and that we want everything else that we want for the sake of this, then it seems that we have identified the ultimate end or goal of human life. But have we? Actually, not quite. The problem, as Aristotle points out, is that while we can all agree that we want to be happy, people have very different ideas about what happiness involves. So he launches into a detailed investigation of the nature of happiness. In chapter 5 of Book I, Aristotle distinguishes three sorts of human life that correspond to three different understandings of happiness. The first type is the **life of enjoyment**, and people who live this way tend to identify happiness with pleasure, as though the ultimate goal of human life were to satisfy the appetites we share with other animals. Aristotle dismisses such a life as vulgar, slavish, and not reflective of the dignity of human nature. But notice that later in the *Ethics* he spends a good deal of time discussing pleasure, and clearly regards pleasure as important for the good life; Aristotle thinks that the truly happy life is in fact the most pleasant life, but he is emphatic that happiness does not *consist in* pleasure. The next way of life Aristotle considers is the **political or active life**, in which a person pursues honour as the supreme value. People living in this way seek to accomplish good deeds in society in order to be recognized (honoured) by others. This, Aristotle believes, is an improvement over the life of enjoyment, as it reflects a superior set of values. Nevertheless, honour cannot really be what happiness consists in, because honour depends on the fickle attitudes of other people and can easily be lost if those attitudes change. Further, Aristotle claims, people want not only to be acknowledged by others, but to be acknowledged *as good people*, which shows that actually *being* good is a more fundamental value than merely appearing to be good.

Along the way, Aristotle also rejects the life of money-making, which equates the storing up of wealth with happiness. He dismisses this way of life as unsatisfactory on the grounds that money is purely a means to other things. No one values money for its own sake, but rather because of what she thinks she can get with it, which shows that these other things are actually more important. So money lacks one of the key characteristics of happiness in that, unlike happiness, it is only extrinsically good, and not good in itself (intrinsically). Aristotle also (in chapter 6) dismisses Plato's notion that the Form or Idea of the Good is the key to ethics and to the discernment of the good life. In the *Republic*, Plato taught that wise rulers would need to keep their mental eyes fixed on the Form of the Good to use it as a pattern to make laws and guide human life well. According to Aristotle, this road leads to a dead end, mostly because the things that are good come in such a broad diversity that it seems hopeless to think there is one single "form" that is common to all of them (1096a19–33; 1096b21–26). Aristotle's own preferred explanation of why we call these diverse things 'good' has to be sought out in his *Metaphysics*, and it relates to his theory of focal meaning or analogy, which we considered in the previous chapter regarding the term "being." In a rare personal remark, Aristotle explains his divergence from his teacher, Plato, as follows: "while both are dear, piety requires us to honour truth above our friends" (1096a16).

This leaves what Aristotle calls the **life of contemplation**. He does not say here what this way of life involves, but he develops it at considerable length in the rest of the work (and we will return to it later on). The life of contemplation is the genuinely good human life for Aristotle, and, in a nutshell, this way of life sees happiness as linked with attaining knowledge. But happiness is not just knowing any old thing—it consists in contemplating the highest things. If you recall Aristotle's discussion in the *Metaphysics* of ultimate knowledge involving the causes of things, and of the Prime Mover as the ultimate final cause and the cause of all causes, it is only a short jump to the conclusion Aristotle draws that happiness consists in the contemplation of God. But there is much to say in the meantime before we reach these conclusions in the final book of the *Ethics*.

THE FUNCTION ARGUMENT

In Book I, chapter 7, Aristotle lists some of the attributes of happiness. We do everything we do for the sake of happiness, so happiness is the most "final" of all the ends we pursue. Happiness is, then, "always desirable in itself and never for the sake of something else" (1097a33–34). Happiness is also commonly understood to be self-sufficient in the sense that "when isolated [it] makes life desirable and lacking in nothing" (1097b15). The idea here is that if we are truly happy, we won't need anything else. Aristotle will qualify this later on (see chapter 10 of Book I and chapter 10 of Book 9), and it will turn out that in fact we need a wide variety of things to be in a genuinely, self-sufficient and happy condition. For instance, to be happy we will need a decent share of luck or good fortune; a person who has fallen into misery due to sickness or financial ruin or relational breakdown or other hardships can't be called happy in the full sense. We need friends, some cash and a relatively peaceful existence if we are going to be happy, and good looks can't hurt our prospects either. And, Aristotle thinks, whatever happiness itself consists in, a person will have to be able to ensure that he or she has it not just for a day or two, but for an extended period of time—ideally over an entire life, or as close to that as possible. Yet these things remain more or less extraneous to the essence of what makes a human life happy, for Aristotle.

How can we get more specific about what happiness really amounts to? Aristotle suggests that we could do so "if we could first ascertain the function of man" (1097b25). The "function" of a thing is simply its purpose; the function or purpose of a sculptor is to produce sculptures; the function of an axe is to cut; the function of an eye is to enable its possessor to see. Aristotle performs a kind of inductive generalization over various things that have functions, and then asks whether human beings themselves do not have a function, just *as* human beings. Aristotle's inference is somewhat sketchy here—why should it follow from the fact that carpenters and firefighters and secretaries have purposes that human beings *as human beings* should also have a purpose? Each of these job titles denotes a certain role we fill in society, and so of course they can be understood as functional concepts. But being human does not seem to be a job title or role of that sort. To our modern worldview, this argument will likely sound strange. To see where he is coming from, recall that for Aristotle, the cosmos in its entirety is imbued with teleology or purpose. As we saw in our earlier consideration of the *Physics*, Aristotle takes final causes very seriously. So for him it is quite natural to suggest that human beings, as part of this ordered cosmos, have their own distinct purpose just like anything else.

If we are willing to follow Aristotle this far, we can next ask, "What might the purpose of a human being *be*, and how can we know what it is?" Here is Aristotle's

146 | CHAPTER 7

answer. A human being is a type of living being, and the distinctive feature of human life and activity is *rationality*. Now, the good of a thing has to do with it performing its distinctive function well (with excellence). So, Aristotle locates the human good in the activity of the rational soul performed in accordance with the best and most complete virtue (excellence) (1098a16–17). This is Aristotle's general outline of the human good and human happiness. Happiness, for human beings, is to live and act in a way that is good for us, given the kind of being we are. It involves the fullest realization of our distinctively human capacities in vibrant activity. The Greek word for happiness (*eudaimonia*) is probably better translated as "flourishing" since, as we use the word in English, "happiness" refers to a feeling or emotional state, rather than the energetic exercise of our distinctively human capacities in the most excellent (virtuous) way possible.

From here, it is only a few short steps to the further conclusion that human happiness consists in contemplation. Contemplation involves the exercise of what Aristotle sees as the highest human faculty, namely reason or intellect (*nous*), which realizes itself most fully when it grasps the highest objects—the ultimate truths. For a more complete discussion of this, we have to jump all the way to the last book of the *Ethics*, where Aristotle says this:

> ... the activity of reason, which is contemplative, seems both to be superior in serious worth and to aim at no end beyond itself, and to have its pleasure proper to itself (and this augments the activity), and the self-sufficiency, leisureliness, unweariedness ... and all the other attributes ascribed to the supremely happy man are evidently those connected with this activity, [so] it follows that this will be the complete happiness of man. (1177b14–24)

Aristotle is aware that given the kind of beings we are, with all sorts of practical needs, we have to pay attention to many other things as well to sustain a life of contemplation. We cannot simply spend all our time contemplating—we also have to get our groceries, do our laundry, and fulfill our obligations to our families and to the society we are part of. Nevertheless, Aristotle believes we

> must, so far as we can, make ourselves immortal, and strain every nerve to live in accordance with the best thing in us.... This would seem, too, to be each man himself, since it is the authoritative and better part of him. It would be strange, then, if he were to choose not the life of his self but that of something else.... [F]or man, therefore, the life according to reason is best and pleasantest, since reason more than anything else is man. This life therefore is also the happiest. (1177b34–1178a4)

For Aristotle, the best human life will be one that includes whatever we need to support a life that provides us with as much opportunity to engage in the pursuit of the truth and the exercise of our reasoning faculties as we can manage.

Do you agree with Aristotle that the best thing in you, and the thing that most of all makes you what you are, is your ability to know and to reason? If so, you may be inclined to buy his argument. There are, of course, other options. For instance, a person might think that what makes us most fully ourselves is our capacity to love, and so might see a life of love as higher than a life in the pursuit of truth. Someone else could identify the awareness of beauty as the highest thing in a person, and claim that the pursuit of beauty is therefore more fully human than the pursuit of knowledge. Or maybe a happy life requires all three: knowledge, love, and beauty. Again, maybe people are sufficiently different that happiness isn't a one-size-fits-all sort of thing. Maybe one person's function, and corresponding happiness, can differ from another's. Even if we differ from Aristotle on what the highest and most excellent human activity consists in, we might still find the way he answers the problem of happiness compelling. The idea that our happiness lies in the greatest possible fulfillment of our best capacities remains a powerful one.

b) Virtue and Character: Aristotle's Vision of a Good Person

Having noted that Aristotle takes human happiness to consist in contemplation, understood as the human activity that most fully realizes our highest abilities, we need to try to make sense of why he then spends so much of the *Nicomachean Ethics* (Books II through V, and Book VII to the middle of Book X) talking about other things. The *Ethics* includes two books on friendship, and significant portions of two different books on pleasure. In particular, Aristotle spends an enormous amount of time detailing what he calls the moral virtues, or virtues of character. These differ, for Aristotle, from the intellectual virtues (covered in Book VI), which naturally seem more relevant to the life of contemplation. Why are these other topics so important for Aristotle? To begin to explain this, we need to develop an understanding of what the moral virtues are.

Book I, chapter 13, begins, "Since happiness is an activity of the soul in accordance with perfect virtue, we must consider the nature of virtue; for perhaps we shall thus see better the nature of happiness." What, then, is a virtue for Aristotle? Simply put, a virtue is a positive, stable character trait. In the most general sense, a character trait is a way a person is, or is disposed to act. It is something like a personality trait. When we call a person an introvert or an extrovert, for instance, we mean that the person in question has a tendency to act or to respond to circumstances (such as being in a group of people) in certain regular ways. Like personality traits, moral character traits can be more or less stable. A person who always (or nearly always) acts in a certain way can be said to have a stable disposition or trait. If a stable character trait is also *positive*, that is, if it contributes toward the individual's flourishing or happiness, then it is a **virtuous** disposition. At 1106a23, Aristotle describes virtue as a state of character that "makes a man good and which makes him do his own work well." Accordingly, a stable disposition to act *negatively*—in ways that undermine one's ability to flourish—is a vice, or a **vicious** character trait. Many (or maybe most) people have character traits somewhere in between purely virtuous and purely vicious. We act in good ways some of the time, but we also act in bad ways some of the time. For Aristotle, the person who usually acts in positive ways (but sometimes messes up due to weakness or instability) is **continent**. By contrast, the **incontinent** person is the one who acts in negative ways most of the time, but occasionally—maybe by chance or because a stab of conscience breaks through—acts in the ways a virtuous person would act.

We need the virtues, Aristotle thinks, if we are to attain happiness. And it turns out that there are many different virtues that we need. The virtues can be classified according to the different parts or components of the soul which they perfect. For Aristotle, the soul contains a rational element, and a non-rational element. Human beings share the non-rational part of the soul with all living things—it is responsible for our organic life-functions of nutrition and growth. Since this is not distinctively human, Aristotle sets it aside as far as virtue is concerned. Aristotle's claim, in Book III, that virtue and vice, as well as moral praise and blame, have to do with *voluntary* human activity, is relevant here. Voluntary actions (unlike, say, the digestive processes governed by the non-rational part of our soul) spring from a moving principle within us that is under our conscious control. More than this, distinctively human activity that can be evaluated morally has to involve deliberation and choice (for his treatment of these topics, see especially chapter 3 of Book III). In Aristotle's view, we deliberate about different possible ways of achieving our goals, and we choose whatever seems to us to be the best course of action (the course of action that will most likely enable us to achieve our goal). Action that results from this process is distinctively human because it involves the rational part of our soul, which, for Aristotle, constitutes each person's self. Since virtuous and vicious states of character are the result of our deliberate and voluntary choices and actions, we are responsible for our own moral character.

Returning to the point about how Aristotle classifies the virtues, notice that he distinguishes two sub-parts within the rational part of the soul. One of these is reason itself, or the intellect, and the other is something that "shares in reason" but is not itself rational. Aristotle describes this as the part of the soul that has appetites and desires (1102b30–31). It is at least very similar to what we would refer to today as the will, so I will call it the "volitional" part of the soul (from the Latin word *voluntas*, which can mean "will," "desire," or "inclination"). The volitional part of the soul shares in reason insofar as it can listen to and obey reason, so that it can come under our rational control. Unlike the circulation of our blood and our digestive processes (which work entirely apart from our rational control), our emotions, attitudes, and desires can be influenced and directed by reason, at least to some extent, and this is how they share in reason. Both the intellectual and the volitional parts of the soul have their own virtues. Aristotle calls the former the **intellectual virtues** and the virtues of the volitional part he calls the **moral virtues**, or virtues of character; I will follow him by focusing more attention on the moral virtues.

He begins Book II by stating that we develop the virtues of the intellect mostly by learning and being taught, but the moral virtues arise from habit (1103a15–17). We are not born with the moral virtues, though we have the capability of developing them if we cultivate the right habits. This explains the strong emphasis Aristotle puts on having a good upbringing if we are to become good (virtuous) people—bad habits learned early on can make it very hard to change later in life, even if we want to! In order to form good habits, according to Aristotle, we have to repeatedly do the sorts of actions a virtuous person would do.

At this point, we might ask Aristotle, "How are we supposed to know what actions a virtuous person would do if we ourselves are not yet virtuous?" If I can only become virtuous by doing virtuous things, but I would only know what is virtuous if I were already virtuous, then trying to become virtuous seems hopeless. Aristotle tells us to look for a virtuous person and imitate his or her activities. But we might ask, once again, how can I tell who the virtuous people are if I myself am not one of them? Maybe Aristotle's claim that we have the capacity to become virtuous from birth indicates a sort of natural tendency toward virtue in us. And maybe that capacity itself gives us some sort of natural awareness of what is good and what is bad, at least enough to identify who the virtuous people are. But this possibility takes us beyond what he in fact says. I am not sure that Aristotle ever provides a satisfactory answer to this problem.

THE MAIN MORAL VIRTUES AND THE DOCTRINE OF THE MEAN

Many see Aristotle's famous **doctrine of the mean** as the key to his teaching on the moral virtues. The basic idea of the "mean" is that in many areas where virtue is possible, virtue is found between more and less of something. For example, the virtue of **courage**, one of the four classical cardinal moral virtues, has to do with how we manage fear. Aristotle understands courage mainly in the context of warfare, so his main picture of a courageous person is the soldier who stands his ground in the face of danger in battle. But we can extend the idea to any situation where we have to maintain our position to fight for a good cause at the risk of possible harm to ourselves. It is possible to have too much fear, to be afraid of the wrong things at the wrong time, and to run away or back down instead of standing firm when we should. People who tend in a stable way to let themselves be overcome by fear have the vice of cowardice. But there is another vice that is opposed to courage, namely the vice of recklessness. Reckless people throw themselves needlessly into danger, risking harm without good reason. We can say that they do not have enough fear, or do not fear the things they should. So we can describe recklessness as a deficiency in fear, and cowardice as an excess of fear. The virtue of courage then, attains the mean between excess and deficiency—the courageous person is not the one without fear, but the one who fears the right things at the right time. She stands her ground and risks harm to herself when she should, but does not do so for no reason (see Book III, chapters 6 to 9, for a detailed treatment of courage).

Aristotle discusses many other moral virtues that display this same structure, depicting virtue as a mean state in between two vicious states that can be described as an excess or deficit in some area. Consider the virtue of **temperance** or self-control, another cardinal virtue (see Book III, chapters 10 to 12, for a detailed account). A temperate person knows how to engage with her appetites and manage pleasure in a way that leads to health and happiness. In the area of food, she does not overeat and give in to indulgence, as does the glutton, whose vice is on the side of excess (too much indulgence in food). But she does not starve herself either, as does the "insensitive" or ascetic person whose vice is on the side of deficiency (a lack in the area of eating and drinking). As Aristotle puts it, the virtuous states of "temperance and courage, then, are destroyed by excess and defect, and preserved by the mean" (1104a25). Aristotle's thorough analysis of character and the moral virtues deals with many other areas of human life. In anger management there is a mean between being too easily angered (the term for this is irascibility) and not getting angry when one should (inirascibility). In the area of giving money also, a person can have an excess (the prodigal person who gives more than is right) or a deficiency (the stingy person who withholds giving when it is right to give). Concerning honour, a person can be ambitious (the vice of excess desire for honour) or unambitious (the vice of not caring enough about honour). The virtue of pride or magnanimity ("greatness of soul") is also related to honour in a way, but more precisely has to do with one's self-assessment (see Book IV, chapter 3, for details). The magnanimous person is "great" in the sense that she possesses all the virtues; further, she knows that she is great and carries herself accordingly, by contrast to the vain person (excess) and the overly humble person (deficiency). Aristotle also discusses social virtues, like truthfulness, which has to do with how you present yourself to others and rests in between boastfulness and false modesty. Wittiness is the mean in giving amusement that lies between being a buffoon and a boor.

Does every human virtue fit into this framework of excess, deficiency, and mean? It is certainly not the case that every human *activity* has a virtuous mean state. There is no "right amount" of murder, for example. And you can't make adultery a virtuous act by committing it with "the right people at the right time in the right way." But these actions can be drawn into Aristotle's scheme if we describe things properly: an act of adultery, for instance, is a matter of the sexual appetite going wrong, and so it results from an excess in the area of sexual desire and is a violation of the virtue of self-control or temperance. It is not as easy to see how **justice**, another of the cardinal virtues, consists in a mean between excess and deficiency. Aristotle defines justice as the "state of character which makes people disposed to do what is just and makes them act justly and wish for what is

Table 5: Virtues and Vices in Aristotle's *Ethics*

	EXCESS	MEAN (VIRTUE)	DEFICIENCY
Fear and confidence	Rashness	Courage	Cowardice
Pleasure and pain	Licentiousness	Temperance	Insensibility
Getting and spending (minor)	Prodigality	Liberality	Illiberality
Getting and spending (major)	Vulgarity	Magnificence	Pettiness
Honour and dishonour (major)	Vanity	Nobility	Timidity
Honour and dishonour (minor)	Ambition	Proper ambition	Lack of ambition
Anger	Irascibility	Patience	Lack of spirit
Self-expression	Boastfulness	Truthfulness	Understatement
Conversation	Buffoonery	Wittiness	Boorishness
Social conduct	Flattery	Friendliness	Cantankerousness
Shame	Shyness	Modesty	Shamelessness
Indignation	Envy	Proper indignation	Spite

just" (1129a7–9). This is obviously not much help unless we know what "just" and "justly" mean. He devotes the entirety of Book V to the topic of justice, and much could be said about it. For the purposes of our overview of the moral virtues, a few brief points will suffice.

Aristotle calls justice "complete virtue, but not absolutely, but in relation to our neighbour" (1129b25). Unlike the other moral virtues, which have to do with moderating ourselves, justice has to do with standing in a right relationship to others. He distinguishes two senses of "justice." The just person in the broad, general sense is the person who follows the laws (assuming that the laws are good and promote the happiness of the political community). In what Aristotle calls the particular sense of justice, the just person is fair. Aristotle focuses on this second, particular sense, and divides it into its *distributive* and *rectificatory* forms, which have to do, respectively, with how common possessions are divided up among citizens, and with making right the wrongs committed by one person against another. Given this, Aristotle describes justice as a mean between the extremes of "acting unjustly and being unjustly treated" (1133b33), which, he admits, is a different sort of mean than in the other virtues. The idea here is that the just person does not assign too much or too little of what is useful or harmful either to herself or to others, but assigns the right amount in accordance with what is due to each person. It will often be the place of political leaders or judicial officers to determine what distribution of goods is just, and what is required to amend wrongdoing, so in a way, the virtue of justice belongs most properly to people in those positions. But insofar as we participate in social and political interactions with fellow citizens, we are all capable of pursuing justice in our own relationships and in the state more broadly. As we will see, in Aristotle's understanding of democracy or (speaking more in line with his usage) constitutional rule, all citizens participate in the assembly, so all require the virtue of justice.

Aristotle makes the following summary statement at 1106b18–27:

> both fear and confidence and appetite and anger and pity and in general pleasure and pain may be felt both too much and too little, and in both cases not well; but to feel them at the right times, with reference to the right objects, towards the right people, with the right motive, and in the right way, is what is both intermediate and best, and this is characteristic of virtue.

If the mean or intermediate state is the characteristic of all moral virtue, the question arises how we are to discern and attain this intermediate state in the various areas of life. To do so is difficult, which is why you will only rarely find a person who is comprehensively virtuous. Aristotle offers us some practical advice: If you find yourself leaning toward an excess or a deficiency in one of the areas described, the way to get yourself closer to the middle is to aim for the opposite extreme. Then, like a stick that is crooked in one direction we will come out closer to straight if we bend ourselves in the opposite direction (1109b6). If, for instance, you struggle with letting your temper get out of control, aim to be completely unmoved by anger, and you will hopefully end up somewhere closer to the virtuous mean state. Ultimately, we cannot identify the mean in any of these areas without possessing what Aristotle considers to be the master moral virtue, namely **prudence or practical wisdom** (*phronesis* in Greek). Prudence is the fourth classical cardinal moral virtue, and in a way it is the most important, since all the other moral virtues require that we possess practical wisdom. Why is this the case? It is because practical wisdom is the excellence of soul that enables us to deliberate and choose well (in ways that contribute toward our own flourishing and that of others), and without this ability we cannot act well, since all genuine human action flows from deliberation and choice. But acting well is the heart of all moral virtue. Aristotle classes practical wisdom with the intellectual virtues, but it has a foot in the camp of the moral virtues as well because unlike the other intellectual virtues which perfect our ability to grasp truth, practical wisdom perfects our ability to act well. To deliberate and choose well, we need a grounding in the truth about what is good for human beings (this is part of the province of what Aristotle calls speculative or philosophical wisdom), but we also need to know how to achieve these goals, and to have our will set on pursuing them. The virtue of practical wisdom begins in grasping the truth about the good that should be done to attain happiness, and ends in issuing commands to our will to do that good.

c) Friendship and Pleasure: Two Further Components of Happiness

The good life, according to Aristotle, does not consist only in the cultivation of the virtues discussed in the overview presented above. Part of what makes Aristotle's *Ethics* particularly human and realistic is that he finds within it a very significant place for friendship and pleasure. This section will complete our picture of Aristotle's ethics with a sketch of what he says on each of these topics.

GENUINE FRIENDSHIP AS A KEY TO THE GOOD LIFE

Just a few lines into Book VIII, Aristotle makes the poignant claim that "without friends no one would choose to live, though he had all other goods" (1155a5–6). After listing a number of reasons why friendship is important and necessary to individuals at every stage of life, he says that friendship is what holds states together, and is even more important than justice. This is high praise for friendship; Aristotle clearly sees it as essential for human happiness. Indeed, he devotes two whole books of the *Ethics* to the subject of friendship. From 1155b16, Aristotle begins his discussion of the kinds of friendship that can exist. In all friendship there is mutual love and reciprocal goodwill. Friends see one another as good and wish good things for one another, and friendship arises between two people when both of them know that they feel this way about one another. But the different kinds of friendship are based on the different sorts of things people love; for Aristotle the lovable is threefold, consisting of the good, the pleasant, and the useful. There are then friendships based on virtue (goodness), friendships based on the pleasantness of one another's company, and friendships based on the utility (usefulness) each derives from the other. In a sense, friendship based on virtue is the only true friendship because in it the friends love *each other*, while in friendship based on utility they love the benefits they derive from the relationship, and in friendship based on pleasure they love the enjoyment they get from being together rather than loving the other person for who he or she is. In these last two types we can say that the friends really love *themselves* and are ultimately in it for themselves.

The friendship of those who are good (virtuous) is more enduring than the other sorts, Aristotle tells us, because it depends on stable character traits and does not dissolve when the utility or pleasantness of the relationship diminishes (1164a10–11). But true friendships are also rare, because not very many people are truly virtuous, and friendships of this sort only emerge gradually, once the friends have come to know one another well and to trust one another. And for such friendships to be fully realized, the friends must live together and pursue activities together. They must also be equals to each other; friendship among unequals (e.g., between parents and their children, or between those at different levels of social status) cannot be realized as fully. One helpful way to understand Aristotle's view of friendship is to note that for him, a true friend is "another self" (1166a31). Just as we desire our own existence, life, and goodness for our own sake, we desire these things also for our (true) friends, for their own sake. But again, Aristotle says, this is only possible among those who are good, because a bad person will not love even himself but, living with all sorts of inner conflict and turmoil, will seek to escape from and forget himself. For this reason, Aristotle concludes, "we should strain every nerve to avoid wickedness and should endeavour to be good; for so and only so can one be either friendly to oneself or a friend to another" (1166b28–29).

In Book IX, chapter 8, Aristotle makes a paradoxical statement about self-love. The more a good person loves herself, the better it will be not only for her but also for others. This is because the good person strives for what is truly the best, and what is best is the life of virtue, which will often involve acting for the sake of our friends and our country even when it involves great personal sacrifice. The truly good person is selfish, but in a good way; she takes for herself what is truly best and highest. Such people "will throw away wealth too on condition that their friends gain more; for while a man's friend gains wealth he himself achieves nobility; he is therefore assigning the greater good to himself" (1169a27–29). In conclusion, the truly happy person, says Aristotle, needs friends. In fact, "no one would choose the whole world on condition of being alone, since man is a political creature and one whose nature is to live with others" (1169b18). Whether you consider the happy person from the point of view of the active life, or from the point of view of the contemplative life, we live better when we live with friends. Friends enable us to accomplish more good things, and stimulate us to think and contemplate more effectively as well. The goodness of a good person is multiplied by the presence of good friends.

"Without friends no one would choose to live, though he had all other goods." (*Nicomachean Ethics*, 1155a5–6)

TRUE AND FALSE PLEASURES

Back in Book I, Aristotle dismissed the life of pleasure as beneath the dignity of human beings. But this is not the end of what he says about pleasure, because he also notes that the truly happy life is in fact the most pleasurable life. The *Ethics* contains two substantial treatments of the topic of pleasure; the first comes in chapters 4 to 14 of Book VII, and the second in the first five chapters of Book X. Aristotle consistently maintains that although pleasure is not *the* good for human beings, it is nevertheless an important marker of what is good, especially when we distinguish among different sorts of pleasure. There are base and disgraceful pleasures which stem from doing wrong and are agreeable only to people with vicious characters, and then there are the pleasures that arise from a truly flourishing life that is consonant with the virtues. There are pleasures of the body, which we share in common with animals, and then there are pleasures of the soul, which are more properly human because they spring from the activity of what is higher or more noble in us. In fact, for Aristotle, all pleasure is the result of activity, so that the better the type of activity, the better the pleasure that comes along with and completes it. Aristotle makes a very important point at 1174b17–23, which is worth quoting fully:

> [I]n the case of each sense the best activity is that of the best-conditioned organ in relation to the finest of its objects. And this activity will be the most complete and pleasant. For, while there is pleasure in respect of any sense, and in respect of thought and contemplation no less, the most complete is pleasantest, and that of a well-conditioned organ in relation to the worthiest of its objects is the most complete; and the pleasure completes the activity.

We take the most pleasure in our senses of taste, or hearing, or sight when they are engaged with the best objects—deliciously prepared food, or beautiful music or visual artwork, for instance. The same goes for contemplation, which is the activity of that which is highest in us, our reason.

From here it is only a short jump to the conclusion Aristotle made in Book I, and which he repeats and develops in chapters 7 and 8 of Book X: Perfect happiness, for human beings, consists in contemplative activity. This is not only the best activity we can engage in, given the sort of being we are, but it is also the most pleasant. And given Aristotle's claim that the best activity of one of our knowing powers requires engagement with "the worthiest objects" to which that power is open, we note once again the conclusion that Thomas Aquinas and other medieval Aristotelians were to make so much of: The truest happiness and the highest pleasure for human beings consists in the contemplation of God. Recall that for Aristotle, God is the highest cause, the final cause of the entire universe, and the ultimate explanation for everything that happens. It follows that the pursuit of the ultimate truth must in the end lead us to God (but keep in mind that Aristotle, who did not know of the personal God of Judeo-Christian faith, understood by "God" the ultimate metaphysical principle he referred to as the Prime Mover). Contemplation of the highest truths is our highest activity and aim, but contemplation and the pursuit of truth is best pursued together with friends who will stimulate, challenge, and encourage us. And without the moral virtues, no genuine friendship of this sort is possible. We come, finally, to the answer to our earlier question of why Aristotle spends so much time on these topics: both friendship and the moral virtues are necessary to sustain a life ordered to that most pleasant activity of contemplation. The social nature of human beings that Aristotle already emphasized so much in the *Ethics* comes to the forefront all the more in his other treatment of practical philosophy in the *Politics*, to which we now turn.

3. *POLITICS*: THE MASTER SCIENCE

Aristotle opens his treatise on politics with a concise argument to the effect that the goal or aim of the state or political community is the highest good. The good of the individual, explored in so much depth in the *Ethics*, turns out to be subordinate to the higher good of the community, in Aristotle's thought. For him, the smallest unit of human community is the household. Individual human beings form families in order to meet their needs. And households join together to form villages. But neither the household nor the village is sufficient to meet the needs of human beings. Only when multiple villages link up to form a city-state does the complete and self-sufficient unit of community emerge, the community that is capable of fully meeting the various physical, mental, and social needs of its members. Aristotle argues that the state or "political community" is the highest form of human community, since it "embraces all the rest," and so the state aims at the highest human goal, or the highest good (*Politics*, 1252a5). This point recalls Aristotle's remark at the end of the second chapter of Book I of the *Ethics*: "though it is worthwhile to attain the end merely for one man, it is finer and more godlike to attain it for a nation or for city-states" (1094b9). Political science is, for Aristotle, at the top of the hierarchy of sciences, since its job is to realize the good for the whole community. Every other good thing human beings pursue, whether as individuals or in groups, and all the arts and sciences they use to achieve these various goals, will be subordinated to political science and its goal, which is the common good of the entire community.

"Though it is worthwhile to attain the end merely for one man, it is finer and more godlike to attain it for a nation or for city-states."
(*Politics*, 1094b9)

Political science is, then, the "master science" because it determines what other sciences will be operative within the state, and what goals they will pursue. To see this point, think of the way government funding achieves a similar sort of purpose in our own time. If there is no funding for certain sorts of research, then unless the researcher is independently wealthy or finds a private sponsor, that research simply won't happen. And it is often government agencies that make decisions about what sort of research is worthy of financial support. For Aristotle, such decisions will be made well only if they are made with an eye to the common good of the whole community. Aristotle sees the state as naturally prior to the individual (1253a19); he compares individuals to the parts of a body, and the city-state composed of those parts to the whole living body itself—hence the expression "the body politic." The parts are for the sake of the body, and without the body the parts lose their meaning. Once again, pursuing the good of the whole state is a higher goal than pursuing the good of the individual. And the pursuit of the common good is the goal of political science.

The parts of the body politic exist for the sake of the common good. In the frontispiece to Thomas Hobbes's *Leviathan* (1651), the governing body is presented as constituted by its individual members.

a) The Nature and Purpose of the City-State

We also need to see that the good of the state is deeply intertwined with the individual good, in Aristotle's thinking. The *polis* (city-state) is necessary, he tells us, not only because it enables an efficient division of labour and the possibility of a more comfortable life, but also because without the context of the city-state, a human being cannot be fully human. He writes at 1253a30–39,

> A social instinct is implanted in all men by nature, and yet he who first founded the state was the greatest of benefactors. For man, when perfected, is the best of

animals, but, when separated from law and justice, he is the worst of all.... [I]f
he have not virtue, he is the most unholy and the most savage of animals, and
the most full of lust and gluttony. But justice is the bond of men in states, for
the administration of justice, which is the determination of what is just, is the
principle of order in political society.

The way Aristotle sees it, the full flourishing and virtue of individuals depends
on the existence of a state that is capable of administering justice via good laws.
So there is a close link between the goals of the *Ethics* and those of the *Politics*—
the happiness of individuals depends on the constitution of the state they belong
to. People in a modern liberal democracy like Canada will likely find it difficult
to know what to make of Aristotle's claim that the government should focus on
trying to make its citizens into virtuous people (see 1099b30–31). The idea of laws
designed to shape our character and habituate us into acting in certain ways strikes
us as an undue intrusion into our freedom to pursue our own personal versions
of happiness. But for Aristotle, the crafting and instituting of such laws is *the
whole point* of political science. Just as the purpose of studying ethics is to become
a better person, the purpose of studying political science is ultimately to form
better states, and no state can be good if its citizens are not good. Further, as we
saw above, no individual can attain to complete virtue unless he or she is part of a
well-organized political state. From this point of view, the question of what makes
a political state good takes on a great deal of importance.

To answer the question of what makes a state good, Aristotle thinks, we have
to answer the question of who should rule in the state. He distinguishes the six
different basic kinds of state from each other on the basis of who has the governing
authority (we will consider the types of state in the next section). In Book I, he
explains that ruling a state differs in important ways from ruling a household. This
leads him into a lengthy investigation of the relationships that make up a household (husbands and wives, parents and children, masters and slaves) whose details
we cannot go into fully in our brief treatment of the *Politics*. We do need to point
out that Aristotle's discussion here raises some deep concerns for contemporary
readers. We cannot excuse Aristotle's views on women and slavery, even if we can
understand them as a product of his time and place. Aristotle states that some people are "natural slaves" in the sense that they are good at following the direction of
others but lack the ability to direct themselves. He further believes that women by
nature are inferior to men, and those who are inferior by nature are fit to be ruled
by their superiors, he tells us. To be sure, not everyone is a born leader, and many
will inevitably be followers in various spheres of society. But on the basis of the
inherent dignity of every human being, we have to reject Aristotle's justification
of the ownership of slaves as property, and his depiction of women as second-class
citizens. We can only bemoan the fact that Aristotle's ideas have given support,
historically, to the justification of oppressive sexist and racist practices.

But even while firmly rejecting these problematic views, we can arguably still learn a great deal from other parts of Aristotle's *Politics*. To point out just one instance, Aristotle insists that the rule of law is superior to the rule of persons, because of the impartiality of the law (see 1287a29–32). Many nations in our time have adopted this stance as constitutionally foundational. Aristotle also challenges the unlimited pursuit of wealth, which motivates many people in the contemporary developed world. He argues in chapter 9 of Book I that while household management clearly requires us to acquire resources and engage in trade, those whose lives are focused on the unbridled accumulation of money have made a serious mistake. Instead of trying to live *well* (that is, virtuously), they have taken up the unworthy goal of merely living, and have thereby undermined their own happiness. In a related point in Book IV, Aristotle argues that neither the very rich person nor the poor person is likely to be happy, but only the person of moderate wealth. This is because the wealth of the rich tends to make them arrogant and contemptuous toward the poor, while the envy of the poor tends to cause them to be bitter and even malicious toward the rich. But contempt and envy both distract us from following reason, which is necessary for a truly good life. Applying Aristotle's common-sense reasoning about such things could help us to reduce the social tensions and dramatic conflicts that continue to plague human society in our own time.

b) Examining Kinds of States

Beginning with Book II, the rest of the *Politics* centres on the question of what makes a state good, which (as we have already pointed out) Aristotle links to the question of who should rule in the state. He explores these questions by considering both actually existing states, and models of the ideal state proposed by the great thinkers up to his time. Aristotle had empirical information on at least 158 different city-states on hand when he turned to the investigation of the question of what sort of political state is best. And his conclusion was that all existing states are flawed. The main proposals for an *ideal* state also fall short in various ways. Once again, Aristotle comes to the intellectual rescue by indicating where these flaws lie, and what a truly ideal state would look like.

As we saw in chapter 4 of the present book, Plato's argument in the *Republic* involved him in a long discussion of the nature of the ideal political state. Whether or not Plato meant his *Republic* to be taken as a serious proposal is an interesting question—Aristotle at least takes it quite seriously, and subjects it to critique. (He also critiques Plato's second, more realistic proposal for a good state outlined in the *Laws*, but we do not have time to cover that here.) Aristotle's critique of Plato's *Republic*, in chapters 1 to 5 of Book II of the *Politics*, focuses on Plato's idea that to ensure unity and harmony in the state, it would be necessary to abolish private property. Aristotle argues that instead of increasing unity in the state, the abolition of private property and the sharing of all things in common—including wives and children—would have the opposite effect. By destroying the bonds of what Aristotle calls "natural affection" within the family, the architects of Plato's proposed republic would only sow the seeds of discord. Although it is true that inequalities in wealth and possessions are the source of many human conflicts, removing private property will not resolve the problem because it does not address its root. And what is the true root of human conflict, for Aristotle? It is the disordered desires of human hearts that seek after wealth and honour instead of virtue. The real solution, then, is to inculcate properly ordered desires by means of laws that form citizens in virtue (1266b29–30).

Book III, chapter 7, lists three relatively good kinds of state, distinguished from one another based on who holds ruling authority. In a **monarchy**, one man (the most virtuous among all the citizens) rules over the entire city-state in the interest of the common good. This, according to Aristotle, is the best form of government possible (so long as a person like this can be found). In the second-best form, an **aristocracy**, the relatively few members of the social elite ("the best," which Aristotle understands as the most virtuous) rule for the good of the whole. And in a **constitutional government**, third in the rank of true forms of government, the citizens at large hold the ruling authority and exercise it for the common good. Aristotle then distinguishes three forms of perverse or corrupt government that result when the rulers rule in their own interest rather than for the good of the whole: **democracy** is the corrupt form of constitutional government; **oligarchy** the perverse form of aristocracy, and **tyranny** the degraded version of monarchy and the worst sort of government possible. For those living in the modern west today, where democracy is held up as one of the most important values, it may come as a surprise that Aristotle considers democratic rule to be a corrupt form of the third best type of government. The reason for this ties into Aristotle's belief in an objective purpose (*telos*) of human life—letting policy and governance follow the whims of the majority who have neither a virtuous character nor a clear conception of the good will not likely lead the city-state or the individuals who constitute it to fulfill their highest purpose (Aristotle discusses different kinds of democratic states in Book VI).

Democracy and oligarchy can be described as the rule of the poor and the rule of the rich, respectively, since in any sufficiently large society the many are relatively poor, and there are relatively few wealthy people. The world of today is certainly no exception; 1 per cent of the world's population owns half of the total global wealth. Aristotle devotes a great deal of space in the *Politics* to the comparison of democracy and oligarchy, in part because the conflict between rich and poor is a major causal factor of political instability (Book V treats this conflict at length in the discussion of "the causes of revolutions in states"). When he comes to his own characterization of the best state from a practical point of view (in Book IV), Aristotle argues for a constitutional government that blends features of democracy with features of oligarchy. His reasoning, in a nutshell, is that in this way we can avoid the oppression of the poor by the wealthy and vice versa, and that will remove the motivation from either class to revolt against the other. To the same end, if one class is more in control, the class that is not should be given the greatest involvement in governance that is possible. Another way to mitigate the conflict between the rich and the poor is to ensure that those of moderate wealth (what we might call today the "middle class") play a central role in the governance of the state to arbitrate between the interests of rich and poor (1296b35–1297a13). Aristotle also appears to advocate some sort of social welfare system when he recommends following the example of the rich citizens of Tarentum, who gained the good will of the poor by "sharing the use of their own property" with them (1320b10).

Table 6: Forms of Government (Aristotle)

	TRUE FORM	CORRUPTED FORM
Best	Monarchy	Tyranny
	Aristocracy	Oligarchy
Worst	Constitutional	Democracy

c) *The Best Political Organization*

We have considered some of the key features of what Aristotle thinks is the best political constitution that is practically possible. In Book VII, he gives his account of what the best state would look like under ideal circumstances. The best state will be a reflection of the best human being, and will possess the same virtues:

> [T]he happy state may be shown to be that which is best and which acts rightly; and rightly it cannot act without doing right actions, and neither individual nor state can do right actions without virtue and wisdom. Thus, the courage, justice, and wisdom of a state have the same form and nature as the qualities which give the individual who possesses them the name of just, wise, or temperate. (1323b30–36)

We have here a very general principle, which is interestingly reminiscent of the way Socrates depicts the virtuous individual and the virtuous state as analogous in the *Republic*. But what does this principle entail, as far as the concrete features the best state will possess? After discussing practical considerations of what size the ideal city-state will be and what sort of territory and geographic considerations are best suited to sustaining it, Aristotle goes on to make some further points that also look suspiciously Platonic. For instance, Aristotle distinguishes the citizens who rule from the producing or working class (the farmers, merchants, craftsmen, and other manual labourers), who are not really citizens, because for Aristotle, real citizenship involves a partnership among people who are equals. The work of the working class ensures that the rulers will have sufficient leisure to cultivate virtue and engage in the deliberations necessary to run the state well. These rulers will serve as warriors when they are young and as councillors and legislators when they are older. And they will take turns in governing the city, further reflecting their equality (1332b26–28). Furthermore, the education of children into the spirit of the laws of the city will be the concern of the government (not the family), and the government will have further control over the age when men and women are permitted to reproduce, to ensure the children produced are in the best condition possible. Aristotle's ideal state looks more like an aristocracy than a monarchy, and this accords with what he says earlier on: "aristocracy will be better for states than royalty ... provided only that a number of men equal in virtue can be found" (1286b7–8). Monarchy is only the best form of government when there is one person who is markedly superior in virtue to all others and like a god among men. This happens only rarely, and given the danger of a slide into a tyrannical government, should be avoided if a genuine aristocracy can be established.

4. CONCLUSION

Aristotle presents ethics and politics as two deeply intertwined aspects of practical science. While his *Ethics* focuses more on the sorts of virtues individual human beings need to cultivate in order to realize their *telos* and attain happiness, the *Politics*, by examining the sort of constitution and laws a good state will embody, achieves a higher goal. A good state will provide the necessary context for individual realization of happiness. The two disciplines are tied together, in Aristotle's view, by the fact that the purpose of the legislator or statesman (who needs most of all to study political science, and therefore ethics as well) is to craft laws for the state that will form its citizens in the virtues. It is unsurprising, then, that in the final book (VIII) of the *Politics*, Aristotle deals with the subject of the education of the citizens from their youth, to which "the legislator should direct his attention above all" (1337a11). To reiterate, the good of the state depends on the virtue of its citizens, and the virtue of those citizens depends on the laws of the state which form and habituate them in the right direction. These laws will be made well if they are made by virtuous rulers in the interest of the common good. In Aristotle's thought, therefore, ethics and political science must work together to realize the human good for both the individual and the political community.

In both Plato and Aristotle, morality or ethics is an objective matter, and centrally involves the cardinal virtues. The role of wisdom plays a key role in guiding and coordinating the virtuous life for both of these thinkers. As usual, however, we find Aristotle turning away from Plato's exalted speculation about the Form of the Good as the non-hypothetical first principle, toward a more concrete understanding of the way reason governs individual human life and political states. Nevertheless, Aristotle cannot avoid the basic Platonic idea that a view of the common good ought to guide the law-makers who must rule with the aim of ensuring that the citizens are formed in virtue. In the next and final chapter, we will turn our attention from the mainstream Platonic-Aristotelian tradition toward alternative schools of ancient philosophy.

Chapter 8:

HELLENISTIC PHILOSOPHY, CHRISTIANITY, AND NEOPLATONISM

HISTORICAL CONTEXT

Culturally speaking, Western civilization stood for many centuries on two major pillars: the heritage of Greco-Roman science and law, and the Judeo-Christian religion. I've said a good deal about Classical Greek philosophy already, and have pointed out that in the later, Medieval period, we encounter a type of philosophy very much influenced by Plato and Aristotle, but at least equally affected by the monotheistic faiths of the Abrahamic religions. To understand the Medieval period, which can be said to begin with Augustine, we need to take account of what took place between the death of Aristotle in 322 BCE and the birth of Augustine in 354 CE. Although these six and three-quarter centuries brought many important cultural and political shifts, I will focus on three particularly significant movements in the history of Western philosophy: First, philosophy during the Hellenistic era (roughly 323–30 BCE); second, the origins of Christianity in the first century CE; and third, the philosophical movement known as Neoplatonism, founded by Plotinus, who lived between 205 and 270 CE. Because there is so much ground to cover here, I'll be giving more historical detail than usual in this introductory section.

Scholars commonly place the beginning of the Hellenistic period at the death of Alexander the Great in 323 BCE. The period ends with the rise of the Roman Empire in 31 BCE, following the battle of Actium, where Julius Caesar's nephew and adopted son Octavian defeated Mark Anthony and Cleopatra to begin his rule as Augustus Caesar, the first Roman Emperor. The schools of Plato (the Academy) and Aristotle (the Lyceum) continued to operate during the Hellenistic period—though not without significant disruptions and transformations—and well into the common era. But various rival philosophical schools and movements also emerged in Athens, the most influential of which were (1) the **Garden of Epicurus**, a school started in 307 BCE; (2) **Stoicism**, founded by Zeno of Citium around 300 BCE; and (3) the **Skeptical movement** that traces its origin to Pyrrho, who lived between 365 and 270 BCE. Epicureanism, Stoicism, and Skepticism all had Greek and Roman adherents in the centuries that followed. Marcus Tullius Cicero, a powerful Roman orator, philosopher, and politician who lived at the end of the Hellenistic period (106–43 BCE), famously summarized the views of the three movements in Hellenistic philosophy in his dialogue *On the Nature of the Gods*. Cicero was another of the classical philosophical figures who would exert a profound influence on Western Christian thought from its earliest beginnings up until at least the nineteenth century.

Christianity began as a movement within Judaism, the religion of Israel (the Jewish inhabitants of ancient Palestine), which traces its origins all the way back to Moses (born c. 1600–1393 BCE) and Abraham (born c. 2000–1800 BCE). Jesus, who was born around 4 BCE and died around 30 CE, understood himself to be the fulfillment of the promise of God to Israel to send a Messiah. The Hebrew Word "Messiah" gets translated as "Christ" in Greek, and carries connotations of being the King of the Jews and the Son of God, the Creator of the heavens and the earth. Jesus's early followers claimed to have met him personally after he had been crucified and buried, and they understood his resurrection from the dead to be the proof of his identity as the Son of God. Christians ever since have followed Jesus Christ as Lord, looking forward to his return from heaven, where they believe he ascended after rising from the dead. His second coming would bring the judgement of God and would herald the transition from the present age of the world into the age to come, in which true justice and peace would be established. Christians refer to this as "the coming of the kingdom of God." Although Christians experienced horrific persecution in the first three centuries after Jesus's life on earth, by an amazing turn of events, Christianity became the official religion of the Roman Empire by 381 CE, setting the stage for well over 1,000 years of Western **Christendom** (the political and cultural dominance of the Christian religion).

Plotinus was born in Egypt around 204 CE, and may have had Christian parents but seems to have abandoned that path at some point. He is best known as the founder of a school of thought which has come to be called "Neoplatonism," though Plotinus saw himself as simply a follower and interpreter of Plato. Plotinus taught philosophy in Rome between 245 and 271 CE, presenting Plato and Aristotle as philosophically compatible despite their disagreements, some of which we have already noticed. As we will also see when we come to examine his work more closely, Plotinus's philosophy is quite openly mystical, in the sense that it invites the reader to experience the divine realities under discussion, rather than resting content with abstract argumentation. In Plotinus, and in Neoplatonism more generally, we have a philosophical bridge between Classical Greek thought and monotheistic spirituality and mysticism. Neoplatonism was one of the major forces that shaped philosophy throughout the Medieval period and well into the Renaissance.

INTRODUCTORY BIG QUESTION: HOW DO WE NAVIGATE PLURALISM?

Our own cultural time and place is undoubtedly pluralistic. By "pluralistic," I'm referring to the multiplicity of diverse ways of living and thinking reflected in the many cultures and ethnicities that converge within much of the Western world today, without losing their distinctiveness. Today, most people possess a sense of the variety of religions the great human civilizations have produced, and we encounter expressions of Hinduism, Buddhism, Islam, and various other traditions as a common experience. The Hellenistic period in the ancient Greek—and increasingly Roman—world was also a time in which a person could come across a bewildering variety of diverse systems of belief and ways of life. Because of the expansion of the Greek and then Macedonian Empire under Alexander, people living during the Hellenistic period could come into contact with ideas from Persia, Egypt, and other parts of the Mediterranean world, and even from places as far as India.

The experience of radical and profuse diversity raises the basic question of which system of beliefs or way of life a person ought to choose. The questions of what beliefs one should hold, and of how one should live, have been basic to philosophy ever since its origin. But these are the same questions that the great religions have also sought to answer. While we can find substantial overlap in the answers given by different philosophical, scientific, and religious systems, we also find points of sharp disagreement, which sometimes manifest in intense political, cultural, and even military conflict. Is there a God to whom we can relate, or are we alone in the universe? If there is a God of some sort, which conception of God is correct (or are they all somehow correct)? Can everything be explained by appealing to natural, material facts, or is there a supernatural or at least immaterial side to the universe, or at least to human life? Do we have any real control over what takes place, or are our choices determined by events that are outside the scope of our will? Furthermore, how could we come to know which of the possible answers to these questions are correct? What method for investigating such questions is the right one?

The different philosophical schools and the different worldviews offered by human religions of the Hellenistic world, like those of our own day, provided divergent answers to these and other questions. While all this diversity of perspective swirls around us, and the possibilities make our heads swim, we nevertheless keep on living our lives, and we do so based on our convictions about the way things are, and about what is good. Which of the many possible ways of seeing the world do you ascribe to, and why? In other words, what do you think the world is basically like? And what way of life is best, and what makes it good, according to you (or do you think all ways of life are equally good)?

1. HELLENISTIC PHILOSOPHY

The three main philosophical movements of the Hellenistic period, Epicureanism, Stoicism, and Pyrrhonian Skepticism, gave their own set of answers to questions about logic, natural science, and ethics, and each set of answers taken together as a package yields a distinctive philosophical system. Of the readings that represent these schools, only the first two to be discussed in this chapter (Epicurus's *Letter to Menoeceus* and *Principles*) are written by the founder of a movement. Epictetus, a philosopher from the first and early second centuries CE, will be our representative of Stoicism, and the reading that represents the Skeptical school was authored by Sextus Empiricus, who lived in the second or third centuries CE. The fact that (in the case of Stoicism and Skepticism) we have classic presentations of these movements from thinkers several centuries removed from the originators of the movements they represent speaks to the extent of the influence these movements held in ancient intellectual culture.

Do the three main Hellenistic philosophical movements have anything in common? They do show continuity with the Platonic and Aristotelian philosophies in their overall preoccupation with questions concerning how to think rightly (logic and epistemology), how to understand what the world is like (natural science), and how we should live (ethics). In general, each understands philosophy as a way of life and not merely as an intellectual exercise. But Hellenistic philosophy, in each of the three main schools, deviates from the Platonic-Aristotelian framework in significant ways. The most relevant deviation lies in the denial by all three Hellenistic schools of the existence of certain immaterial entities that were centrally important for Plato and Aristotle. The Hellenistic thinkers can be called **materialists** in that they rejected immaterial Forms, immaterial souls, and immaterial gods. But as we have seen, for Plato and in a qualified way for Aristotle, philosophy culminated in the contemplation (by the immaterial soul) of just such immaterial entities—the Forms and the Good for Plato, and the formal and final causes along with the Prime Mover for Aristotle. To get rid of substance as immaterial form and of immaterial supernatural beings would be to tear out one of the vital organic components of the Platonic-Aristotelian philosophical system. The materialism of the Hellenistic schools also helps explain the strong preference of the later medieval theologian-philosophers for Platonic and Aristotelian modes of thought. Lastly, although this oversimplifies things, one can fairly characterize Epicureanism, Stoicism, and Skepticism, despite their differences, as centrally concerned with **tranquility** (*ataraxia* in Greek), that is, with achieving a state of mental peace or freedom from trouble. Part of the reason for this focus on reaching tranquility may have had to do with the relative political instability in which these philosophical systems developed and operated.

a) Epicureanism

The goal of the Epicurean philosophical system is the attainment of happiness, understood as a state of existence that is maximally pleasant. Although Epicurus identifies happiness with pleasure, we have to take care not to interpret him as advocating some sort of abandonment to indulgence in luxurious food and lots of sex. For Epicurus, the most stable and enduring happiness consists instead in the state of being free from trouble or pain. To achieve the state of happiness, Epicurus and his followers believed, one must learn how to manage one's desires. And desires come in different kinds. Some of the things we desire are natural and necessary for life and happiness, as, for example, is the desire for water and the desire not to be torn apart by a wild animal. Other desires are natural but not necessary, and we could take as an example the desire for a particularly rich slice of cheesecake. Although the desire to eat

Epicurus (341–270 BCE)

is natural, cheesecake goes outside the bounds of what is needed to fulfill that desire. Finally, there are what Epicurus calls "groundless" desires. Call me a spoilsport, but I have always felt that the desire to ride on a rollercoaster is rather groundless—what natural appetite does such a want fulfill? Epicureanism tells us to avoid desires that are groundless and those that are natural but not necessary, and to focus on fulfilling only desires that are natural and necessary, and we will find it an easy thing to be happy.

Certain kinds of pleasures bring about a great deal of pain and disturbance in the end, outweighing the initial pleasure. Anyone who has experienced a hangover will be able to understand this. Epicurus writes,

> For it is not drinking bouts and continuous partying and enjoying boys and women, or consuming fish and other dainties of an extravagant table, which produces the pleasant life, but sober calculation which searches out the reasons for every choice and avoidance and drives out the opinions which are the source of the greatest turmoil for men's souls.[1]

In order to be happy, we must be free from disturbances. Epicurus thought that one of the greatest sources of disturbance was certain beliefs that human beings tend to hold. For instance, the beliefs that divine beings will judge us for our wrongdoing and punish us in the afterlife tend to cause a good deal of fear and anxiety in human hearts. Relatedly, people are troubled by the thought of death, thinking it is something bad. The solution, Epicurus says in his *Letter to Menoeceus*, is to stop believing in such things. Although he believes in gods, like everything else they are ultimately just collections of atoms, even if the atoms that compose the gods are particularly fine and subtle. And the gods, being always in a state of blissful happiness, never do anything to disturb their tranquility. But this entails, Epicurus thinks, that the gods remain blissfully unconcerned with human affairs, so that we need not fear them.

His argument against fearing death[2] goes as follows:

1. The good is identical to pleasant experience, and the bad is painful experience.
2. When we exist, death is not present.
3. When we die, we no longer exist and do not experience anything.
Therefore,
4. Death is nothing to us, and in particular is not a bad thing for us.

The practical corollary of Epicurus's argument is that to fear death, the gods, and judgement is irrational. You will never experience death, since when you die, there will be no one around to experience anything anymore. Why be afraid of something

---

1 Cahn, p. 333.
2 Cahn, p. 332.

you will never experience, and which therefore can never be bad for you? Clearly, this argument rests on some assumptions. For one thing, might we not fear death because it represents the loss of possible outcomes or goals we would have been able to achieve if we had remained alive? Epicurus also assumes that human bodily death amounts to *annihilation*; his argument depends on the claim that there is no afterlife (no immortal soul, no resurrection of the body, etc.). Obviously those who belong to religious or philosophical traditions that involve belief in some sort of afterlife aren't going to be content with this part of the argument. Epicurus feels confident in assuming that death is annihilation because of his atomistic worldview: Since we are ultimately nothing but collections of atoms, once the arrangement of atoms that constitutes our bodies has disintegrated, there cannot possibly be any "us" anymore. Strictly speaking this sort of reasoning does not rule out the possibility of the continuation of a *material* soul that disengages from the body upon death, or the possibility of a resurrected body. But Epicurus's world is one governed not by divine providence but by chance; it is the result of random collisions of atoms falling through a void. And in such a world, the likelihood of one's body being reconstituted after death is slim.

Given certain things he says, it is hard to avoid wondering if in the end Epicurus's materialistic natural philosophy isn't motivated in part by practical, ethical considerations. For instance, in the *Principal Doctrines*, Book XI, he writes, "If our suspicions about heavenly phenomena and about death did not trouble us at all and were never anything to us, and, moreover, if not knowing the limits of pains and desires did not trouble us, then we would have no need of natural science."[3] Epicurus seems to be saying that we engage in natural science, not purely to know what is true, but because we want to liberate ourselves from fears and reach tranquility of mind. Elsewhere, he gives arguments for his claims that only atoms and empty space (the void) exist,[4] but he also seems to side with materialism not because he *knows* that there is no immortal soul or life after death but because he wants to rule these out in order to avoid worrying about them. Does the goal of mental tranquility legitimate the sacrifice of objective enquiry?

b) Stoicism

Another philosophical system that makes the attainment of tranquility central is Stoicism, a Hellenistic movement that derives its name from the Greek word *stoa*, the covered porch structures found in Athens where the Stoic adherents met in the early days of the movement. We have only fragments of the writings of the first founders of Stoicism—Zeno of Citium (344–262 BCE), Cleanthes (331–232 BCE),

---

3 Cahn, p. 335.

4 See for instance his *Letter to Herodotus*, section 39, in which he says that "the totality is made up of bodies and void," and "beyond these two things nothing can be conceived" (Inwood and Gerson, pp. 6–7).

Epictetus (c. 55–135 CE). From Edward Ivie's *Epicteti Enchiridion Latinis versibus adumbratum* (1715)

and Chrysippus (280–207 BCE). The text we are considering is from Epictetus (55–135 CE), one of the later Stoic thinkers who lived in the Roman imperial period, along with Seneca (4 BCE–65 CE) and Marcus Aurelius (121–180 CE), who was one of the Roman Emperors. Epictetus was a slave who had been set free, and who taught Stoic philosophy in Rome and later in the Greek city of Nicopolis, where he set up his own school.

Epictetus begins his *Encheiridion*, a title meaning something like "Manual" or "Handbook," by distinguishing between the things that are "up to us," namely our own opinions and desires, from what is "not up to us," such as our bodies, possessions, and success. While what happens to the things not up to us is surely affected in part by our choices, we do not ultimately have control over them. Epictetus offers the promise of complete security and freedom from harm to all who keep clear in their minds what is up to them and what is not. To avoid all misfortune, he urges us, "detach your aversion from everything not up to us, and transfer it to what is against nature among the things that are up to us."[5] In other words, if you stop wanting to avoid natural misfortunes, then when they happen you won't be upset or disappointed by them. One of my favourite applications of this comes in paragraph 3: "If you kiss your child or your wife, say that you are kissing a human being; for when it dies you will not be upset." We might naturally respond to a saying like this by asking, "Isn't it good and fitting for me to be upset when I lose my child or spouse?" Epictetus, with typical Stoic coolness, would reply in the negative; it is never a good thing to be moved from mental tranquility. Death, even the death of a loved one, won't make us upset if we have firmly decided in our own mind not to take a negative attitude toward it.

While his particular interpretation of Socrates can be questioned, the fact that Epictetus takes Socrates as his moral hero and exemplar is clear. He urges his reader to ask herself, "What would Socrates or Zeno have done in these circumstances?" and elsewhere says, "You, even if you are not yet Socrates, ought to live as someone

---

5 Cahn, p. 340, paragraph 2.

wanting to be Socrates."[6] In places, Epictetus's manual reads like a practical self-help book focused on positive thinking, or a set of common-sense rules for dealing with a variety of situations a person might encounter. He nicely summarizes the general perspective he is advocating in paragraph 8: "Do not seek to have events happen as you want them to, but instead want them to happen as they do happen, and your life will go well." Try applying this principle to sports: When you watch a football or a basketball game, don't hope that the home team will win. Instead, want the outcome of the game to be whatever it is, and you will never be upset. Clearly this would undermine team spirit, and maybe even competition in general. The teammates themselves, if they were properly Stoic, would not want their own team to win rather than their opponents. The whole sports industry would probably go bankrupt if Stoicism were to become widespread. Would not the overall result be that no one would even *try* to win any more? Why try to win if you don't care about the result? In general, why care about anything that happens? Would such an attitude not undermine much of the progress and achievements of which human beings are capable? Maybe so, but Epictetus points out: "'This is the price of tranquility; this is the price of not being upset.' Nothing comes for free."[7] And the alternative is to live as a slave to "external things," namely to things that are outside of your control.

Many of the metaphors Epictetus uses to describe life imply the control or oversight of a higher power and intelligence. For instance, in paragraph 17 he depicts life as a play, such that we must play the parts that are assigned to us by the playwright. Whatever we have, we must see as having been given to us, and when we lose it, we are to regard it as having been given back to the giver. When the captain calls, we must be ready to go even if we have to leave everything we have been interested in behind. In other places, Epictetus is more explicit about the common Stoic conviction that the universe is governed by a benevolent and supremely rational God (Zeus, to be specific), and that as a result everything that happens is both good and rational.[8] As far as the *Encheiridion* is concerned, Zeus is mentioned specifically only in paragraph 53: "Lead me, Zeus, and you too, Destiny/Wherever I am assigned by you;/I'll follow and not hesitate...." Nevertheless, the idea is apparent elsewhere, for instance in paragraph 31: "the gods ... [are] beings that arrange the universe well and justly." In the much longer *Discourses*, of which the *Encheiridion* is a kind of summary, Epictetus clearly depicts Zeus as the designer and governor of the universe, who is in some sense personal, but is also not fully distinguishable from the rational order that underlies the universe. Our goal, in bringing ourselves into "accord with nature," is to participate in the good

---

6 Cahn, p. 347, paragraph 33 and pp. 350–51, paragraph 51.

7 Cahn, p. 342, paragraph 12.

8 See for instance Book I, chapter 16, of Epictetus's *Discourses*. A good recent edition can be found in *Discourses, Fragments, Handbook*, trans. Robin Hard (Oxford: Oxford University Press, 2014).

rational order established by (or identical to) Zeus. The conception of a rational order in nature was the basis for "natural law" theory, which medieval thinkers like Thomas Aquinas would later develop at length, and which also had notable modern adherents in John Locke and Immanuel Kant.

c) Skepticism

Like Stoicism, the third major school of Hellenistic philosophy we are considering has a long and complex history. Pyrrhonic Skepticism claimed to have originated with Pyhrro of Elis, whose dates are approximately 360–270 BCE. Another branch of Skepticism, the version that came out of the later Academy of Plato, was developed by Arcesilaus (316–241 BCE) and later Carneades (214–129 BCE), both of whom served as leaders of the Academy. Academic Skepticism was a logical outflow of the Socratic method of refutation. The Socrates of the early Platonic dialogues was constantly engaged in subjecting the views of his conversation partners to refutation. The Academic skeptics, in the Socratic spirit, focused on the critical examination of views held by themselves and others. Pyrrhonic Skepticism—represented by Sextus Empiricus's *Outlines of Pyrrhonism*—defined itself in part by contrast to the other philosophical schools by rejecting **dogmatism**, a term that referred to the definite acceptance of a given position as true. Skepticism took a stand directly against the Platonic-Aristotelian tradition, and also against the Epicurean and Stoic philosophical schools. Each of these other movements held definite beliefs about what was true and what was good, and part of what it meant to be an Epicurean or a Stoic was to adhere to the core doctrines of the relevant movement. Not so with Skepticism.

Sextus Empiricus was a late Hellenistic figure about whose life very little is known. Like Epicureanism and Stoicism, the Skepticism described by Sextus sees the entire purpose of philosophy as the attainment of the state of mental tranquility. But unlike the dogmatic philosophers who think tranquility comes from the mind's adherence to certain beliefs, the skeptic sees the path to tranquility in the suspension of judgement and the cessation of the urge to hold beliefs at all. Suspension of judgement in turn arises from the activity of setting up conflicting appearances, judgements, and arguments against each other. Once one realizes that the arguments for and against a statement are equally forceful, one will naturally refrain from either

Sextus Empiricus (c. 160–c. 210 CE). From a 1692 copper engraving based on an ancient coin

believing or disbelieving the statement. I might wonder, for instance, whether it is objectively good or objectively evil to evade paying my taxes. The dogmatic thinker tries to sort through the reasons in order to reach the truth of the matter, and ends up believing that one or the other of the statements is true: "Tax evasion is evil" or "Tax evasion is good." The skeptic, on the other hand, looks at arguments for both sides and, noting the equal credibility of the arguments, ends up withdrawing from making a judgement one way or the other. While the dogmatic thinker continues to be disturbed and emotionally affected by the arguments against her preferred conclusion, the skeptic finds mental tranquility by withdrawing from the whole project of determining the truth about the matter. Skepticism, then, is merely the ability to engage in this activity of opposing arguments which leads to suspension of judgement and consequently to mental tranquility.

The skeptic thinks that we never possess any knowledge with certainty, at least not about non-evident things (that is, things that go beyond our immediate sense impressions). As a result, all dogmatic assertions about what reality is like are at best uncertain, and at worst necessarily false. In fact, Sextus seems to see the falsity of all claims as following from their radical uncertainty—since we have no way of making judgements with certainty about non-evident things, we have to conclude that any assertions made about them are untrue. But if the skeptic asserts that

(1) All assertions are false

then the question must be raised about the assertion the skeptic has just made: Is (1) true or false? The skeptic thus faces a dilemma: If (1) is true, then it stands as a counter-example to the skeptic's claim that all assertions are false, and it turns out that the skeptic believes that at least one assertion is true, namely assertion (1). If, on the other hand, the skeptic claims that (1) is false, it would be reasonable to ask what the skeptic was trying to accomplish by asserting it in the first place. Isn't the very act of asserting an act of presenting some claim as true? Sextus takes hold of the second horn of this dilemma, and states emphatically that when the skeptic says all assertions are false, she includes that assertion itself.[9] In other words, the skeptic never dogmatizes, that is, she never presents anything as definitively true. According to Sextus, in making statements like (1), the skeptic is merely "saying what appears to him and ... reporting on his own feeling, without indulging in opinion or making positive statements about the reality of things outside himself."[10]

The bulk of Sextus Empiricus's *Outlines of Pyrrhonism* consists in an account of the ten modes by which we attain suspension of judgement. Without going into details, I will simply point out that Sextus, in good skeptical fashion, does not claim that these are comprehensive or even valid. Nevertheless, they seem

---

9 Cahn, pp. 355–56, chapter VII.
10 Cahn, p. 356, chapter VII.

to be good exercises for shaking oneself out of a dogmatic mindset. Each of the ten modes presents one sort of reason for thinking we can't justifiably go beyond appearances to make judgements about the way things are in reality outside us. The first mode, for instance, points to the plausible claim that different animals receive different impressions through their sense organs, which differ in various ways from our own sense organs. But we can't step outside of our own sense impressions to judge whether our impressions are more accurate than those of other animals. And so we have to conclude that, while we know how things appear to us, we don't know what they are really like. The other modes draw similar conclusions from the facts that different people perceive things differently, that our different senses present things to us in different ways, that things appear different under different circumstances, etc.

d) Concluding Remarks on Hellenistic Philosophy

The adherents of the Epicurean, Stoic, and Skeptical schools of thought, all throughout the period, engaged in conversation and debate with one another. As a result, Hellenistic philosophy should be seen as a large-scale conversation. The topics of debate were problems inherited from their Socratic, Platonic, and Aristotelian forbears, but the solutions each school arrived at differed in significant ways from those of the Plato and Socrates we know from Plato's dialogues. The perspectives represented by each of these schools continue in one form or another up to the present day. For instance, like the Epicureans, utilitarians in ethics take pleasure as the foundational ethical value. Stoicism continues in the rationalism of Immanuel Kant and his followers, and the skeptical impulse finds expression in contemporary epistemology inspired by the great modern skeptic David Hume (who argued against many common beliefs, but certainly did not withdraw judgement in general). The contemporary materialistic understanding of the universe, and of the human being within it, also has Hellenistic philosophy as an ancestor. But as we move closer to the Medieval period, the Hellenistic schools lose their influence on Western thought in favour of a philosophical outlook that could be more easily synthesized with Abrahamic monotheism. Though not by any means completely suppressed in the centuries between the fall of Rome and the Renaissance, Epicureanism, Stoicism, and Skepticism lost their dominance for at least a millennium.

2. CHRISTIANITY AND NEOPLATONISM

An interesting passage in the biblical book of Acts tells about an encounter between Paul, the Christian apostle and author of more than one third of the New Testament, and some Hellenistic philosophers. The encounter takes place in Athens:

Saint Paul Preaching, by Raphael (1515)

A group of Epicurean and Stoic philosophers began to debate with him. Some of them asked, 'What is this babbler trying to say?' Others remarked, 'He seems to be advocating foreign gods.' They said this because Paul was preaching the good news about Jesus and the resurrection.[11]

This group of philosophers then invites Paul to a meeting of the Areopagus council, wanting to hear more of Paul's teaching. The author comments parenthetically in verse 21, "All the Athenians and the foreigners who lived there spent their time doing nothing but talking and listening to the latest ideas." In the end, most of these philosophers sneer at Paul's message, but a handful followed Paul and became believers, and Dionysius, a member of the Areopagus, was among them. The name Dionysius is important for the Medieval period because of the powerful influence of a Christian Neoplatonist from Syria who wrote using his name in the late fifth or early sixth centuries. Now known as Pseudo-Dionysius the Areopagite, this unknown monk combined the Christian tradition with Neoplatonism as it had come down from Plotinus to Proclus, who lived between 412 and 485 CE.

---

11 Acts 17:18, NIV.

a) From Jerusalem to Rome

As I noted in the introduction, Christianity began as a Jewish religious movement. Jesus himself was a Jewish carpenter from a small town called Nazareth, who became well known as a holy man, teacher, and worker of miracles, and gathered a small band of dedicated followers before being crucified under the Roman Governor Pontius Pilate on charges of insurrection against Rome. Jesus called his twelve closest male followers "apostles," and these men claimed to have encountered Jesus again after his gruesome death, testifying that they had walked and talked and eaten with him over a period of forty days before Jesus ascended to the right hand of God the Father. Following this, one of the Jewish religious leaders named Saul (later known as Paul, the one referred to in the passage from Acts cited above) took it upon himself to destroy the Christian sect. But as he was doing so, he claims to have encountered the risen Jesus in a blinding flash of light. Realizing that the one he had been persecuting was in fact his Lord and the Messiah, Paul began to speak boldly for the cause of Christianity, and largely through his influence the Christian faith spread out from its Jewish roots throughout the entire Greco-Roman world. By the time we reach Augustine in the fourth century (the late Classical/early Medieval period), the Roman Empire had adopted Christianity as its sole official religion.

Much could be said about the history and core beliefs of Christianity, which was the main religion of the Western world for over 1600 years, and continues to claim large numbers of adherents even today, growing exponentially in Asia and Africa even while declining in the West. I will focus here on the two central Christian doctrines that have come to define Christian orthodoxy at least since the Councils of Nicea in 325 and Chalcedon in 451. These two doctrines were symbolized in the fingers of the cosmic Christ as depicted for instance in the Hagia Sophia in Istanbul—the two raised fingers signify the dual nature of Christ as God and man; the two other fingers and thumb touching each other signify the three persons in the Triune Godhead, a reference to the **doctrine of the Trinity**. According to Christian teaching, God has existed from all eternity in three persons (*hypostases* in the Greek): the Father, the Son, and the Holy Spirit. Each of these persons is fully God, and is really distinct from the others even though they fully interpenetrate each other so that in reality there is only one God (hence Christianity is a monotheistic religion). The second core doctrine of Christianity is the **doctrine of the Incarnation**, which teaches that God took on human flesh in the person of Jesus Christ, so that the man Jesus was fully human and fully God at the same time, the only begotten Son of God. The practical thrust of these teachings could be summed up in the Christian motto: "Jesus Christ is Lord," which was a very controversial thing to be proclaiming in the early days of Christianity, when the pagan Roman Emperors called themselves sons of God and the bringers of good news and peace to the world. But such language became much more comfortable once the Holy Roman Emperors themselves were Christians, which began with the Emperor Constantine. The development of Christianity and the political history of the Holy Roman Empire is fascinating, but unfortunately extends beyond the scope of this book. Still, the Medieval period in the history of philosophy would be unintelligible without a basic appreciation of the Christian religious and political background of the Western world.

b) Plotinus: The Descent of the Soul

The main continuation of classical Platonic and Aristotelian philosophy into the late Classical period took the form of Neoplatonism. As a period in the history of philosophy, Neoplatonism denotes a Platonic school often said to have been founded by Plotinus (204–270 CE) and to have ended with the ban of pagan (non-Christian) philosophy in 529 by the Christian Roman Emperor Justinian, a date which many see as the starting point of Medieval philosophy. But Neoplatonism, as the attempt to systematically interpret the thought of Plato, began much earlier than Plotinus (after all, there were about six centuries of reflection on Platonic thought between Plato and Plotinus). And through thinkers like Proclus (412–485) and Pseudo-Dionysius (late fifth or early sixth century CE) Neoplatonism would later exercise a powerful influence all the way through the Medieval period, the Renaissance, and beyond. The theological traditions of Judaism, Christianity, and Islam all found in Neoplatonism a philosophical language well suited to the articulation of their positions.

Since Plotinus played a key role in Neoplatonism's flourishing, and in transmitting the thought of Plato to Augustine and other early medieval thinkers, he serves as an ideal representative of the movement for our purposes. Plotinus's major work, the *Enneads* (Greek for "Nines") is actually a collection of shorter treatises composed by Plotinus and collected and thematically arranged by his famous student Porphyry the Phoenician (234–305 CE) into six groups of nine treatises each. *Ennead* IV 8 and V 1 present with particular clarity Plotinus's view of the soul and its descent and way of return, as well as his understanding of the emanation of all being from three transcendent principles: the One, the Intellect, and the Soul. As these are Plotinus's central teachings, we will focus on these portions of the *Enneads* here.

Plotinus (c. 204–270 CE)

As is clear from the beginning of *Ennead* IV 8, Plotinus is not simply writing a dry philosophical treatise:

> I have many times awakened into myself from the body when I exited the things other than myself, and entered into myself, and, seeing a marvelous and great beauty, I was then especially confident that I belonged to the better part and that I was engaging in the best life, and that I had come to that activity having identified myself with the divine and having situated myself in it, that is, having situated myself above all in the intelligible world. After this repose in the divine, descending from Intellect into discursive reasoning, I am puzzled how I have now descended and how my soul has come to be in the body....[12]

The personal tone and the language of inner experience indicates that Plotinus is offering us something akin to a mystical manual intended to guide us on a spiritual journey. In Plotinus's view, all human souls originate in and are truly part of the divine, and we need to remember this and enter on the ascent back to our divine source. His identification of the divine with the intelligible world, and his clear preference for life on the intelligible plain over life in the body echo the sort of things Plato said in the *Phaedo*, for instance. Indeed, to account for the "descent" of the soul from its proper home with "the One" into bodies, he appeals to different aspects of Plato's thought on the subject. This leads into a dual explanation for the descent: On the one hand, the soul is to be blamed for its descent, which implies that its choice to turn from the One was *voluntary*. But on the other hand, he describes the descent as *necessary*, something intended by "a good craftsman" (presumably God) who sent our souls into the sensible universe in order to govern it and to make it intelligent.

The rest of *Ennead* IV 8 is dedicated to showing how these two reasons for the descent are not contradictory. The key to understanding this, Plotinus thinks, is to realize that soul can deal with and care for bodies in two different ways. The first is modelled by the way in which the Soul of the world (one of the three divine principles) cares for the world (the material, sensible cosmos) beneath it. The Soul rules over the universe of bodies without direct contact with them; it does not penetrate far into bodies but orders them "with royal oversight," all the while keeping its gaze fixed on what is above itself, namely the divine Intellect which encompasses the totality of the intelligible world.[13] This mode of governance is not blameworthy, and our individual human souls can participate in it. When a human soul does this, it "travels on the heights and directs the universe" along with the world-Soul, like a king ruling together with but under the high king.[14] But there is another way our souls deal with bodies, and this way is blameworthy and results in the soul becoming

---

12 Cahn, p. 405. *Ennead* IV 8.1.
13 Cahn, p. 406. *Ennead* IV 8.2.
14 Ibid. See also Cahn, p. 407; *Ennead* IV 8.4.

chained up in a cave-prison (note the allusion to Plato). This takes place when our souls turn their gaze away from what is above us—from the world-Soul and the divine Intellect, and ultimately from the One that is the source of all being and intelligibility. In turning away from our origin, we become engrossed in the world of bodies that is beneath us and we forget what we truly are and where we came from.

c) Plotinus: The Return to the One

If you read through that last paragraph you might be asking yourself, "What am I reading? What exactly is this all about? Does the world have a Soul? What would the experience of ruling the universe together with the Soul of the world be like?" To progress in understanding what Plotinus is up to, we need to get a handle on the metaphysical framework he is working with. Plotinus takes seriously Plato's talk about the Form of the Good (recall this from Plato's *Republic*, Book VI, 508b–509a), together with the long treatise on "the One" in the late dialogue entitled the *Parmenides*. For Plotinus, the One and the Good refer to the same thing (if you can call it a *thing*, which you really can't). Following Plato, this indescribable "entity" is the source of all being and all knowledge. But the One itself is neither a being nor an intellect—it is beyond these, and is the absolutely simple source of them.

Plotinus's reason for claiming these things—other than the fact that he believes Plato taught them—is that to explain complexity and multiplicity we need to trace it back to what is simple and one. We do this, for instance, in science, when we explain a multiplicity of phenomena, like various bodies falling toward the earth, by appealing to a simple law or set of laws, in this case, the law of gravity. But if all complexity must be reduced to simplicity, then it follows that the ultimate explanation for things must be something that is completely and perfectly simple. So we speak of a One-beyond-being that produces all being and intelligibility. The first product of the One (though we must understand "first" not in a temporal sense, but in the sense of causal dependency) is the Intellect. The Intellect is just like the One, except that it involves some complexity. Plotinus tells us that the One generates the Intellect as follows: "In turning toward itself The One sees. It is this seeing that constitutes the Intelligence" or Intellect.[15] The "complexity" of the One seeing itself (brought about by the distinction between the knower and what is known) is what manifests in the Intellect, the highest divinity besides the One. And the Intellect contains within itself the entire realm of the intelligible Forms or Ideas. Scholars have seen in the Intellect a combination of Aristotle's Prime Mover (recall the divine Thought thinking itself from the end of our chapter on the *Metaphysics*) and the Demiurge of Plato's *Timaeus*.[16]

---

15 I am using Elmer O'Brien's translation here: *The Essential Plotinus: Representative Treatises from the Enneads* (Indianapolis: Hackett, 1984).

16 In the *Timaeus*, a late dialogue, Plato gives an account of the creation of the universe by a divine Intellect or Craftsman (the Greek word is *demiourgos*). See *Timaeus* 28a–29a for the initial account of how this Demiurge orders the cosmos according to an eternal model.

The generation of Intellect by the One is something that happens necessarily, since something which is as perfect, powerful, and all-around good as the One cannot help but give of itself. This self-giving involves the production of the Intellect by the One, but Intellect in turn, also being good, must also produce, and as a result we have a third "hypostasis" (substance or underlying reality), namely the Soul. As the Intellect is the image of the One, so the Soul is the image of the Intellect. The Soul is slightly less perfect than the Intellect, and has a dual nature—on the one hand it contemplates the Intellect, but on the other hand it governs the universe of things below itself. The lowest of all things, in Plotinus's hierarchy of realities, is matter. Unlike Gnosticism, a movement which held that matter was intrinsically bad, Plotinus did not think matter itself was evil. Instead, evil comes from the undue attachment of the soul to matter, which hinders the soul's ability to maintain its unity with the world-Soul, and thereby to dwell in the intelligible world and be connected to the One. And this brings us back to the point that got us started on this excursus into Plotinus's metaphysical worldview, namely the cause of the descent of the soul into bodies.

Plotinus is not philosophizing purely for the sake of abstract speculation. He genuinely believes that we are lost souls, who have forgotten our true value and our true origin, and need to be recalled back to the unity with the One that properly belongs to ourselves. In fact, for Plotinus, our true self is simply a part of the intelligible world and a fragment or spark of the divine. But by pursuing things beneath us in the realm of bodies, we have come to despise our true selves. Plotinus compares us to

> children who at birth are separated from their fathers and, being raised for a long time far away, are ignorant both of themselves and of their fathers. Since they no longer can see their father or themselves, they dishonor themselves, owing to ignorance of their lineage, honoring instead other things ... it is honor of these things and dishonor of themselves that is the cause of their complete ignorance of god.[17]

Plotinus strove to act as a philosophical guide to such wandering souls, pointing them to the way of reunion with the Father of all, the One. It does not take a great deal of effort to see how the early Christian thinkers would be attracted to the philosophy of Plotinus rather than to rival schools of thought like Epicureanism and Stoicism. Although not himself a Christian, Plotinus's thought contained elements that resonated profoundly with the Judeo-Christian vision of the world as created by a transcendent God who exists beyond space and time. Christian thinkers could even find traces of the doctrine of the Trinity in Plotinus's emphasis on the three primary realities, even if they could not accept his way of ranking them so that the Soul and the Intellect were inferior to the One. In Christian teaching, the Son and the Holy Spirit are no less fully God than the Father.

---

17 Cahn, p. 409. *Ennead* V i.i.

3. CONCLUSION

We have covered a lot of ground—over 850 years of the history of Western philosophy. We broke up Classical philosophy into three parts: (1) philosophy before Socrates, (2) the golden age of Socrates, Plato, and Aristotle, and (3) philosophy after Aristotle up to the border of the next major period in the history of philosophy, the Medieval era. It is conventional to give Plato and Aristotle pride of place in treating of the Classical period, and we have not deviated from this, though we have sought to provide more information about what came before and after them than is sometimes done. I have emphasized that each of the philosophers we covered did his thinking in critical engagement with his predecessors. Socrates and Plato took up the major themes of the Presocratic thinkers, and Aristotle wrestled with the main epistemological, metaphysical, and ethical doctrines of Plato to produce his own comprehensive philosophical system. The Hellenistic schools that followed continued to engage with the big ideas propounded by Socrates, Plato, and Aristotle, but branched out into their own directions, providing a further multiplicity of options for those who would follow the way of philosophy. Finally, in Plotinus's Neoplatonism we get a masterful development of Platonic thinking that has room for key insights from Aristotle as well. Emphasizing the high-level metaphysical principles taught by both of these thinkers, Plotinus inclines toward a philosophical-spiritual mysticism that sought to blend theory with practical experience of the divine. The continuity within the Western tradition, which I have been emphasizing, extends far beyond Plotinus, running all the way through the Medieval era and well into the Modern period.

The Road to the Medieval Era

If you were planning to go on to study the next major phase in the history of Western philosophy, the present chapter would serve as a sort of bridge between eras. In particular, the work of Plotinus represents a crucial link between the Classical Age of philosophy and the Medieval Period because of its profound influence on thinkers like St. Augustine and Pseudo-Dionysius, thinkers who served as major authorities for the most important medieval philosophers. Plotinus's thought brings out just that emphasis on the religious or mystical elements of Plato and Aristotle that made those Greek thinkers so appealing to the minds of the medieval philosophers, as they found there a rational approximation to the truths which they accepted already on faith, on the basis of Judeo-Christian revelation. Plato's doctrine of the Good and Aristotle's Prime Mover appeared as the end result of the best reflection by natural human reason on the ultimate causes of all things. It was hard for the Medievals not to see the greatest of the Classical philosophers as a providential preparation for the coming of Christ, who manifested the fullness of divine truth. The Classical philosophical tradition was carried on not only by thinkers in the Christian West; there are important medieval philosophical developments in the Jewish (Maimonides and Gersonides, for instance) and Islamic (Averroes and Avicenna being two of the greatest) traditions as well.

St. Augustine of Hippo (354–430 CE), from Gerard Seghers's *The Four Doctors of the Western Church: Saint Augustine of Hippo* (17th Century).

The Medieval period proper begins with the fall of the Roman Empire (between 410 and 476), and ends around the time of the Protestant Reformation in mainland Europe. During this period, the relationship between reason and faith, and the related connections between natural knowledge and revelation, or philosophy and theology, stand out as central themes and questions. On the one hand, the medieval thinkers viewed philosophy through the lens of faith, but at the same time they saw the object of faith (the divine reality) through the lens of philosophy. The pioneering Christian philosopher in whom these two ways of seeing collided with spectacular results is St. Augustine of Hippo, also known as Aurelius Augustinus (354–430). Augustine ingeniously synthesized the Classical Greco-Roman philosophical inheritance and infused it with Christian theological content to lay the foundations for medieval philosophy.

A tradition over three hundred years long of Greek and Roman Christian thinkers leads up to Augustine. The Christian thinkers of the Patristic period (roughly 60–400 CE) varied in their attitudes toward pagan philosophy. Some, like Justin Martyr (100–165), embraced aspects of pagan philosophy and used it to formulate their own ideas and defend Christianity intellectually. Others, like Tertullian (160–240) rejected it completely. Tertullian famously asked, "What indeed has Athens to do with Jerusalem? What concord is there between the Academy and the Church?"

Augustine himself had not always been a great Christian saint. We know a great deal about his life because of his classic autobiographical work, the *Confessions*. Raised by a pagan father and a Christian mother in a small North African town, Augustine left his mother's religion in his teenaged years and spent a good deal of time enjoying the pleasures of the body and the sights of the Roman theatres. He cited his reading of "the books of the Platonists" (most likely Latin translations of Plotinus and Porphyry) as a key to his intellectual conversion to Christianity. In Neoplatonism, Augustine found philosophical concepts and vocabulary that enabled him finally to make sense of the Christian God.

Well, enough said, at least for now! I hope you've enjoyed this introduction to the great conversation that is Western philosophy. Having gone back to examine the roots of this conversation, it is now up to you whether or not to pursue it further. Whether or not you choose to do so, I wish you well, and I hope that this book has begun, or has spurred on, a reflective process in your own heart and mind on some of the most important human questions that face us all.

Image Credits

Adapted from a series of paintings of the theological and cardinal virtues, by Sandro Botticelli and Piero del Pollaiolo (c. 1471).

Plato's Divided Line, adapted from footnote 5 of Plato's *Republic*, 2nd edition, translated by G.M.A. Grube, revised by C.D.C. Reeve (Hackett, 1992).

Plato's Allegory of the Cave, from Jan Saendredam's 1604 print of Cornelis van Haarlem's painting *Antrum Platonicum*.

CHAPTER 5

The School of Athens, by Raphael (1511).

Bust of Alexander, by Anonymous (2nd–1st C BCE). Image licensed under the Creative Commons Attribution-Share Alike 2.0 Generic License. Uploaded to commons.wikimedia.org by Maksim.

Porphyry's Tree, from Edmond Pourchot's *Institutiones Philosophicae* (1730) (adjacent modernized image, copyright © Broadview Press).

CHAPTER 6

Figure of the Heavenly Bodies, by Bartolomeu Velho (1568).

Image of finches, by John Gould (1845). From Charles Darwin's *Journal and Remarks* (The Voyage of the Beagle).

CHAPTER 7

Sisyphus, by Matthäus Loder (19th C).

Frontispiece by Abraham Bosse, from *Leviathan* (1651) by Thomas Hobbes.

CHAPTER 8

Bust of Epicurus, by Anonymous (date unknown). Image licensed under the Creative Commons Attribution-Share Alike 3.0 Unported License. Uploaded to commons.wikimedia.org by Keith Schengili-Roberts.

Epictetus, from Edward Ivie's *Epicteti Enchiridion Latinis versibus adumbratum* (1715).

Sextus Empiricus, by Anonymous (1692), from a copper engraving based on an ancient coin.

Saint Paul Preaching in Athens, by Raphael (1515).

Bust of Plotinus, by Anonymous (3rd C CE).

The Four Doctors of the Western Church, by Gerard Seghers (c. 1600–50).

Index

From the Publisher

A name never says it all, but the word "Broadview" expresses a good deal of the philosophy behind our company. We are open to a broad range of academic approaches and political viewpoints. We pay attention to the broad impact book publishing and book printing has in the wider world; for some years now we have used 100% recycled paper for most titles. Our publishing program is internationally oriented and broad-ranging. Our individual titles often appeal to a broad readership too; many are of interest as much to general readers as to academics and students.

Founded in 1985, Broadview remains a fully independent company owned by its shareholders—not an imprint or subsidiary of a larger multinational.

For the most accurate information on our books (including information on pricing, editions, and formats) please visit our website at www.broadviewpress.com. Our print books and ebooks are also available for sale on our site.

broadview press
www.broadviewpress.com